For —

Jennifer

With warm regards —

John Cutler

Make the Bold Move

Bobbie Cutler

John Cutler

Make the Bold Move

John Henry Cutler

VANTAGE PRESS
New York

To Bobbie

CONTENTS

FOREWORD

"Every person who writes for newspapers has two ambitions," John Cutler says. "One is to be syndicated; the other is to own his own weekly. I've been fortunate enough to have done both."

Plus a whole lot more.

Among other things, his writing brought him a friendship with the late Gene Tunney that spanned their adult years; gave him a chance to rub World War II shoulders with the late Ernie Pyle and the late Robert Sherwood; once made him a thinly veiled short story character drawn by an angered John P. Marquand; and turned him into perhaps the most knowledgeable living chronicler of the political history of Boston and Massachusetts.

The strains that have dominated his life—brilliance, humor, the desire to write, and the ability to express his opinions forcefully—showed up early. As did legendary James Michael Curley, several-times mayor of Boston, four-time congressman, governor of the Commonwealth—and twice a prisoner in jail.

As Cutler's mother would later tell him, when he was five and growing up in Boston, they were present when Mayor Curley dug the first shovelful for a subway that ran from Kenmore Square to St. Mary's Street in Brookline. Curley, she said, took off his top hat and let it drop over the boy's ears.

Forty-two years would pass—and a long writing apprenticeship would be served—before their paths would cross again.

At the age of fifteen, Cutler was writing "little profiles" of young people who showed up each Friday afternoon when his mother held open house. Two years later, when his first published piece appeared in the Boston Latin School *Register,* he'd begun to read "hundreds of biographies," collecting little intimate glimpses of people which he'd "write down on an envelope and stuff in a drawer. Things like, whenever Napoleon went off to campaign he usually took along a gallon of cologne."

That habit continued while he earned his bachelor's, master's, and Ph.D. degrees in romance languages and literature at Harvard. "By then, I'd collected so many little-known facts I cross-indexed them into categories— like 'rain.' "

Those little-known facts were soon destined to change his own life.

Dartmouth followed Harvard, and Cutler taught French and Spanish for five pre–World War II years. In 1940 he gave a lecture course on Rousseau and Voltaire. Though he was a popular instructor and liked teaching, "I wanted to write, write, write!"

One day, armed with a few features he'd written of little-known facts, he walked into the old *Boston Evening Transcript*. The editor liked them, turning the biographical ones into a later syndicated column. Then feature stories began to flow in newspapers here and abroad, the *Boston Post* one Sunday running six simultaneously, and articles began appearing in national magazines like *Reader's Digest, Esquire, Collier's,* and more.

While a World War II naval lieutenant stationed at Recife, Brazil, headquarters of the South Atlantic Fleet, he edited the *South Atlantic News*. At the conclusion of an interview with Senior Vice Admiral Jonas Ingram (which would later result in a *Liberty* magazine article titled "Boss of the Atlantic"), Cutler was asked, "Is there anything else I can do for you?"

With the bravado of innocence, he said he'd like to interview Brazilian president Vargas—and all the cabinet ministers. No sooner said than he was on a PBY Mariner, flying to Rio. "Me! Alone! . . . in this huge plane . . . getting paid extra, per diem!"

Learning that Commander Gene Tunney, who was in charge of the physical fitness and athletic programs of the U.S. Navy, was coming to Brazil, John wrote a welcoming editorial, telling how Tunney during World War I had slept on a plank in the mud at the Battle of Verdun, and how, knowing he'd have to back up when he fought Dempsey, he'd practiced running backwards. Their friendship began when Tunney asked how he'd known this.

Those little-known facts again.

Through Tunney, he later met a "very pompous John P. Marquand," angering the writer "when I told him he reminded me of the late George Apley." Several months later, a Marquand story appeared in *Harper's* "about a brash, young Navy lieutenant. It even had some of the phrases I'd used!" John said, laughing.

If writing has been Cutler's life, for the last twenty-nine years the *Duxbury Clipper* has been his lifeblood. One night in 1950, while he was teaching languages at Boston University (he'd added Italian and Portuguese during the war), his wife, "Bobbie," casually suggested that what their town needed was a weekly paper.

Together they have watched the *Clipper* grow from a shaky, six-page giveaway to a thriving, sometimes fifty-two page edition, printed on their own presses and sent to forty-nine states ("all except the culturally deprived state of Wyoming," said Cutler) and seven foreign countries. . . .

Almost everybody in Duxbury reads the *Clipper.* One reason is Cutler's editorials, which can be pungent and heated. Said the *Gardner News* (Massachusetts) in 1965: "Duxbury is his town, his hobby, and in a special way, his friend," and Cutler doesn't hesitate to speak out when he feels something is amiss.

Interwoven through the *Clipper* years, other writing continued, some fabulous characters marching from his typewriter onto the pages of four books he "doctored" for others and several others he authored alone.

In 1957—ironically to help keep the *Clipper* afloat—Cutler ghosted Curley's autobiography, *I'd Do It Again!* Except for a book on Woodrow Wilson, it subsequently sold for the highest amount of second serial rights, $32,000.

A runaway bestseller followed the Curley book, the humorous *All about Men,* which Cutler fleshed out from an outline of Dr. Joseph Peck, "who had written nothing but prescriptions for thirty years"; then intrigue with *Secret Diary from Red China,* which had been written interlinearly, between the lines of another novel, and smuggled out of Red China. Chosen as one of the best one hundred books of 1961, Cutler had expanded the Chinese author's typescript, falling "madly in love" with the novel's heroine en route.

There was even more drama in 1963 with Caryl Chessman's *Face of Justice.* Chessman, the "Red Light Bandit" and convicted murderer, who up to that time had spent the longest time on death row in U.S. history, had already written *Cell 2455* and *Trial by Ordeal* in his trilogy on the causes of crime, the treatment of criminals, and the ineffectuality of capital punishment.

When the warden of San Quentin forbade him to write any more books, he pretended to be typing legal briefs, would then tear up his originals, flush them down the toilet, and save the carbons—which were smuggled out.

Cutler, through the publisher and unknown to Chessman, "unwrote" the book, improved his English, and was the entire editor. "I read in *Time* magazine that Chessman warned whoever was working on his book not to cut it (Cutler did, by half) or he'd take care of them. And also that the warden couldn't understand where it was or how it got out.

"It was in *my* living room!"

But Cutler's greatest literary mark—and one that reflects the massive research into Massachusetts politics and Boston folklore begun by the Curley book—has been with three formidable Massachusetts personalities.

In 1962 he wrote *Honey Fitz: Three Steps to the White House,* the biography of John F. Fitzgerald, Rose Kennedy's father, grandfather of President JFK—and archenemy of James Michael Curley. Active in Democratic politics for sixty-four years, Honey Fitz had been a rollicking mayor of Boston, congressman, presidential aspirant—and the man who introduced Mother's Day, the municipal picnic, and Boston Common's official Christmas tree.

"I think writers of contemporary biographies have the most fun," and Cutler had just that with the other two: 1970's *Cardinal Cushing of Boston,* and '72's *Ed Brooke: Biography of a Senator* . . .

"I take the anecdotal approach, and the anecdote must illumine the personality," he says. "For example, Cushing was harsh-voiced and austere but had a terrific sense of humor. One night, speaking at a banquet for the Red Sox baseball team, who were all dressed in street clothes, he quipped, 'I'm the only guy here who's in uniform!' "

By Cushing's time, the Irish had made a lot of progress, and he was highly respected by the top layers of society. "There are three kinds of aristocracy," says Cutler. "Of birth, of intellect, and of character—and Cushing had character."

Of former Senator Brooke, Cutler says, "One of the most brilliant persons I've ever known personally, and except for James Michael Curley, the most charismatic. Brooke, up to then, had consistently refused publishers' pleas, so it took a great deal of persuasion," says Cutler.

"At first," said Brooke himself, "I didn't want a book because I thought I was too young, hadn't accomplished anything, and thought it premature. Mr. Cutler didn't get in contact with me until after he'd talked to a lot of people. Then when I heard about this man . . . who he was . . . what he was . . . and his scholarship, I was really quite flattered, frankly, that he would write about me."

What has all his writing brought Cutler?

"Fulfillment! I never wrote primarily for money. I wanted to know people who did things, and just look at the people I've met!"

Cutler retains much of that enthusiastic boy who read so prodigiously and collected those little-known facts. Along the way, he's lived a few of his own, becoming a man whose writing life is almost as colorful as some of the characters he's portrayed. Like Curley, he could say—only this time in words of his own—"I'd do it again!"

Nancy Anne Dawe

(These excerpts are reprinted with permission from the November 4, 1979, issue of the *Boston Herald Magazine*.)

Make the Bold Move

Chapter One
28 FULLERTON

It was a steamy July day in 1990, with the temperature hovering in the nineties, when Bobbie and I left Duxbury, Massachusetts, to drive to Boston. Less than an hour later, we parked at the Harvard Club of Boston on Commonwealth Avenue. Taking a cab, we headed toward Fullerton Street, which is roughly halfway between Fenway Park and the former Sears, Roebuck building on the corner of Park Drive and Boylston Street. I wanted to revisit haunts of my early days.

Bobbie left me at the corner of Brookline Avenue and Fullerton Street, then continued on to nearby Harvard Dental School, where she had an appointment. As I walked down Fullerton, a dead-end street which extended to the MBTA tracks at Fenway Station, I marveled at the drastic changes in the neighborhood in which I was born in 1910. Concrete buildings lined both sides of the street.

The Fullerton Street of my childhood was bordered by a large field sparsely studded with trees on one side and underbrush and woodland on the other. I remembered patches of asparagus, strawberries, and wild blackberries which I used to pick. At the end of the street were the Boston and Albany Railroad tracks, now replaced by the rapid transit lines which run from Riverside to Park Street. On the woodland side of Fullerton was a three-story, straw-colored brick town house with a stable in the rear. Two other vertical houses were part of this block, which stood like a lonely sentinel in its sylvan setting. According to legend, this house, which had basement living quarters, had been built by a wealthy sportsman who was apparently interested in horses, for there were four stalls in the stable. Our rent was thirty-five dollars a month.

Our house, which had fourteen rooms and one and a half baths, had a granite porch in front. It faced a stand of birch trees across the street, which sloped down to a field bounded by Brookline Avenue and Burlington Avenue.

Burlington Avenue, another dead-end street, was a residential neighborhood with a row of red brick houses that extended to the railroad tracks. The third parallel dead-end roadway was Overland Street, which was a

1

three-minute walk to Fenway Park, which had been built in 1912 on Jersey Street. It has been renamed Yawkey Way. The only landmarks that remain from my childhood days are Fenway Park and the Buckminster Hotel in Kenmore Square. The hotel, which is now a lodging house, was built in 1903.

At the end of Fullerton Street, a vacant lot was all that remained of a livery stable, nestled against the railroad tracks. I have a vivid memory of Gypsies who made their annual summer visit to pick dandelions near the site of the livery stable. Other pleasant memories were the hurdy-gurdy organ grinder with his friendly capuchin monkey, who collected the nickels and dimes thrown by the neighborhood kids. A less frequent visitor was the scissors grinder, carrying on his back a rack of tools which included knife sharpeners. An unexpected thrill came when I was ten years old and the Ringling Bros. Circus parked their train right at the end of Fullerton Street. One day I saw, walking right past our house, a flabby and paunchy Jess Willard, who had been dethroned in 1919 by Jack Dempsey as world heavyweight boxing champion. Jess Willard, who was six feet, six inches tall, looked even taller in his sombrero. Right behind him was the black-bearded lady, looking big, burly, and exotic in her white turban. Clowns and assorted circus performers followed her. I wondered whether they walked all the way to the Huntington Avenue grounds where the big tent was pitched.

The Boston and Albany Railroad tracks separated Fullerton and Aberdeen streets. Aberdeen, another dead-end street, fronted on Beacon Street. Aberdeen played a major role in my life all through grammar and high school, for here lived many of my childhood friends, both boys and girls. Since there was no recreation area in their neighborhood, they made Fullerton Street's open space the focus of their athletic and recreational activities.

Friday afternoons, especially, was open house at 28 Fullerton. After school, ten or twelve boys and girls—most of them from Aberdeen Street— hopped the fence and crossed the tracks. They made themselves at home, entering the front door without knocking. Our house had a slate-roof porte-cochere with an iron staircase winding up from the driveway to what we called the sitting room. This room I remember as the "House of Mirth," because in it I had read my first novel, Edith Wharton's *House of Mirth*. The sitting room was separated by portieres from the parlor, where I had taken piano lessons twice a week for seven years beginning at the age of eleven. I remember how irked I used to get because my mother always served the piano teacher a steak and mushroom dinner. I was irked because this extended what was supposed to be an hour-long session.

In the sitting room we had a Victrola (we called it a gramophone) on which we played records after winding up the machine. I remember how thrilled I was by the sound of Caruso's booming voice. We also had an album of John McCormack. I also remember "Brighten the Corner Where You Are," which I learned later was a Salvation Army Song. Some of the musical hits of my early boyhood years were "Ah, Sweet Mystery of Life," "Down by the Old Mill Stream," "Let Me Call You Sweetheart," and "A Perfect Day." On most Friday afternoons we danced in the sitting room or played games like checkers or Parcheesi, and my favorite game, post office. I clearly remember the first girl I kissed. During these informal gatherings, my mother always served hot chocolate and cookies in the winter and cool refreshments in the summer.

The sitting room and parlor were directly over the basement kitchen and dining room. The coal furnace was down a few feet from the adjoining hallway. I remember looking through a gap in the steps leading to the cellar and seeing the dark residual water which was once a part of the Back Bay. I remember the sound of anthracite coal rumbling down a chute from a basement window. I also remember tending the furnace and carrying scuttles of coal up to our coal stove in the kitchen.

One night my sister Ann—two years younger than I—and a friend, Elizabeth McKenna, were sitting at the kitchen table playing cards. I forget what I said that infuriated the girls, but I'll always remember their revenge. As I left to go up the dark staircase, they gave a bloodcurdling scream that scared me out of my wits. I have from that day on been afraid of the dark.

I remember, a few years later when we were staying in Hull in the Kenberma section of Nantasket Beach, where we spent several summers, I had to leave on the night boat to get to my job in a small ice cream factory in Brookline. I found the house at 28 Fullerton frighteningly empty and dark. I opened the front door and ran as fast as I could up two flights of stairs to my bedroom on the top floor. Without taking off my clothes I dived into bed and pulled a sheet over my head. A few minutes later I recovered enough to take off my clothes and slip into pajamas.

Another terrifying experience was the first and only time I tried to swim at Magazine Beach in Cambridge (another vanished landmark of my youth). I got into water over my head and frantically tried to get ashore. I made it just before I went down for the third time. My inability to swim was still with me when I joined the Boy Scouts at the age of ten or eleven. I never

3

got past second class because I couldn't swim fifty yards, a requirement for first-class Scouts.

Around this time an adult friend on Aberdeen Street, Walter Kett, gave me a set of boxing gloves for Christmas. My older brother Chris, who used to say I was Walter's "pet," remembers what happened when we first tied on the gloves in the Kett living room. Chris says I hit him so hard I knocked him over the sofa.

This brings me to the fun times we had under the arc light in front of our house on Fullerton Street. Our neighborhood was often the scene of nightly fun as we played relievo, duck on the rock, and red light. We were all poor kids, sons of a working class that included chauffeurs, custodians, one coal "heaver," and a fruit dealer. We improvised our fun. My favorite sport was boxing, and at the risk of being immodest I'll say I was the champ, even though I was a year or two younger than any of the other kids.

By this time Fullerton Street was a busy recreation center. We boys played baseball in the summer, football in the fall, and skated and played hockey in the winter on the sandlot baseball field across the street from my house. In the winter we often flooded the field by opening the steamer of the hydrant near the arc light. How well I remember the day I was carrying a kettle of boiling water out of the kitchen to thaw out the steamer when I saw Joe Reisman, a mounted cop, trot down the street on his handsome horse. I rushed back to the kitchen, and for a while there was no more hydrant tinkering. Our gang felt bad when Joe was shot to death while investigating a housebreak on Jersey Street.

We were all in high school when we bought purple and white hockey uniforms and called ourselves the Aberdeen Athletic Club. We were good enough one year to make the finals of an informal amateur league. In a game played at the Boston Arena we lost to the Maiden Athletic Club, 8–3. I remember that game especially because of the shiner I got while playing left defense.

In the fall we played football on the gravelly surface where we had built our baseball field. The boys called me "the Flying Turk." We built a crude backstop and found flat stones which became first, second, and third bases and home plate. We chipped in to buy bats and balls. When a ball had its cover knocked off, we wound black tape around it. Once in a while I tried to remedy the situation by sitting on Jersey Street, just outside Fenway Park, hoping a player would hit a ball over the roof. I spent several futile days waiting for this to happen. Some days when a Red Sox game became lopsided and the fans started leaving the park early, we were allowed to

4

climb into the bleachers. I saw such stars as Ty Cobb, Tris Speaker, and Harry Hooper. One afternoon I saw Hooper leap halfway up the right field wall to rob a batter of a home run. Another day, I was shocked when Babe Ruth, who had been traded to the Yankees a year or two earlier, lumbered out of the players' exit on his way to his black Packard roadster, which he'd parked on Jersey Street. During the walk to his car, I was shocked to hear him use the word "f——" twice. I was not used to this language, since our Aberdeen gang rarely used profanity. Once in a while, someone might get teed off and invite you to "piss up a rope," but that was about all.

My brother Chris and I are the only two survivors of five children, and neither of us knows much about our parents' background. My father was born in Megalopolis, Greece, my mother in Mount Rath, near Dublin, Ireland.

My father had studied English before he left Greece at the age of twelve. He used to say he had been a shepherd on his father's sheep farm. He came to America by way of Montreal and later joined relatives in Boston, including two stepbrothers, a stepsister, and a few cousins. Some of them had adopted the name Cutler, which was passed on to my father, who was born Aristides Canteles, a name my children wish he had retained. In time Aristides became Ari and Ari became Harry. His stepsister, Panayiota, died in 1989 at the age of ninety-three, leaving eight of ten children whom she and her husband, Charles Coniaris, had raised. My father's two stepbrothers had died several years earlier.

All the Coniaris children were well educated—two at Harvard and one daughter at Radcliffe. One of the sons is a psychiatrist.

Although my father had little formal education, he was of a philosophical turn of mind. He took everything in stride but was especially proud of his children—especially their athletic achievements. He was also proud of his heritage. I remember how he beamed one day when I told him my ancient history teacher had said, "A thousand years after the Age of Pericles, the Germans were still sitting on bales of hay."

My mother, Margaret Burke Fitzpatrick, was one of fifteen children. Her father was a schoolmaster who, she said, became superintendent of the school district. (When Bobbie and I visited Mount Rath in 1970, we thought it must have been a pretty small district.) Margaret Fitzpatrick, who had red hair and blue eyes, lived on Long Island with her aunt, Elizabeth Fitzpatrick, who had "brought her over." She was sixteen years old at the time. She did not remember the exact year she came to Boston, but in later years she told me she remembered a parade in Boston honoring Admiral George Dewey, of Spanish-American War fame, so it must have been around the turn of the century.

When I was seven years old the Postal Annex, a huge concrete building, replaced some of the brick houses on Burlington Avenue. Its loading platform was close to the Boston and Albany Railroad tracks. I remember going back and forth on hot summer days selling the construction workers lemonade I had made by the pitcher for three cents a glass.

When I was a high school sophomore, S.S. Pierce built its headquarters, which spanned almost the full distance between Fullerton Street and Burlington Avenue. It encroached on our sandlot baseball field and a batter could have easily hit the wall of the building.

The kids in our neighborhood used to skate and play hockey on nearby Hawes Pond, in Brookline. It was a big thrill for me when my father took me downtown to the Wright and Ditson store and bought me a pair of Blue Streak skates. But he never bought me a bicycle. I remember trading an old baseball glove for a wheel to put on a battered bike that never functioned.

My father's two stepbrothers, James and Philip, owned the Norway Spa on Massachusetts Avenue across the street from the old Loew's State Theater. It wasn't far from Huntington Avenue, where Chris and I, and sometimes our sister, Ann, went to the Strand Theater on Saturdays. That is, when we could dig up the fifteen-cent admission fee. The program usually included a double feature, Fox Movietone News, and occasionally a cartoon. My favorite cowboys were William S. Hart and Tom Mix. I especially enjoyed the thrilling serial starring Pearl White, *The Perils of Pauline*.

After the movie, we always stopped at the Norway Spa for free banana splits.

My earliest memory of school was chasing a boy around the schoolyard when I was in the kindergarten of Longwood School, just over the line in Brookline. I went there because there was no other primary school in the area. I remember my kindergarten teacher, Miss Wentworth, with her tightly wound braided hair. My next memory came soon after I entered the first grade. A teacher took me by the hand and led me upstairs to a second-grade classroom. I had no clear recollection of anything else that happened in primary school, but I must have been a docile student, because I never had to be sent to the office of the principal. Miss Marsh was a tart, flinty person who often rapped the knuckles of recalcitrant pupils.

* * *

As I headed back to the Harvard Club on that hot summer day in 1990, I was passing Burlington Avenue when another incident from my childhood came to mind. I had been sent to the store by a housewife on Burlington Avenue to buy a few items, including a dozen bananas. While crossing the street on my way back, I was hit by a small truck owned by Foy's Fish Market. When a passerby picked me up, he asked where I hurt. "The bananas," I sobbed, "they're all crushed."

Another incident involved my young sister, Ann. We raised a few chickens and had a chicken coop and pigpen beside the barn. The only occupant of the pen was "Johnny," who became my pet. I refused to eat any of the roast pork when he was slaughtered.

One morning Ann took Johnny some swill, and she fell over the side of the pen and landed right in the muck. Hearing her shriek, my mother rushed out and turned the garden hose on her. By the way, I was never called Jack and rarely called Johnny. My nickname was "Blackie," because of my black hair.

As I kept walking down Brookline Avenue I was amazed at how the entire area had changed. I saw an office of the *Boston Phoenix* and a radio station, WMAX, along with restaurants, bars, and parking lots—most of them for Fenway Park fans. There was also a bank, a printing establishment, and souvenir shops, also for Red Sox fans. As I approached Kenmore Square, I remembered how I shivered in the cold of winter while earning less than a dollar a night selling newspapers. Later I had a plush job: I peddled the *Boston Daily Post* and was paid seven dollars a week for going back and forth on street cars between Kenmore Square and Cottage Farm Bridge, now renamed Boston University Bridge.

Continuing on my way to the Harvard Club, I passed the Somerset Hotel on Commonwealth Avenue. Here pretty Betty Pembroke, of Aberdeen Street, took me to her junior prom. On the railroad tracks behind the Somerset was a trestle that kept my memory stirring. During World War I, when I was nine years old, I used to see an American soldier patrolling back and forth guarding the trestle. One day in a burst of patriotism I brought the soldier two sandwiches and an apple. He seemed so appreciative, I brought him more food later.

After Bobbie and I had a late lunch at the Harvard Club, we drove back to Duxbury. Bobbie asked me how my morning went.

7

"*Rus in urbe,*" I said.

"What are you talking about?"

"You studied Latin, Bobbie. It means 'country in city.' "

She smiled.

"I get it. Now it's just *urbe.*"

Chapter Two
SCHOOL DAYS

The section of Back Bay extending from the Public Garden to Massachusetts Avenue, and bounded by Beacon and Boylston streets, was called the most elegant rectangle in America early in the century. In this area, at the corner of Newbury and Exeter streets, was the less elegant Prince School. In the late 1980s the school was renovated and now houses luxury condominiums and exclusive shops. The elegant rectangle is today overrun with students, secretarial schools, and offices for professionals.

I entered the fourth grade at the Prince School along with children from all walks of life, including sons and daughters of the domestics and coachmen who worked in the stately houses in the rectangle.

By this time my latent stubborn streak was beginning to show. One afternoon Miss Field, my fourth grade teacher, asked me to come out into the corridor, where I expected to be rebuked and taken to the principal's office, where "Old Man Ripley," the bald-headed tyrant, would probably give me a few whacks with his favorite weapon—a rattan. Instead, Miss Field gave me a macaroon wrapped in tissue paper and said, "Now you be a good boy, John." I also remember wondering one morning why Miss Field kept using the word *verb*. For heaven's sake, didn't she know the correct word was *herb*?

The following years passed uneventfully except that I was getting more rebellious.

"Listen to the bully," my fifth grade teacher, Miss Reynolds, said one day. Another teacher in the sixth grade, who used to discipline me gently, said to me two or three times, "It isn't you, John. It's the little man inside of you."

I met my match one day in the eighth grade, when Harold James, a husky student who was taller than I, joined the class in midterm. I challenged him to a wrestling match during our lunch hour, which lasted from noon to one-thirty. Harold and I spent most of that time on the Commonwealth Avenue Mall trying to pin each other down. It was a draw. We shook hands and became good friends. We returned to school with our shirts hanging out, dirty and disheveled.

9

I was interested in other things besides roughhousing. Girls, for instance. I remember walking a fifth-grade blonde home during the lunch hour, then waiting outside with only a pickle for lunch until Dorothea came out of her house. Often during the lunch period I wandered over to the Museum of Natural History, which was a few blocks away on Berkeley Street. Later it became a Bonwit Teller shop, and today it is a fashionable store for men. Culture was waning in Boston.

In good weather I went to school on roller skates. I remember seeing those quaint "electrics" on Commonwealth Avenue. They were always black, slow moving, and driven by elderly ladies wearing dignified hats that were anything but chic. Since the electrics' batteries had to be recharged after being driven about twenty miles at fifteen or eighteen miles an hour, they soon disappeared from the scene.

After graduating from the Prince School I went to the High School of Commerce, which was in the Fenway, a ten-minute walk from Fullerton Street. By this time I had caught up with Chris; I had skipped one grade, and he had had to repeat another because of a prolonged illness that included pneumonia and the mumps. Our sibling rivalry, which had begun in the eighth grade when we each captained baseball teams, intensified during the four years at Commerce.

We both lacked motivation for learning, but we had a successful interest in athletics. In our freshman year I won the Boston City junior shotput championship. My certificate was made out to "Christopher J. Cutler." That error was never corrected.

The subjects we studied the first year included bookkeeping, accounting, algebra, English, and Spanish.

I remember distinctly my surprise when a Spanish teacher gave me an A. At Prince School I hated homework and most of my grades were Bs with a few Cs. When I got that A in Spanish, it dawned on me that I was potentially a good student. It was an impetus that helped me compile a straight A record during the last three years at the High School of Commerce.

My whole outlook suddenly changed. I was no longer a bully, no longer so disputatious. You could almost call me a nice boy. In my sophomore year my English teacher, who used to give student test papers to me to correct, said I belonged across the street at Boston Latin School, which in those days outranked even Groton, St. Mark's, and Andover on college board exams. In my third year I began to think seriously about going to college.

From our sophomore year on, Chris and I played on the varsity hockey, baseball, and football teams. Chris made Boston's All-Scholastic City

Baseball Team as leftfielder. One Boston newspaper noted that he had a "big-league" arm. He showed it one afternoon when, after hitting a home run himself, he threw out a Boston Latin player at home plate after chasing a long fly ball that had been hit over his head. Commerce won the game 1–0. I played centerfield and did no damage, defensively or offensively. Chris was also a much better hockey player than I. My best moment came in the game played at the Boston Arena against Boston Latin when I passed the puck to Chris, who scored, giving us the 2–1 win.

That year, Lawrence Jackson, who taught English, invited me to take a special course in Latin. He said the course was being introduced primarily for my benefit, and that two other students also were taking the course. In my senior year, instead of reading *Julius Caesar*, we read a book written by Cornelius Nepos.

In midterm of that year I was chosen the best scholar-athlete at Commerce, and I was asked to give some academic advice to the junior class in the assembly hall. I was given only ten minutes warning to prepare my speech, and I flunked it.

"If you are interested in advancing your education I suggest this curriculum: Spanish, Latin, English, math, and . . ." Here I became flustered; I couldn't think of a fifth course. I tried again. "Spanish, Latin, English, math, and . . ." Again I was stymied. (I meant to add "history.")

The following year I took a postgraduate course at Boston Latin. Since I had so many subjects to make up, I had to work harder than most of the other students. I took Latin (Cicero), physics, American history, ancient history (after school), and three years of French, moving from first-year French to second-year French and, a couple of months later, into third-year French class. My French teacher was "Maxie" Levine, who I learned was loved and admired by generations of Latin School students. Toward the end of the semester he called me up to his desk.

"Cutler," he said. "I want you to promise not to take the college boards in French. I have never lost a student in all my years of teaching, and remember, they had three years of French before they took the boards. You had only one." Several years later I ran into Maxie at the Yale Bowl.

"I didn't take your advice, Mr. Levine. I took the college boards in French and almost got honors with a 75." That was the lowest grade I received on my boards. That postgraduate year was tough but rewarding. I took piano lessons twice a week, tutored a Commerce student once a week in algebra and plane geometry, and, during my free periods at Boston Latin, I studied trigonometry with Harold Garland, my old math teacher at the

11

High School of Commerce. I also worked at the Boston Public Library after school and all day Saturdays.

During that postgraduate year, while recovering from the flu, I read the classic Greek story "Atalanta and the Three Golden Apples." Boston Latin had a literary magazine called the *Register*. I was laid up long enough to rewrite the story in what was meant to be Homeric prose. My title was "Atalanta and the Three Golden Bananas." The narrators of the story were Vestal Virgins, "who often, for want of better diversion, gossiped among themselves." In any case, the wooer of Atalanta, Hippomones, slipped into the good graces of Atalanta and married her, thus complying with the edict of her father, the king, that he would give her in marriage to any youth who could beat his daughter in a foot race. In the original story Atalanta paused three times to pick up the golden apples which Hippomones dropped to slow her down. In my account she slipped on three golden bananas.

After I passed the college boards I was admitted to Harvard, Holy Cross, and the Massachusetts Institute of Technology. My preference was Harvard, but there was little money in the family till. Meanwhile, Lawrence Jackson, a graduate of Holy Cross, arranged for me to enter the Jesuit college with a full scholarship: free tuition, room, and board for the entire four years. Father John Fletcher of St. Cecelia's Church, where we attended Sunday School and Mass every Sunday, "conspired" with Jackson to pressure me into accepting the Holy Cross offer. After wavering back and forth between Harvard and Holy Cross for several weeks, I went to Holy Cross with gifts of stationery and stamps from Father Fletcher.

In September of 1928 I took the train to Worcester and registered at the college. A junior who was taking down information looked up, obviously surprised, when I casually mentioned that I had been admitted to Harvard. This gave me the first clue that I had made the wrong move.

That afternoon I learned that my roommate would be Felix Talbot, who had been a star catcher on the same Boston Latin baseball team that my brother Chris had defeated almost single-handedly two years earlier. We were delighted to room together. I wrote my mother what I thought was a cordial letter, telling her how happy I was.

The next morning I went to my first class. My professor of Greek was a handsome man with a beard, but he seemed austere, and he looked forbidding. My second class was in English. When I saw the same professor sitting at the desk I made a bold but impulsive move. I walked up to him. "Father," I said, "may I be excused? The dean wants to see me."

A few minutes later I was trying to explain to Dean Bull why I was

12

leaving Holy Cross. I half listened while he gravely informed me, between puffs on his pipe, that I would be violating canon law if I went to a non-Catholic college.

I rushed to my dormitory room, packed my clothes, left a letter of apology for Felix Talbot, and took a taxi to the Worcester train depot. About an hour later I called my mother from South Station and told her what I had done. With her usual acumen and good humor, she laughed. To my amazement she said, "I could tell from your letter, John, that you were not happy there."

From South Station I took the rapid transit to Harvard Square, went to Memorial Hall on the Harvard campus and was literally the last freshman to register. One registrar testily told me to hurry up. Registration was closing.

My mother drew four hundred dollars from the bank that year to pay my tuition. During the rest of those happy years at Harvard, I didn't ask for another cent from my family.

Meanwhile, my brother Chris entered Boston College on a baseball scholarship that carried him through all four years.

Chapter Three
817 BEACON STREET

In 1928 life abruptly changed. Sears, Roebuck and Co. had bought the land fronting on Brookline Avenue from Park Drive, formerly Audubon Road, to Fullerton Street. Audubon Road had its name changed because of the unsavory reputation of some of its houses which were not homes, to paraphrase Polly Adler. Reluctantly we moved from 28 Fullerton across the tracks to a second-floor apartment at 817 Beacon Street, now part of a parking lot which is adjacent to the Massachusetts Turnpike. We had much less space for comfortable living in our five-room apartment, especially since two children had been added to the family. By 1928, Henry Shannon was eight years old, and James Philip was six. I always felt sorry for Jimmy and Harry, who missed most of the fun, games, and excitement we older children had had on Fullerton Street.

Gone were the happy, carefree days of my childhood, but the memories remained. Aunt Nan, a trained nurse, who was one of my mother's older sisters, spent three years with us in the early 1920s before returning to her nursing duties in England.

"When I was growing up in Ireland," she said, "I heard about the wild Indians in America, but I never met any until I got to know the Cutler kids." We knew, however, that Aunt Nan really loved us and we were distressed to see her go. But she had a point. When my mother visited Bobbie during the Second World War, she said, "We never could do anything with John." When she spanked me, I used to laugh and say, "That didn't hurt." Then she would laugh.

Later we had another Irish visitor, Finton Quigley, a nephew of my mother's. Fint, who was six feet, four inches tall, worked for two years as a landscape gardener in Chestnut Hill before he got homesick and moved back to England, where he had been living. Bobbie and I never heard much about him again until we visited Fint's uncle in Mount Rath in 1970. Fint's uncle was a butcher who closed his shop during the "siesta hour."

What early memories there were: setting off fireworks under the arc light on the Fourth of July; watching Peter Trivoulidas dance in a neighbor's living room after he won the Boston Marathon in 1920; the foot races we had on Fullerton Street, which my father always won; games we played under the arc light; the hockey rink we built alongside the driveway of my house. The wooden sideboards had been construction forms given to us by an engineer who was foreman when the S. S. Pierce headquarters building was built on Brookline Avenue. My mother, always ready to improvise to help the family finances, "took in" a dozen boarders who were construction workers. Those were carefree days, when none of us had ever heard about marijuana or cocaine or whiskey. We could have fun without needing the uplift of drugs or alcohol.

I particularly remember Sundays, when we often had a friend or neighbor in for lunch after my sister, brothers, and I attended Mass and Sunday School at St. Cecelia's Church. Our favorite guest was Emily Kett, a sister of Walter Kett, who had given me the boxing gloves years earlier. Emily was a pretty, amusing, and spirited young lady who had been a family favorite for years. She occasionally took Chris and me to the zoo at Franklin Park, and I still have old photographs of Chris and me wearing white sailor suits. My mother, who was the soul of generosity, prided herself on her cooking, and those Sunday meals were always happy occasions.

Other things changed when I enrolled in a highly competitive college. I had less time for extracurricular activities. I hated to give up piano lessons, especially because I was learning to enjoy playing the classics—composers like Bach, Chopin, Rachmaninoff, and Schubert. But one thing I knew: my choice of Harvard had been wise. It was a haven for underprivileged boys like me. It awarded scholarships to needy boys who got good marks. But I remember feeling diminished when a mathematics professor named Julian Coolidge called us day students "untouchables," a derogatory term used in India to describe the lowest class.

My parents—especially my father—had always considered me fractious, but a hard worker. In the summer of my junior year in high school I had earned money working in an ice cream factory in Brookline owned by Mr. Wadsworth, who made gourmet ice cream and sold it at two or three outlets. Even though I was only fifteen at the time, I used to unload bags of sugar that weighed 250 pounds. Wadsworth ice cream was made of pure heavy cream, fresh fruit, and granulated sugar. I had to cull entire crates of strawberries for my favorite flavor, and often lunched on a quart of strawberry ice cream.

The following summer I had a tougher job, working for the Golden Dome bottling plant in Roxbury. I used to carry two cases of quart bottles of soda or tonic water up a high ladder and stack them up against the wall almost to the ceiling. During the school year I still worked after school and Saturdays at the Boston Public Library.

After I completed the postgraduate year at Boston Latin, I had a better paying summer job working for the Boston Ice Company. How I dreaded those four-deckers in Dorchester, with signs in the windows indicating how much ice was needed. I regularly had to lug on my back chunks of ice weighing up to a hundred pounds. We also sold ice to retail stores where the ice blocks were much heavier.

When I entered Harvard in September I saved money by walking more than two miles to college. I also saved money by taking my five classes on Mondays, Wednesdays, and Fridays. Then, skipping lunch, I had an hour of compulsory exercise. My choice was boxing. I remember the spirited tussles I used to have with an amateur boxer from Puerto Rico. When we met at our twenty-fifth reunion, we were both heavyweights, not all of it flab. I was too heavy in college to make the varsity boxing team, but in my freshman year I sent our middleweight champ to the doctor with a split lip. I don't think I could have made the second round with our Harvard light heavyweights.

While a freshman, I began working Saturdays for Morgan Bros. Creamery. Four of the creameries were in Brookline, and there were several others in Greater Boston communities. In summers I worked full time at a Morgan creamery in Dorchester.

My favorite subject as a freshman was History I, which covered the period from the fall of the Holy Roman Empire to the beginning of the First World War. I was jolted when I got a D on the first quiz I took in this course. But it taught me a lesson. We had a syllabus which prescribed about ten hours a week of reading, and we attended two lectures a week by professors who were authorities in their field. On Fridays we split into small sections where we had quizzes.

In my ignorance I had not realized it was necessary to take notes on the lectures and reading. I soon caught on, and by the end of the year I was delighted when my history instructor told me he expected me "to write the best final." I must have, because I got a B-plus in the course, after a slow start. My grades were good enough to merit a Dana Scholarship for my sophomore year—the first of several scholarships I was to receive during my undergraduate career and four years in the Graduate School of Arts and Sciences.

I hit stride as a sophomore. Although other student friends advised me against it, I elected English II, the famous course taught by Professor George

Lyman Kittredge. One of the many legends, probably apocryphal, surrounding this imperious white-bearded professor, who always wore a gray suit with cutaway and gates-ajar collar, involved his visit to Oxford University, in England, to clear up a disputed passage in Shakespeare. He was told there was only one man in the world who could answer his question—Professor Kittredge of Harvard University. I took this course, not realizing how difficult it would be.

In the second semester Kittredge told the class of about three hundred that no undergraduate "had ever received an A in this course." This puzzled me, because I had had an A at midyears and felt sure I could retain this grade in the second semester.

"Kitty" was unique. A cartoon in the *Lampoon* showed William Shakespeare sitting in his class taking notes. He told us that the correct name of the Bard of Avon was spelled "Shakspere," "because that's how he signed his name." He also said the same author could not have written Bacon's *Essay on Love* and *Romeo and Juliet.* At a banquet one night he told his audience that, by using the same technique which scholars used to prove that Shakespeare's plays were written by the Earl of Oxford, he could prove that Keats wrote the dinner menu.

Since it was possible to elect English II for two years, I did so, after completing the first year with an A. During the latter part of the second year Kittredge repeated his comment that no undergraduate had ever received an A in his course. I concluded that he thought I was a graduate student.

English II demanded a good memory, but that was only the beginning. In his three-hour examination, Professor Kittredge listed about fifty excerpts from one of Shakespeare's plays—some of the excerpts as brief as three words. Students had to identify who said them, to whom they were said, in what context, and what they meant. I used to fill three bluebooks for these exams. Students also had to memorize passages from various plays.

For the final exam in our junior year, I tutored three of my friends on *Othello.* We stayed up all night and were exhausted by dawn. Suddenly I remembered, about a half-hour before the nine o'clock exam, that I had not memorized the one passage which Kittredge whimsically had asked for among various other passages every year for several years. Frantic, I memorized these lines while running from a friend's apartment on Remington Street, about a half-mile away from Harvard Hall, and I made it there just in time for the exam. Just as I suspected, Kittredge asked for this passage.

As I look back on these undergraduate years, getting an A for two years in English II was by far my proudest achievement. When Kittredge retired, in 1936, no other undergraduate had ever received an A in the course, which he had taught for about forty years.

During my last years at Harvard, where I majored in Romance languages and literature, I made Group II three consecutive years.

Minimum requirements for Group II were two and a half As and one and a half Bs. Group I required three and a half As and half a B. I would have made Group I as a sophomore if my economics professor had given me the A he said I deserved. "But it is my policy never to give undergraduates As." I wasn't satisfied when he said I was the best student in the class. I needed scholarships, not praise.

My sister, Ann, who was never interested in her studies, had switched from Girls' High School to Notre Dame Academy in the Fenway, next to Emmanuel College, for her senior year. Here she met a pretty student named Mary McGillicuddy, who became her best friend and spent a lot of time after school at our house on Fullerton Street. I was at Boston Latin that year. Mary was my first date when we saw Buddy Rogers and Richard Arlen in *Wings*. Her parents were both doctors, and one of them, with a single remark, changed the course of my life. I was still seeing Mary when she entered Radcliffe College and I was a senior at Harvard. That year I had been admitted to Harvard Law School and was planning to go. One night Dr. Helen I. McGillicuddy made a casual remark.

"You don't want to be a lawyer, John," she said. "You like to talk. You would be happier as a professor." That did it. I decided to go to Harvard's Graduate School of Arts and Sciences. As if lawyers don't talk.

At the end of my junior year at Harvard, Jacob Cantor, a junior Phi Beta Kappa, told me I was next on the list to be elected to Phi Beta Kappa in my senior year. At the time I did not know the dilemma I faced. Graduate students are not allowed to take elementary courses and prospective Phi Beta Kappas are not allowed to take an elementary course as seniors. The Dean of the college explained this to me when I complained of not making Phi Beta.

"I wouldn't worry," he said. "You got a magna cum laude, and there are about the same number of magnas as there are Phi Beta Kappas." Paul Vail, who was elected to the honor society in my place, had never, during all four years, even made Group II.

Later I learned that I missed summa cum laude when my tutor, Guillermo Rivera, told me the vote against me was three to two. But I felt upbeat when I received the Susan B. Anthony prize for writing the best essay on the Golden Age of Spanish Literature.

I always wished I could have afforded to "live in" at Harvard. I didn't feel the stigma later, when, after working for Morgan Bros. Creamery that summer, I entered graduate school, for there were no "houses" for graduate students, and many students lived off campus.

One incident lingers in memory. One night I was vice chairman of a formal dance at the Hotel Vendome. I was wearing a chesterfield over my dinner clothes and was approaching my car when a derelict from nearby skid row accosted me with outstretched palm. Before he could say a word, I said, "Brother, can you spare a dime?" Never will I forget the look of stupefaction on his face as he reached into his pocket and pulled out a dime. I returned it, of course, adding a half-dollar. He was still numbly gaping at me as I got into the car.

Chapter Four
GRADUATE SCHOOL

Jacob Cantor and I were the only members in our field of the class of 1932 to enter the Harvard Graduate School of Arts and Sciences in the fall of that year. It was an exhilarating experience. There were no "gentlemen's Cs" here, and a B-minus had a stigma attached to it. There were a few female students along with candidates for a master's degree or doctorate from all over the world. They ranged in age from early twenties to late thirties.

When I attended my first class on the history of the novel I got an idea of the scope of graduate work at Harvard. Professor Hawkins filled the blackboard with titles of books for collateral reading and said there would be more reading assignments later. In the next two class sessions he filled the blackboard again. It was a fascinating lecture course that traced the evolution of the novel from fabliaux in the Middle Ages to Marcel Proust and Henry Fielding.

All went well until the midyear examination. In my first year of philology I panicked in the middle of the three-hour exam. My memory failed. I scribbled a note to Professor J. D. M. Ford, saying my mind had suddenly gone blank. I sat there disconsolately, certain that my graduate career was over before it had even begun. Suddenly, fifteen or twenty minutes later, my mind cleared, and I hurried to complete the exam.

At midyears, Professor Ford, head of the Romance languages department, called me into his office. Glancing up, he tersely said, "Bring that B-plus up to an A." He said nothing more. I wound up the year with four As. I had a straight-A record during my four years in graduate school except for one B-plus in a course on Dante.

One requirement for a master's degree is a reading knowledge of German, and since I had taken no German as an undergraduate, I spent the next two summers taking courses in the language. For this reason I didn't get a master's degree until 1935.

My financial situation was much better. I received scholarships the first two years and spent three afternoons a week working in the French Library on the top floor of Widener Library. Since the tuition in graduate school was half of what it was in Harvard College, and because I was working Saturdays at Morgan Bros. Creamery, I was actually saving money. The third year was the most exciting, for Professor Ford appointed me a Radcliffe tutor. The tutorial system was an integral part of both undergraduate and graduate work at Harvard.

I was assigned to Agassiz House on the Radcliffe campus to tutor six undergraduates. It was more fun than work, for my students were bright and attractive. Their assignments included plays by Molière, Racine, and Corneille, and other French works.

One afternoon I leaned too far back in my chair and toppled over on my back. As I picked myself up, I repeated what Professor George Lyman Kittredge had once told a class when he slipped off the dais: "This is the first time I have ever been on the same level as my students."

That year Professor André Morize offered an optional course—lecturing to Harvard undergraduates. He assigned me to lecture on Jean Jacques Rousseau. I spent several hours preparing for the lecture, but when the day came I was so nervous at the thought of facing more than three hundred students that I decided I needed a stimulant. If Professor Morize knew I had downed two whiskey sours before giving the lecture he probably would have canceled it. As it turned out he complimented me on the lecture, criticizing me only for using distracting gestures.

To qualify for a Ph.D., candidates had to have a comprehensive knowledge of French literature from the *Chanson de Roland* to modern authors, along with the same requirements for either Spanish or Italian literature—that is, from the *Poema del Cid* or *Orlando Furioso* to modern Spanish and Italian authors. Having taken elementary Italian in my senior year at Harvard, I took all the courses offered in Italian, as well as in Spanish and French. I also took half a year's course in Portuguese, in which we read the Portuguese epic poem, *"Os Lusiades."* We were required to learn Portuguese grammar on the side.

Meanwhile, I had begun research on the book-length dissertation to qualify for a doctorate. One morning early in 1935, Dr. Isaac Goldberg, with whom I was taking a course in Spanish-American literature, mentioned a Peruvian author who, he said, "was an apt subject for a doctoral dissertation." I read an article on this author in the *American Mercury*, which was written by Dr. Goldberg, and immediately became enamored of Manuel Gonzalez-Prada. I decided to follow Goldberg's advice. I wasn't interested in the kind of subject most doctoral candidates chose. They reminded me of the legendary Cornell professor who spent fourteen years studying the vowel *e*. Asked if he had any regrets, he said, "Yes. I should have confined myself to short *e*." I wasn't interested in transferring literary bones from one cemetery to another. Prada was virgin terrain.

Prada was a poet and a vigorous writer, who reminded me of H. L. Mencken. I remember one of his metaphors: "Peru is a sick organism. Everywhere the finger touches it, it spurts pus." During my research I discovered in an obscure Spanish magazine (*Nosotros*) that one of the pseudonyms Prada used in his poetry was "Merida." Later his son, Alfredo Gonzalez-Prada, who was in the diplomatic service in Washington, D.C., helped me with the thesis. He invited me to the Hampshire House in New York to discuss the project, and over a scotch and soda he said, "How did you ever find out about Merida? I've been trying to find that pseudonym for years."

Alfredo was a delightful person. I enjoyed our visit, although I was embarrassed when I knocked over my drink, which he refilled. Alfredo later committed suicide, and I never came to understand why. He was such an accomplished and cultured gentleman.

The night before I was to take the three-hour oral examination for my Ph.D., I was too nervous and frightened to sleep a wink. In the morning I took the rapid transit to Harvard Square, having made up my mind that I couldn't take the exam that was scheduled for nine o'clock. In despair, I went into a drugstore and drank four cups of black coffee. Suddenly my mind cleared and I felt completely revived. Twelve professors were waiting to quiz me. Professor Ford opened the inquisition by asking me to trace the morphology of the French word *sermon. Here I go, down the chute,* I thought. "I know the word is connected with the Latin word *sanctimoniam,* but I can't think of the exact word." Ford helped me. "The Latin word is *sacramentum,*" he said. I then had no trouble tracing the evolution of the word. I easily answered all questions during the first hour of philology, and had no trouble during the second hour, which was based on French literature. At the end of the two hours Professor Ford asked if I wanted to be examined on Spanish or Italian literature. I said it made no difference because I felt equally prepared in both. Fortunately, I chose Spanish.

My biggest ally during the final hour was Professor Guillermo Rivera, who had been my tutor for three of my undergraduate years. He asked me to trace the evolution of the picaresque novel from Roman to modern times. Rivera knew very well that years before he had asked me to write a thesis on this subject, thus it was easy for me to trace the history from the Latin era through Middle and High German, during which I mentioned Til Eugenspiegel; then on through Gil Blas, in French and Spanish literature;

and culminating in *Moll Flanders*, *The Adventures of Joseph Andrews*, and *Tom Jones*, in English literature. Thanks to Rivera, I used up almost a quarter of the last hour on this question.

Words cannot describe the elation I felt when that ordeal was over. Professor Ford shook my hand saying, "Welcome into the fellowship of scholars." On the way to 817 Beacon Street I was stopped by a police officer for speeding. "I don't care if you give me a ticket," I said. "I just got my Ph.D." He waved me on.

During my Radcliffe "tutorial" year I was guest at a tea given by the French Club. Among the charming young students was Penelope Young, who invited me after the reception to share a beef stew at her home. Penelope later graduated from Radcliffe summa cum laude and was easily the most beautiful girl I had seen on the Radcliffe campus. I dated her for several months, even though I knew her serious boyfriend was Jack Dawson (whom she would marry), who was in his last year at Harvard Law School. Penelope was the daughter of an architect who had been born in Scotland, and she herself had a delightful Scottish accent. I almost cried many years later when I heard of her tragic death. She'd been traveling in Africa with her husband and her older sister, Doreen. Doreen had been given a trip around the world by Concord Academy, where she had been dean, when she retired in the 1980s. I read in a Boston newspaper that Penelope, Doreen, and Jack had been incinerated in a small airplane taking off from Nairobi, headed for Sri Lanka. It was a terrible loss.

By this time, my friends called me the "five o'clock scholar," because I rarely studied after leaving Widener Library at that hour. One day I saw a photo of "Miss Massachusetts" in a Boston newspaper. I called her, identified myself, and asked her out to dinner. Although not as beautiful as Penelope Young, she was one of the prettiest girls I have ever known. We dated for almost a year and continued to be friends until our paths diverged.

During the first three years of graduate school I continued to work Saturdays at Morgan Bros. This led to an amusing incident when the mother of two Radcliffe girls, Dorothy and Elaine Bevan, whom I had often visited for bridge games in their Newtonville home, came into the creamery at Coolidge Corner in Brookline. When she saw me in a white apron working behind the counter, I could see her jaw sag. She couldn't imagine a Radcliffe instructor masquerading as a clerk in a creamery.

After getting my Ph.D. in June 1936, I had a choice of three colleges at which to teach. I picked Dartmouth and was invited to Hanover, New Hampshire, for an interview. After having tea with several members of the

Romance languages staff, Professor Harold Washburn, chairman of the department, suggested I attend the Spanish School at Middlebury College during the summer to improve my fluency.

The summer I spent at Middlebury was delightful. I felt recharged as my fluency in Spanish gradually improved. My "literary" Spanish had always been good, but I was almost a colloquial illiterate. I couldn't say things in Spanish like "Pass me the spinach, please," or "Ted Williams hit a homer in the top of the eighth." But by the end of the seven-week course I felt at home in the language. I could even play bridge and tennis in Spanish. My profanity was barely adequate.

I remember asking a student, after leaving Middlebury, what course she would be taking at Smith. Instead of saying "taking," I asked what course she would be "following." I was still thinking in Spanish—a good sign, since I was scheduled to teach the language at Dartmouth beginning in September. I also taught elementary French, and the following summer I attended a French-speaking semester at the University of the South in Sewanee, Tennessee.

Theoretically we were not allowed to speak English during these sessions at Middlebury and Sewanee, but we occasionally broke the rule. One afternoon at Middlebury I was talking to Professor Louis Solano, whom I was surprised to see at Middlebury, since at Harvard he was considered a linguistic legend who had command of twenty-seven languages. In graduate school I once met him in the stacks at Widener Library while he was studying Gaelic. I presumed this was his twenty-eighth language. At Harvard I had taken elementary Italian with him in my senior year. He told me he was more interested in linguistics than literature. Odd!

During our conversation we lapsed into English for a moment. "You will love teaching at Dartmouth," he said. "You'll find that facing your first class will be one of the most exciting times in your life." He was right.

Chapter Five
DARTMOUTH DAYS

During my first year at Dartmouth I had a good rapport with my students—all of them male, and many of them only a few years younger than I. I used to liven up class sessions by changing the usual routine. For example, I would write ten common words on the blackboard and guarantee that the class, speaking in unison, would mispronounce every one of them. This never failed. Another time I gave them ten common words which I said they couldn't spell. I would ask such words as "anoint," which they would spell with two n's; "inoculate," which they would also spell with two n's. I never met a student who could correctly spell "desiccate." When I gave them a quiz, I would leave the room for ten minutes, and when I returned I would knock at the door. A student told me that none of the boys ever cheated because of my trust in them.

One year Dartmouth had imported several burly football "ringers," and several of them landed in my Spanish class. After winning every game this freshman team was scheduled to play the Boston College freshmen on the following Saturday. I had seen the BC players in one practice session, and I saw enough to tell that BC had also imported some ringers, as they still do.

"You boys are going to lose your first game at BC Saturday," I said. The reaction was not indignant—it was explosive. For a moment I thought they were going to assault me. "You don't want to bet on that, do you, Dr. Cutler," one of the boys said, his voice dripping with sarcasm. "How about a friendly little wager of five dollars?" I knew I was being out of order, but I agreed to make five bets at five dollars each. BC won the game, 14–6. Monday morning one student paid his bet by depositing five hundred pennies on my desk.

Toward the end of my first year of teaching, Gordon Bill, dean of the Dartmouth faculty, called me into his office.

"Dr. Cutler," he said, "I thought you'd like to know that this year you have been named the most popular instructor on the faculty." That buoyed me for a while. I had no idea at that time we would become personal friends soon thereafter and that two years later, his daughter, Mary, would invite me to her engagement party.

The following year I was also pleasantly surprised when the Phi Gamma Delta fraternity invited me to be their faculty advisor. I was too happy to feel lonely that first year, and too lonely to feel happy the following year, when I was boarding in a house off campus, across the hall from an assistant professor of Spanish who shall remain nameless. One night I was invited to speak on Manuel Gonzalez-Prada to the Romance languages professors and their wives. In what I came to believe later was a deliberate attempt to get me tipsy, my friend mixed up several Manhattans, which we shared. It didn't work. I got through the lecture with an eloquence I would not have had without the temporary stimulant.

Alcohol got me in trouble during one of the weekends I spent in Boston. I made the mistake of drinking three bottles of Pickwick Ale, which was known as the poor man's whiskey. When I left the bar to get into my car and drive away I was pulled up short by two men who accused me of going through a red light. I didn't realize they were plainclothes police officers from nearby Station Sixteen. When they pulled me out of the car with the intention of mugging me, I thought, I knocked one of them down. The other burly cop hit me on the head with his billy, and they took me to Station Sixteen, charging me with going through a red light, driving under the influence, driving so as to endanger, and assaulting a police officer. My head was stitched by a doctor at the station. Next morning I was taken to a Roxbury Court where Judge Frankland Miles was presiding. I was the only presentably dressed person on the docket, which was crowded with the usual nightly roundup of bindlestiffs. I heard Judge Miles ask the clerk of court who I was before he turned to me.

"Dr. Cutler," he said. "Do you think alcohol improves your mind?"

"Oh, yes, Your Honor," I said glibly. "At Dartmouth College, I always drink two whiskey sours before I give a lecture."

Immediately the reporters in the courtroom headed for the telephones in the corridor. Judge Miles called them back.

"If any of you report this, I will bar you from this courtroom." He then cleared the courtroom entirely and called me up to the bench.

"There are four charges against you, Cutler. How much money do you have?"

"Your Honor," I said. "I am so broke I had to borrow five dollars from my lawyer."

Earlier I had arranged for three of my friends at Harvard Law School to come to my aid. In the corridor of the courthouse they had conferred with the two plainclothesmen, and one of them admitted hitting me on the head. There was a compromise. If I said nothing to the judge about the incident they agreed to drop the charges of assault and battery.

When Judge Miles asked me how I got the cut on my head, I told him I had hit my head on the curb when I fell. A pleasant conversation followed, which ended when he dismissed three of the charges. He fined me thirty-five dollars—obviously a token amount—and let me go. He was actually smiling. Later his son, Frankland Miles Jr., became a lawyer and settled with his wife in Duxbury. We have often laughed over the incident and are still good friends.

Of course, when Judge Miles had asked me about the potential salutary effects of drinking, in my still befuddled condition I was thinking of those two whiskey sours I had drunk before giving that lecture in graduate school.

Gordon Bill, dean of faculty, who was an excellent bridge player, could usually be found at least two or three afternoons a week at the Graduate Club playing bridge. That brought us together. Bridge had become my favorite card game since I was a junior at Harvard, when a friend in Winthrop House invited a bridge expert to give an exhibition. Walter Leon Hess was a tall, broad-shouldered, imperious-looking gentleman with a shock of white hair and an Edwardian mustache. Hess asked the students to set up two card tables and to deal hands face up from two decks of cards. For less than a minute Hess looked at the twenty-six hands, then was blindfolded. He proceeded to play the hands alternately at both tables: "Table one," he said. "North leads with a three of diamonds, east plays the seven, south plays the queen, and west takes it with the ace. Table two: East leads with the four of spades, south follows with the nine, west with the king, north takes the trick with the ace. Table one . . ." To the amazement of us all, he played out of both decks without making a single mistake. In one respect at least, Hess was a genius.

He had written his own bridge system in a pamphlet, and he had a studio on the top floor of the Statler Hotel in Boston. I memorized the "Hess System of Contract Bridge" and became so taken with the game, I regularly attended Friday night sessions of duplicate bridge at the Statler. The opposition couldn't have been very good because Mary McGillicuddy and I won too many of those Friday night duplicate sessions.

That same year Hess and I often played as partners in Boston tournaments held at the Chess Club and the Somerset Hotel. In one tournament

Hess and I missed by half a match point making the finals in which we would have played against Hal Sims and his partner. We piled up points in one hand when in one three no-trump bid, our opponents could have set us two tricks if they had opened the diamond suit. They had the ace, king, queen, and ten, and our hand was jack high. Their look of consternation when their ace, king, and queen fell on the final plays was something to see. If our opponents had continued in the diamond suit they would have taken four straight tricks. "So, what the hell," I thought, I was going down two, so why not make a stupid play that might confuse our opponents. I led a small diamond from the dummy, north covered, and I went up with my jack. Mrs. Merrill, a distinguished looking lady who was much more expert at contract bridge than I, took the trick with a king. I could see how thoroughly puzzled she was. She had the ace and two other diamonds, but didn't dare lead back a diamond because she felt I had a tenace and was trying to set up the suit. In any case, I made three no-trump, and will never forget the look of stupefaction on Mrs. Merrill's face when she saw her partner's queen and ten of diamonds wasted. She turned to me. "That, young man, was the cleverest thing I ever saw at the bridge table."

In my second year at Dartmouth, I started playing bridge with Dean Bill and other professors two or three afternoons a week. During vacations Dean Bill used to invite a sociology professor named Michael Choukas, a business acquaintance, and me to spend a week playing bridge in a small hotel in Manchester, Vermont, or at another hotel in Newport, New Hampshire. It was our daily ritual to have two cocktails before lunch and two more before dinner. I always made the orange blossoms, and nobody ever had a third drink. In Manchester, one of our players was Fred Howland, president of an insurance company in Vermont, whose daughter was married to Paul Sample, the resident artist at Dartmouth. Fred was a wily old gentleman who, when he learned I was writing a newspaper column for the *Boston Transcript,* said he would deliberately misspell my name in a complimentary letter so the editor wouldn't know it was sent by a friend of mine.

My colleagues in the Romance languages department were beginning to make snide remarks about the time I spent playing bridge. Actually, for a person in my impecunious position it was a profitable pursuit. The few dollars I was making were enhanced when the wives of three professors asked me to teach them contract bridge by playing with them once a week. Each paid me a dollar a session. We would bid the hand, then lay it down, and I would comment on the bids.

I almost got into deep trouble one afternoon when I was playing against Dean Bill and the dean of Dartmouth College, Lloyd Neidlinger. Dean Bill and Neidlinger were obviously not fond of each other. But Neidlinger was one of the protégés of Ernest Martin Hopkins, president of Dartmouth College. On this particular afternoon Dean Bill opened the bidding with three hearts, I passed, and Dean Neidlinger bid three spades. By this time Dean Bill was frowning. "Four hearts," he said. Imperturbed, Neidlinger bid four spades. Bill at this point crossed his legs and shifted uneasily, obviously stirring up a mad. "Five hearts," he said. Neidlinger countered with five spades. I had doubled each heart and spade bid all the way from the bid of four, and now I gleefully doubled the five-spade bid. They went down four, doubled vulnerable. That bridge game ended earlier than usual. Even at a twentieth of a cent a point, this was a traumatic experience for Dean Bill. At least, from his discomfiture I think it was. I remember his salary at the time. Even though he was the dean of the faculty, he was paid only five thousand dollars a year, his daughter told me.

When Ernest Martin Hopkins retired as president of Dartmouth College in 1943, he was succeeded by John Sloan Dickey. Dean Bill became dean emeritus of the faculty in 1947. Soon thereafter he committed suicide in a hospital in Manchester, New Hampshire.

During my second year as an instructor at Dartmouth, Mike Choukas and I had a column in the *Hanover Gazette*. Choukas gave me the material, and I wrote the column, "*The Propaganda Front*," which was "by C and C." One afternoon when Mike and I were playing bridge with Dean Bill, he said with a repressed smile that didn't fool Mike or me, "C and C, I wish I knew who they were." He knew, of course, but we didn't let on that we knew he knew. Later Professor Choukas wrote a book on propaganda.

During the first three years I was getting disenchanted with teaching merely French and Spanish, and I complained to the department head. As a result, during the 1940 calendar year I was allowed to give a lecture course on Rousseau the first semester, and on Voltaire the second semester.

But a lot had happened between 1937 and 1940. On June 6, 1938, I married Elizabeth Bell Kenney in the Boston College chapel. Her father insisted on our being married in a Catholic service, even though he knew I was by this time a lapsed Catholic.

Our marriage was premature. I had met Betty only a few months earlier, and both of us felt that we should wait at least a year, until my financial picture improved. Betty's mother, however, convinced us there was no reason to wait. I was fond of both Mrs. Kenney and her husband, Jack, who was circulation manager of the Hearst newspapers in Boston.

For the previous two years, I had been yearning to write a newspaper column, and Jack Kenney tried to help me. He was a great guy who used to take me to boxing matches at the Boston Garden. He introduced me to Jack Sharkey, the former world heavyweight champion, who owned a bar across the street from the Boston Garden. On the night that Bob Pastor outpointed Tony Shucco, I shook hands with Jack Sharkey, who lived near the reservoir around the corner from the comfortable Kenney home on Lee Street, an attractive Chestnut Hill neighborhood.

It was finally decided that Betty and I would be married. The Kenneys paid all expenses for our honeymoon in France, and Jack Kenney arranged for us to sit at the captain's table on the *Gerolstein*, a one-class German ship. Betty and I stayed in LaBaule, Brittany, with a French family for one month, and later visited the walled city of Saint-Malo, on the Brittany coast. We also visited Quimper, known for its pottery, and Mont Saint-Michel.

On our return trip to Boston, I had a strange experience. At the captain's table I sat next to Monique, a pretty French girl in her early twenties. Monique was on her way to America for the first time, and somehow got the idea that I could help her find a job. We were about halfway across the Atlantic when I returned to my cabin in the early afternoon and saw Monique lying on my bed in her negligee. "I'm sorry, Monique, but I'll have to ask you to leave," I said. I had never thought of her before as being so bold.

In Hanover Betty Kenney got along better with the students than with some members of the faculty. Betty and I were both embarrassed one night at a faculty dinner party when the wife of a French professor asked Betty, "Whom do you prefer, Bach or Brahms?" Betty said nothing, and I didn't have an intelligent answer. I should have said, "Well, I think Bach's music is better than it sounds." I mumbled something inconsequential about our enjoyment of classical music.

I experimented with writing in Hanover during my first two bachelor years, and I was still experimenting during my third year at Dartmouth. Ever since high school days, I had been collecting unusual facts that caught my interest. Voltaire said, "I may not agree with what you say, but I will defend unto the death your right to say it." D'Annunzio once returned to the sender a letter addressed to the "Greatest Poet of Italy," saying he was not the greatest poet of Italy. "I am the greatest poet in the world."

One memorable incident during my marriage to Betty occurred in April 1940, when we stopped at the Hotel Seneca in Rochester, New York, on our way to Buffalo to visit a friend. After dinner we saw a play, *My Dear Children*, starring John Barrymore and his wife, Elaine Barry, who played Cordelia, one of his stage daughters. To appreciate what happened let's dip for a moment into *Damned in Paradise*, John Kobler's biography of John Barrymore.

By April 14, Kobler writes, John and Elaine were barely speaking to each other. During the tour they were traveling in separate Pullman cars and occupying separate hotel rooms. About a week later, Barrymore complained that he wanted Elaine out of the play. On the night train to St. Louis, the next stop, Elaine's mother, Mrs. Jacobs, woke up the producer, Otto Preminger, and said, "If you fire my daughter, I'll tell the reporters that Jack tried to rape me."

When the play opened in St. Louis, Barrymore, near the end of the second act, turned his daughter Cordelia (Elaine Barry) over his knee and spanked her. Kobler writes: "John spanked Elaine hard enough to raise welts. She bit his wrist." The stage manager had no alternative but to fire Elaine.

Betty and I saw the prelude to the altercation. In Rochester, when Barrymore turned Cordelia over his knee to spank her, he walloped her so hard she jumped up and shot a furious look at him. That look was not in the script.

After the show we were waiting in the Hotel Seneca for the elevator to take us up to our room, when Barrymore came into the lobby, following Mrs. Jacobs and Elaine. They obviously were not on speaking terms. John got into the elevator, slouching with his head down, and in the silence that followed, the two ladies looked angry and intense. I can still see Mother Jacobs there, arms folded, with a look of contempt on her face.

Betty and I were amicably divorced in October 1939, but we remained friends who would meet again. I remember how unselfish she was when we divided up our material possessions. She let me keep the car and most of the furniture and books. To this day, I think fondly of Betty Kenney.

After the divorce, time hung heavy when I wasn't in the classroom or playing bridge at the Graduate Club. To banish boredom I sorted my collection of little-known facts into categories. My first story was on people who spent fabulous sums of money on trifles. When I showed it to John Griffin, editor of the *Boston Sunday Post*, he asked if I had any more such material. I did. He paid me fifteen dollars for the first story, and several months later raised the ante to twenty dollars. I wrote under a dozen names.

If the article was about a literary figure, I was Henry Homer; if the subject was science, I was James Sadler; two of the other pseudonyms were Louis Allbright and Calvin Jennison. John Griffin told me I set a record when he published six full-length, illustrated pieces of mine in one Sunday edition, using four different names.

When I read those six pieces I thought I had arrived. To a college instructor earning two thousand dollars a year, six articles at twenty dollars each was a windfall. Things were beginning to click.

I had originally intended to become a full professor, and I knew this would require some scholarly contributions. The first year, I shared an office with Joseph Folger, an assistant professor of Spanish, whom I had met and taken classes with in graduate school. One morning I mentioned my intentions to begin research on a book on the South American novel. Folger said, "Forget a book on South American novelists," while he was retrieving some pipe tobacco I had spilled on the floor of the office. "It would be a thankless job, and besides, there's no money in it."

He dismissed the idea with an emphasis I thought was strange, because later he told a colleague that I was more interested in playing bridge at the Graduate Club than in scholarly research. None of my colleagues in the Romance languages department had ever written anything significant that was original or anything original that was significant. "Why should they expect me to spend my time writing articles or a book about some obscure literary figure who has not yet been written about?" I thought. Primarily because they weren't worth being written about.

Having established myself as a feature writer with the *Boston Sunday Post*, I tried another tack. A weekly newspaper, the *Hanover Gazette*, edited by Earl Hewitt, welcomed the weekly biographical column written by "Jack Henry." My first column was on Napoleon, the second on Theodore Roosevelt.

Early in 1940 I took the train to Boston and slipped past reporters and secretaries into the office of the editor of the now defunct *Boston Transcript*.

There simply were not enough readers to keep the elite paper afloat much longer. A couple of months later a *Transcript* story described what happened:

> On an April morning last spring, a young man walked into the office of Alden Hoag, managing editor of the *Transcript*, with an idea for a short daily column on little-known anecdotes about famous persons.
>   The M.E. read two of the columns.

32

Good stuff, he said, but it lacks something to put it across. Why not write it as a question column and we'll call it "Who Is It?"

It has been a regular feature of the O.E. (opposite editorial) page ever since.

Last week, the young man, John H. Cutler, an instructor at Dartmouth, signed a contract with United Features Syndicate, which services papers throughout the country. The *Transcript* will continue to be the only paper to carry it locally.

The inset sketch for the column was the whimsical work of Paul Sample, still the resident artist at Dartmouth College. An hourglass-shaped dowager is lorgnetting the statue of Moses sculpted by Epstein. A close look makes it clear she is focusing on Moses' genitals! Shocking, really, especially when it is obvious that the lady is a prototype of the Boston dowager who, admitting that Shakespeare was a good writer, said, "I don't suppose there are ten people in Boston who could have written Shakespeare's works."

Years later, when I invited Alden Hoag to the Boston Harvard Club to interview him for my Honey Fitz book, I asked whether he remembered what had caught the dowager's attention.

"Of course," he said. "A lot of Beacon Hill ladies were indignant, I recall, and one canceled her subscription."

A Boston physician wrote the editor a letter asking about the columnist:

We enjoy as a family the "Who Is It?" feature. May we have information as to John H. Cutler, who he is, how come he has such an intimate knowledge of the seamy side of the personalities, is the feature syndicated, and if so, how many papers have it?

S. R. Davis, M.D.

The editor's reply:

John Henry Cutler is an instructor in Spanish at Dartmouth College with a passion for those details about the great that seem to make Napoleon and Jack Johnson of the same biological species. His collection of such details, transcribed from notes on old envelopes, tablecloths, shirt cuffs, and gum wrappers, is rapidly nearing sensational proportions, and he has material to carry on his column for years to come without running out of either notables or scandals. Such is the world's wealth in great men and trivia.

His column is not syndicated, but made its debut and is appearing in somewhat different form in the Hanover paper. But let Mr. Cutler tell Dr.

33

Davis and the numerous other readers who have expressed an interest in "Who Is It?" something of what he is doing.

Here is what I wrote:

Most chronicles of the French Revolution make no mention of the hailstorm—the worst in the memory of man—that occurred a year before the outbreak. King Louis XVI narrowly escaped death as he was returning from a hunt. He little realized that this hailstorm would be instrumental in his being guillotined a few years later.

For crops were ruined, game and cattle killed. A prosperous peasantry— the most prosperous in Europe by the way—faced a winter of starvation. The stage was set for an eruption. The curtain was falling on the divinity of kingship. Materialistic philosophers were pricking the bubbles of tradition. Men like Rousseau had coined symbols to be slung about in crowded Parisian streets. And then it hailed.

But personal glimpses into the boudoirs of the great don't have to be significant to be readable. Isn't history itself a diluted form of gossip? If people can get interested in their neighbor's clothes line why won't they like to hear what an Emperor whispers as he is being crowned? Napoleon turned to his brother and said, "Joseph, if father could only see me now."

In introducing the column, Alden Hoag, editor of the *Transcript*, had noted that it was taking the place of the usual column written by Franklin P. Adams, called "The Conning Tower." F.P.A. was a knight of the Algonquin Round Table.

I was getting into deeper trouble at Dartmouth. Soon after the *Transcript* story, and after I had signed with United Features Syndicate, the *Hanover Gazette* ran another piece on developments:

The humble beginning of "Who Is It?" is of particular interest as a local story. Early in February (1940), Cutler came to the *Gazette* office, told us of his hobby of collecting unusual and little known historical facts and submitted a couple of columns for our use. The earliest was a string of wisecracking facts with little to tie them together and bore the name "Take It or Leave It." We suggested greater unity and together with Dr. Cutler decided that unity would come through making each column a biography of one celebrity.

With this new development worked out on paper, Cutler went to see the managing editor of the *Boston Transcript* last April. . . . The column's popularity grew until one day this fall Cutler returned to the *Gazette* office with a broad grin to explain that he had made the grade. Rights to the column had been bought by United Features Syndicate and it was taking its place across the country with such columns as "My Day" and "Fair Enough."

After four years of college teaching, with raises every year, my salary was flirting with a munificent two thousand dollars. I dreamed of becoming another Westbrook Pegler or Franklin P. Adams.

I cannot describe the glow I felt when I was syndicated. While turning out "Who Is It?" I missed so many bridge sessions at the Graduate Club that Dean Bill asked what had become of me. I spent most of my free time at Baker Memorial Library on the Dartmouth campus. It was fun to skim through biographies—often as many as a half-dozen a day—in search of nuggets of information which, in the aggregate, made an entertaining column, especially if the final clue enabled a reader to identify "Mr. X."

One November day I skimmed through five biographies of Henry Ford looking for items for "Who Is It?" Here are a few of Ford's zany comments:

> I don't like to read books; they muss up my mind.
>
> The best way to remove injustice would be to increase the salaries of Supreme Court judges.
>
> If you will study the history of almost any criminal, you will find he is an inveterate cigarette smoker.
>
> A man learns something even by being hanged.

When, a few months later, I wrote my first "Who Is It?" on Henry Ford, here are some other facts which I included:

> At the age of thirty-six, Ford was making twenty-five dollars a week at the Dry Dock Engine Company. Later he snowballed seventy-five cents, his original capital, into a fortune.
>
> His father wanted him to settle down on the farm, but he was a born tinker. One day he stayed away from Sunday School to show a chum how to take a watch apart and reassemble it. At the age of seventeen he left the farm to work in a factory for two dollars and fifty cents a week. Since that was fifty cents less than his room and board costs, he made up the deficit by repairing watches at night.

The idea of "Who Is It?" was to arouse readers' interest, then make them feel smart by enabling them to guess the identity of Mr. X. Thus the final clue:

He arrived soon after he began manufacturing a 'high-slung, narrow-wheeled and homely machine that had five thousand parts.' He said his customers could have cars painted any color they wanted as long as it was black.

Who Is It?

After spending a few hours in the stacks at Baker Memorial Library, I was heading for the exit when I passed the desk of the librarian.

"Congratulations, John," he said.

I thought he was congratulating me because I had been syndicated. I told him that I doubted the professors in the Romance languages department would have felt the same way.

"When are you leaving?" he asked.

"Leaving?"

"I see you are the first resident of New Hampshire to be drawn for Selective Service."

I was absolutely crushed. Paul was right. My draft number was one. Yes, one.

Not that I was unpatriotic, but the thought of going into military service when we didn't even have a quarrel with Canada or Mexico didn't kindle any ambition of mine to become a hero. I could picture living in a bleak barracks, learning new cuss words. The bell I had rung was beginning to sound like a death knell.

At the time I was drafted, "Who Is It?" was running in several newspapers across the country as well as in the *Boston Transcript*, the *Buffalo Daily News,* and the *Bangor News*. It ran in the *Toledo Blade* and the *Pittsburgh Post-Gazette* until Paul Block, the owner of those two papers, kicked me out for calling Eamon DeValera "a fugitive from a wax museum." But the total income was small, although encouraging for a beginner.

I had been thrilled when the September 1940 cover of *Editor and Publisher* ran a photograph of United Features Syndicate's "fourteen top columnists."

I wondered how Raymond Clapper and David Lloyd George reacted when they saw my photo wedged between theirs on the cover (the arrangement was alphabetical). Journalism makes strange bedfellows.

It was exciting to appear on a magazine cover with such notables as Eleanor Roosevelt, Drew Pearson, Robert Allen, Westbrook Pegler, General Hugh Johnson, and Ernie Pyle.

Before I entered the service Mr. and Mrs. Jack Kenney, who had heard that my column was syndicated, invited me to visit them at the Hotel Shelton in New York City. They must have read about the reception United Features was running on the Starlight Roof of the Waldorf Astoria during my last few days at Dartmouth. After lunching with Betty and the Kenneys, Betty and I walked to the elevator. Betty asked me if I had met anyone I was interested in. I said I had, and that was the last time I ever saw her.

Not all of United's fourteen columnists were at the reception, but I remember meeting a few of them, along with several celebrities. I shook hands with Wendell Willkie, who was running for the presidency against Franklin Delano Roosevelt. It was a big thrill for a fledgling writer.

Chapter Six
IN THE ARMY

Icy dawn streaked over the mountains into Lebanon, New Hampshire, at seven in the morning of that November day when the thirty-eight men chosen to fill the Selective Service quota from District Six in New Hampshire gathered in the draft board office. A motley crew trooped in with bags and bundles. Beneath their chirpiness there was a restrained excitement and eagerness for a new experience.

I half listened glumly as one of my Hanover bridge partners, Professor J. P. Richardson, briefly spoke and, as the name of each draftee was called, shook hands with him. Richardson, leaning on his crutches, told us he hoped we would look back on the year of army training as one of the most valuable and pleasant years of our lives. While he talked I kept thinking of an incident he had once mentioned at the bridge table. During the Sacco-Vanzetti trial, at a Dartmouth football game, he sat within earshot of Judge Webster Thayer, who presided at one trial. He remembered hearing the judge say he would "fix those Communist sons of bitches." I could have done a "Who Is It?" on Thayer, I vaguely thought, hoping that the sixty columns I had sent the syndicate would last long enough to give me time to keep the column going. It would be tough, since I couldn't take Baker Memorial Library with me.

We walked out of the draft board office, past firemen lined up along the walk leading to the bus, which was to take us to the induction station in Manchester, New Hampshire. The firefighters clapped us on the back and wished us luck.

"A Dartmouth college instructor, a postmaster, and a member of the second Byrd Antarctic expedition were among the sixty-three selectees sworn into the Army of the United States yesterday at the New Hampshire induction station," a Manchester newspaper reported. I skipped down to a paragraph where I was mentioned:

> Demonstrating that the draft is no respecter of worldly position, Wednesday's call to the colors brought Dr. John H. Cutler, instructor in French and Spanish at Dartmouth, to the armory for induction. Cutler, the

most interesting personality in the draft to date, is a graduate of Harvard in the class of 1932 and received a Ph.D. degree from Harvard in 1936. . . . The Dartmouth instructor is a native of Boston and is thirty years old. In addition to teaching, he recently signed a contract with United Features, which now syndicates a column by him reaching a million and a half readers.

We decamped at Fort Devens that night. I wished I had sat next to Edward L. Moody of Tamworth, New Hampshire, who had driven a dog sled for the second Byrd Antarctic expedition. He said he hoped the experience would eventually lead him to an assignment with the newly formed Alaskan division of the Army. Moody, I learned, had been in the Antarctic from 1933 to 1935 and took part in the dangerous task of mapping out locations for the various advance bases established by the expedition. With his dog team, he found and marked the trails which were later followed by tractors bearing equipment. Moody also took movies for Paramount and assisted the scientists who made seismographic recordings of glacial ice movements. More recently, Moody had worked for the U.S. Forest Service. He was twenty-nine, unmarried, and as far as I was concerned, the most interesting personality in the draft to date.

At Fort Devens I soon learned that a college teacher or a syndicated journalist didn't impress Army corporals. In the Army barracks where the inductees were quartered, I was almost deafened and nauseated by the vulgar talk that included one favorite chant that was repeated over and over: "Blow it out your asshole."

One gloomy morning at two, a lanky corporal barged into the barracks and yelled, "Drop your cocks and grab your socks." We were then taken down to a medical office to be inspected in the nude to see if any of us had contacted a venereal disease.

After three weeks of intensive training at Fort Devens it was to bed by nine and up for reveille at quarter of six. One afternoon, just after we had received Army fatigues, and just before I could get to a tailor to have my pants shortened by about five inches, a Wellesley graduate whom I had been dating on my occasional trips to Boston made a surprise visit. Her laughter when she saw me in the Army fatigues was easy to understand. I was dangling in my oversized uniform, which would have fit my cousin Finton.

After taking the Army intelligence exam, the four of us who had the highest grades were assigned to the headquarters company of the Sixth Army Corps in the old Hope High School in Providence, Rhode Island. Two of the three selectees were Yale students and the fourth was a Brown graduate, who was a lawyer. I was assigned to GII (military intelligence).

Since I was the first college instructor to be drafted—the first in New England anyway—I suddenly found myself a curio. The *Providence Journal* ran a photo of me sitting in a barber's chair getting a haircut in Providence.

While stationed in Providence, I launched a mimeographed newspaper I named the *Sixth Army Corps Courier*, as an antidote to monotony. The West Point Captain in charge of company discipline took a dim view of the *Courier*, especially when the *Providence Journal* noted that this "sassy Army publication occasionally poked fun at high brass, and contained one editorial citing the futility of war." Under a subhead, "All in Fun," the *Journal* added:

> More adult than most publications of the sort, this new weekly mimeographed newspaper is alert and keen and lively in flavor, and it does not hesitate to give Army bigwigs a little ribbing.

Our drill sergeant was a tough Irishman with a brogue thicker than a Dairy Queen frappe. He was so ill-tempered I used him as a whipping boy in the *Courier*, referring to him always as "Black Mac." When the West Pointer rebuked me for trying to undermine his discipline, I renamed my friend "Sergeant MacBlack."

One morning when the captain came in to inspect our quarters, I was sitting on my footlocker, and when I failed to rise and give him the proper salute, he put me on kitchen patrol for a week. (I hadn't really meant to be disrespectful. I was merely a sloppy soldier.) Sergeant MacBlack rubbed his hands together gleefully when I reported to the galley. He gave me the toughest assignments available. I didn't mind peeling hundred-pound bags of potatoes, but almost gagged when he made me clean out the charnel shed where meat bones were kept in barrels.

When I returned to the more routine life of a private first class I was more discreet when I handed Mac the hot end of the poker. I wrote of a mythical heavy-bearded soldier who deserted from the Irish Republican Army during the 1916 Easter Rebellion in Ireland. I was glad they didn't teach Irish history at West Point.

Meanwhile, the captain's displeasure was unfailingly consistent. One day I went into his office to ask for a weekend pass. The sergeant, whose desk was in the front of the room, asked me why. "Private Cutler is tired," I said. I heard the captain's voice from the other end of the office.

"Give that guy a pass and get him out of here."

Actually, I liked the captain, and I felt bad later when I heard he was killed in action in the European theater.

On one of my leaves, in the spring of 1941, I was invited to a Saturday night party given by Betty Hatch, who lived with two college friends at 193 Beacon Street, in Boston. During the evening she said she wanted me to meet a girl who was the niece of Amie Sumner of Canton, Massachusetts. Betty was Amie's goddaughter.

"John, I have finally met a girl whom I know you'll like. Her name is Roberta Rand Sumner, and she lives at 18 Brimmer Street, on Beacon Hill, right across the street from Rear Admiral Richard Byrd."

"She sounds great," I said. "Any chance of meeting her tonight?"

"Wait until your next leave," Betty said. "I don't know her phone number. I'll have the number next time you come home. I can get it from Aunt Amie, who is living on Pinckney Street with her Aunt May Sumner."

"I may not get another leave for a month," I said. "Let's call Aunt Amie right now."

"I don't know her number either," Betty said.

"I'll call a cab," I said, "and we can drive to Aunt Amie's house and then to 18 Brimmer on a chance that Roberta may be home."

"Well, it's worth a try. She's the most gorgeous blonde I've ever met."

It was around 9 P.M. when we rang the bell at 18 Brimmer. Betty Hatch and her date, John McDonald, whom I had met a few years earlier when he was a student at Dartmouth College, asked to see Roberta Sumner. We could hear the landlady, Mrs. Hindley, going to Roberta's room.

"You have callers, Miss Sumner."

We were ushered into a large room with windows overlooking a courtyard. There was a tiny kitchen adjoining the living room. We sat down. After casual conversation, Roberta apologized for not having any refreshments to offer us.

I suggested that we walk down to Charles Street to get some. It was raining slightly as we headed for a liquor store and bought a bottle of rum. Back in her room, Roberta served rum and Coke. Immediately struck by her beauty, I asked her about herself. During the conversation she said, "My mother is writing a book which has several murders in it." I thought she sounded naive. Roberta told me she was working at the Telepix Theatre, in the Park Square Building, as second in command to the manager, for thirteen dollars a week.

When I asked how she could live on thirteen dollars a week, she said her Aunty May had given her a charge account at S. S. Pierce, the retail store on Tremont Street. Later in the evening, Betty and her friend John spoke about going to New Hampshire some weekend, for skiing. Roberta said she loved to ski. I didn't let her know that I had never done it. It was almost 11 P.M. when I heard a honking outside. It was the staff sergeant who had come to pick me up to drive back to the Sixth Army Corps in Providence. Betty and her date left, and I tried to kiss Roberta goodnight. She pushed me away. The honking continued. Mrs. Hindley came into the room and said, "You must leave at once, it is past eleven." Apparently it was the city rule that men must not be in a single girl's room after eleven. I had tried to hide in the kitchen, intending to try once more to kiss Roberta before I left, but Mrs. Hindley caught me. As I left I asked Roberta, "Will you call me?" I gave her the phone number of the Providence base.

Several days after that, Roberta told me later, she and Aunt Amie were walking across the Boston Common when Roberta told her aunt, "I don't think John Cutler is so great. I met him recently, and I wasn't overly impressed." Aunt Amie had told her earlier that she wished she could meet a man like John Cutler, "a man about town," as she put it. Aunt Amie had told Roberta that I was about to propose to Kitty, the daughter of a Smith College classmate of hers, Ruth McCartney. (I had dated Kitty once and had no intention of proposing to her or anyone else at that time.) Roberta's aunt noticed that she was carrying a copy of the previous night's *Boston Evening Transcript*. She said, "Oh, you want to read John Cutler's column, is that it?" Roberta said she had merely been curious about "Who Is It?" and wanted to read it. It was a brief biography of Cleopatra.

Weeks passed in Providence, and I could not get Bobbie Sumner out of my mind. She was not only beautiful but also intelligent. Her mother was a novelist, Cid Ricketts Sumner, who a few years earlier had divorced Dr. James B. Sumner, a Cornell University biochemist. In 1946 Dr. Sumner would receive a Nobel Prize for isolating the first enzyme. I had by this time learned that Bobbie had done some acting while at Cornell, and had played ingenue and leading roles in summer theater before we met.

But I was disappointed. I had asked Bobbie to call me, and as the days went by she didn't phone. It was difficult for me to call from the Army base, with no telephones accessible. The next time I got leave, I called her from a telephone booth in Boston and asked why she hadn't called me.

"I didn't see why I should," she said. Her tone chilled me, and I was about to hang up when I suddenly said, "I don't suppose you'd like to have dinner with me tonight?" A pause that seemed to last for seconds. "Why, I think that would be very nice."

We drove in her car to the Brunswick Casino, on Tremont Street, and dined and danced. At the end of the evening, when she went to get her wrap from the cloak room, I noticed a piano in the foyer. By this time my skill had deteriorated, but I still remembered a few snatches of some classics. I sat down and played bits of pieces I remembered from my long-ago lessons—a passage from Chopin's Nocturne, and another piece from Rachmaninoff's Concerto in C-sharp Minor. I was still playing the concerto when Bobbie returned, visibly impressed by my performance, which was actually a hoax. From that moment, she seemed to thaw out, and every time I came to Boston I had a date with her. Finally, she let me kiss her, and that was the beginning of a romance that has lasted to this day. It was by far the best thing that ever happened to me. We were married in May of 1941.

Meanwhile, I reported directly to Colonel Gallison, a brilliant officer who was in charge of military intelligence for the Sixth Army Corps, which was headed by Major General Karl Truesdell.

It was a lucky day when Gallison asked me to write a speech for Major General Truesdell. That assignment changed the course of my life.

I kept hounding Gallison to the point where he practically told me to shut up. I would have to wait for a Red Cross check to be sure I was married, he said. Late that same day I jumped out a first-floor window at Hope High and walked down to the Red Cross office in Providence. It took some blarney to convince the woman in charge that I couldn't wait until one of her field representatives checked me out. Reluctantly, she made a few phone calls and made the necessary arrangements.

Three days later Gallison called me into his office and handed me a letter from the Red Cross. "What did I tell you, Cutler? I told you everything would work out."

If I hadn't jumped out the window that morning I never would have made the early September deadline that my language department had given me. As it was, I barely made it.

When I returned to my teaching duties, still an instructor, I found that things had changed. Some of my colleagues didn't greet me with out-stretched arms. Also, I no longer had any enthusiasm for being a professor. I was more determined than ever to stay in the writing business, even though my "Who Is It?" was losing circulation, primarily because I didn't have access to a library while serving in the Army. Originally, the column had appeared in about fifteen newspapers around the country.

Bobbie and I had rented a modest two-bedroom house in Hanover near the football stadium, but she didn't join me until the furniture her Aunt May had given us arrived a couple of weeks later. I picked up a bed, a wing chair (for three dollars), some Chelsea ware, and a desk, a swivel chair, and a typewriter.

With classes just getting under way and little to do, I felt more lonely than ever while waiting for Bobbie to join me.

One rainy afternoon I sat down at the typewriter in the empty house and pounded out all the brain teasers I remembered from my youth. Example: A big Indian and a little Indian are walking down a path. The little Indian is the big Indian's son, but the big Indian is not the little Indian's father. Who is it? The answer, of course, is "his mother." None of my brainteasers was original, but it was the first time twenty had been assembled in one quiz. The title was, "So You Think You're Clever!" I sent them to *American* magazine and received a check for a hundred dollars. In November, Mabel Harding, an editor of *American,* asked if I had any more teasers. I didn't, but using a trap quiz formula I developed, I made some up. This time the magazine called the quiz "Twenty Twizzlers." Miss Harding encouraged me to keep sending twizzlers.

Then came Pearl Harbor, and I was ordered to report for Army duty. I reached for a Navy commission while the Army reached for Private First Class John Cutler. A slight hitch developed when the Navy refused to hand me a commission of lieutenant (junior grade) until the Army gave me discharge papers. The officer at Army headquarters nodded sympathetically when I told him this.

"We'd like to help you out," he said, "but we can't give you your discharge papers until you show us your commission."

This interservice bickering was just getting into gear when the Navy solved the dilemma. A Navy commander drove me to Army headquarters. When he showed a colonel the certificate, I received my discharge papers.

"This is the first time this has happened in our district," the colonel said. The commander agreed.

Chapter Seven
IN THE NAVY

After taking a two-month indoctrination course at Harvard, we were asked to name, in order of preference, the locale of our next tour of duty. I listed sea duty, West Coast, and East Coast, in that order. I was sent instead to a Navy-sponsored school in Chicago to take a one-month course designed to show teachers how to teach. Some of us college teachers concluded that our young instructor had apparently never taught a class before, and many of us considered the course a joke. The instructor took a dim view of a college professor of English, who sat on one side of the classroom, and of me sitting on the other side, because of the silly questions we kept asking to embarrass him. Our questions were contrived, and we had plenty of allies. Came the time when each of us had to give a sample lecture. A few of the co-conspirators dared me to burlesque my lecture on helicopters, and since we knew we weren't going to be graded, I did precisely that. The instructor was not amused when I mentioned the center of gravity and the center of levity. When I spoke of thermal heat, one of the co-conspirators raised his hand.

"Is that word 'thermal' in any way connected with thermos bottle?"

And, as expected, after my "lecture," the instructor told the class how inferior mine was.

After Chicago the Navy sent me to Olathe, Kansas, exactly seven miles from the geographical center of the United States. Thus, my first naval engagement was on a mid-western prairie.

In Olathe I served as battalion commander, then as regimental commander. Navy fliers trained by our flight instructors went from our Olathe Naval Air Station for advance training to bases in Pensacola, Florida, and Corpus Christi, Texas. In Olathe I was also in charge of all official Navy publications, which helped me get similar assignments later.

Then came another exciting day. During all this time *American* magazine had been publishing "Twenty Twizzlers" on a bimonthly basis. Meanwhile, *Reader's Digest* had reprinted "So You Think You're Clever!", paying me $375, or almost four times the original payment by *American* magazine. Later *Reader's Digest* sent me a carton of fan mail, which I have never found time to finish reading.

One success led to another. After the *Digest* reprint, King Features syndicated my brain teasers, and this feature proved much more lucrative than "Who Is It?" King Features paid me not only fifty dollars a week for about a dozen trap teasers, but I also received fifty percent of the proceeds the syndicate received from papers in which the quizzlers appeared later.

During World War II the *London Daily Mirror* bought some of the teasers from King Features and published them to amuse their readers while they were in the bomb shelter. In the introduction to the book, which was published in 1944 by the Hearst Corporation, Clark Kinnaird said that if I had lived in medieval times I might have undergone the direst martyrdom for making the heaviest facts of life light—and fun to know. But, living in more enlightened times, the only torture I must suffer for making Socratean logic, differential calculus, and such, popular elements of an old parlor game, is receiving stacks of mail from argumentative strangers.

Bobbie and I spent a happy year in Olathe, where we made many friends. One was Lawrence Ely, a lawyer who moved to Anchorage, Alaska, after the war. Larry Ely was a former All-American center for the University of Nebraska. We heard from him every Christmas until his recent death. In Olathe, while I was in charge of the regiment, Larry headed the athletic program.

Another old friend was Captain Alan Grinsted, USNR, a former professor of psychology who stayed in the Navy after the war. In 1975 Alan and his wife, Betty, drove into our driveway in Duxbury in their trailer. They are now living in Pensacola, Florida.

While in Kansas I had my first look at America's bread basket. One day Commander Gordon ("Mickey") Cochrane, of the Baseball Hall of Fame, piloted a plane that took us over the flooded plains of Nebraska, where we saw houses and barns completely submerged. I was invited by Captain Dixie Kiefer, the air-base commander, who was captain of the USS *Yorktown* when it was torpedoed by the Japanese in the Pacific. At the time the *Yorktown* was in drydock for repairs.

By the time I went to Brazil I had two syndicated columns going and had written a trunkful of features for the *Boston Sunday Post*.

Chapter Eight
THE BRAZILIAN SCENE

By 1941 Brazil had become a major factor in World War II. President Franklin Delano Roosevelt instructed U.S. Ambassador Jefferson Caffery in Rio de Janeiro to secure air bases from Brazil, for it was clear that Brazilian cooperation was vital to winning the war.

We needed the Belem-Natal "Corridor to Victory" to invade North Africa, Sicily, and Italy, for otherwise Germany might have taken the Suez Canal and fused a union with Japan.

"The plain truth is," said Cordell Hull, "that without this cooperation the course of war in highly essential areas might have been different. For example, consider the situation in the Near East. When Rommel was hammering at the gates of Egypt, it was planes and light tanks and ammunition ferried by northeastern Brazil that helped turn the tide. The value to our cause of these Brazilian airports, and of the cooperation of the Brazilian Army and Navy, cannot be overstated."

Axis ships in ports from Recife to Santos, ready at any time to escape the weak British blockade, were interned. At the embassy's request Brazil stamped out espionage. In March 1942, forty members of Nazi espionage rings, who had been transmitting information to Germany by clandestine radio stations, were intercepted. On July 4, 1942, 383 Japanese diplomats were shipped out on the USS *Gripsholm*, going from Rio de Janeiro to an African exchange port.

The South Atlantic was no longer a happy hunting ground for Nazi submarines, and Hitler's hope of controlling the supply routes was coming to a close.

Topside in the Navy Administration Building at Recife, headquarters and nerve center of the Fourth Fleet, there was a mural in the Officers' Club depicting Vice Admiral Jonas Ingram, commander of the "Fighting Fourth Fleet," kicking Nazi U-boats out of the blue-green waters of the South Atlantic. When the prophetic mural was painted, even optimists dared not hope that the victory over German submarines and surface raiders would be so complete.

Until this time American shipping was sunk almost as fast as it could

47

be built. President Roosevelt and Winston Churchill had sounded grave warnings.

Suddenly the pendulum swung. The convoy system was rapidly improving and U.S. fleet airwings had by 1943 gained indisputable air mastery in both the North and South Atlantic. Flight Air Wing Sixteen played a big role in South Atlantic aerial warfare.

On June 16, 1943, five Catalinas of VP94 reached Belem under the command of Lt. Commander Joseph Tibbetts. At the same time the Headquarters Squadron Detachment was set up with Lieutenant Roy Baske as officer-in-charge. Baske arrived in Belem with his administrative officer, Lieutenant Howard Hart, and machinist Clarence Amos. Most of the maintenance duties fell on the shoulders of Baske and Amos.

Until the first of September 1943, when two bachelor officers' quarters (BOQs) in Belem were completed, Navy personnel occupied Army barracks across the air field. Office buildings, the recreation hall, the Officers' Club, and the dispensary were not ready for use when, on April 16, 1943, I became administrative officer of the Headquarters Squadron (usually called Hedron) of Flight Air Wing Sixteen at its Belem Base. I succeeded Lieutenant Howard Hart, who was transferred to the USS *Barnegat*. My office was in a tent whose floor was flooded precisely at two o'clock every afternoon under a torrential downpour. The daily rains fall so regularly in Belem that it is customary to make exact appointments "after the showers." Showers? No, torrents. But it was so exciting to see lizards, some a foot long, that sought sanctuary in my tent when the rains came.

Belem offered the most impressive and memorable sight of all. As one might expect from a city located in the Amazon region, Belem abounded in multicolored birds, giant butterflies, and wildlife of every description.

We got used to seeing honey bears, sloths, and all kinds of monkeys and snakes, including giant anacondas. One day a Brazilian, dressed only in a loincloth, brought to the base a pregnant anaconda, which he found in the Amazonian Basin about seventy miles away. We watched him kill it, hang it up on a tree branch, and skin it. He sold the skin to an enlisted man for two dollars and fifty cents. An attempt to keep four baby anacondas alive in our dispensary failed.

One officer had a pet ocelot, a pocket edition of a jaguar, and an Army private kept a three-toed sloth in his barracks.

We often visited the jungle in epitome in the famous Belem zoo. There one could see a fifteen-foot, man-eating *jacare* (it resembles an alligator), anacondas, boa constrictors, black panthers, snarling wild boars, tapirs, treacherous emus (they resemble storks), with a sign on the enclosure marked *perigo* (dangerous). And there were birds and anteaters of every description.

High in the wired-in aviary was the arrogant *gaviao*, the large eagle of South America. They looked vicious, perched above lesser winged creatures—even more vicious when they glared at you as they clawed and guttled chunks of raw meat. An ordinary meal for them might be a ten-pound roast. The polychrome collection of parrots, macaws, and other birds, all from the Amazonian basin, would seem unreal in a technicolor production or a Walt Disney animated cartoon.

In the zoo's aquarium was our old friend, the saw-toothed piranha, a deadly creature capable of tearing chunks out of the flesh of swimming animals. We saw the power of those ugly teeth when the warden tossed them fistfuls of hamburger. Also on exhibition was the carnivorous fish called *candiru*. This capsule of death, about as long as a man's forearm, is also deadlier than any toothsome shark.

To relax in Belem we often went shopping and spent the evening in a casino at a time when gambling was legal in Brazil. The first time I played baccarat, I won $250 and thought I had finally found a way to make easy money. One night, after the bank lost fourteen times in a row, I figured it was time for me to jump in. I lost on every deal, and from that night on, I never once beat the bank. Bobbie rebuked me for gambling and refused to send any more of the proceeds from my brain teasers and my other syndicated column, "Who Is It?"

Often the officers stationed at Belem played bridge. One night one of my opponents was Lieutenant Ted Stritter. We all grieved when he was lost the following day while on night convoy coverage. All available planes, including a Brazilian Catalina, three cub planes, and a blimp, combed land and sea for six days. All pilots and crews had turned to the Hedron skipper, including Lieutenant Roy Baske. Navy planes flew over half a million miles seeking a trace of the plane. All that was ever found was a damaged pontoon and some floating parts in the Amazon River.

With Stritter were two other officers. The plane communicated with the base at Belem ten minutes after taking off in a radio check, the last contact. Meanwhile, Flight Air Wing Sixteen made its biggest submarine kills during the summer of 1943.

I was shopping one day with an ensign in the city of Belem when we entered a jewelry store. An attractive senhorita waited on us. My friend told me to ask her if she could have dinner with him some evening. I conveyed the message to the young lady, adding that my friend was known as a wolf (lobo). Her disdainful look puzzled the ensign until I explained what I had said. We tried again, this time seriously, but the answer was still negative.

My second assignment in Brazil was as officer in charge of Hedron at the seaplane base in Aratu, a hamlet about twenty-five miles from El Salvador, better known as Bahia, a city with a population at the time of over half a million. Aratu's scenery entranced me.

As we flew into Bahia I could see the majestic skyline ridged with church steeples and flaunting cupolas against the backdrop of orange and violet clouds spinning tangles against a pure blue sky. I was equally impressed the first time I drove a jeep into Aratu.

In a letter to Bobbie, I wrote:

> I left the States on August 11 and have been in the lush lush land of grow grow ever since. The chief censor, who is myself, won't let me tell you where we are, but in my present location I wouldn't need a speedy magic carpet to get to Rio de Janeiro in a hurry. I am commanding officer of a Hedron detachment, having only recently been promoted. The base is a garden spot of South America, and so strongly resembles my own Duxbury and its bay that I am overcome with nostalgia.

Aratu was a companion operational center to the land base at Ipitanga. Traveling by jeep from Ipitanga along winding steeps and dusty roads, I felt as if I was in Wonderland. I was impressed by the rolling greenery, and for the first time I had a feeling of the proximity of the jungle, especially when two spider monkeys—those tiny gnomes with human faces—scampered off the road, or when macaws and other bright-plumaged birds flitted from bough to bough in a symphony of sound and color. Life seemed so placid, I thought as we drove along. A couple of white Navy planes above looked like lazy giant dragonflies. The twisting road leading into the Aratu seaplane base was banked with red clay and fringed with banana shrubs and palm trees. I saw mud huts with palm-thatched roofs, and near one jungle dwelling, a group of naked children were playing. A woman, balancing a crate of vegetables on her head, was smoking a clay pipe, and behind her comfortably sitting on a donkey was her unchivalrous husband. Man was boss in Brazil.

We passed a deserted monastery tucked into a hillside. I learned later that this monastery had once been occupied by monks who were in cahoots with the Nazis. When a secret short-wave radio set was found, the monks were banished.

You continue along a road that is getting rougher, for the rain has washed away part of it. In cultivated areas you see odd scarecrows. I saw an old-fashioned chamberpot placed on a stick alongside an oxhorn on a stick. Suddenly you see a kind of fairy castle standing out in bold white contrast against the green matted jungle. You are looking at the residence of the Fratelli Vita family, makers of world-famous cut glass and crystal. The officer in the jeep told me to be sure to visit the Fratelli Vita factory in Bahia, where exquisite glassware is manufactured from rock crystal.

Then abruptly I saw the seaplane base, cupped among high red cliffs mantled in green. Such color contrast! Aratu was the most compact base I ever saw in Brazil. It is on the tip of a peninsula jutting into a green-blue bay with white sandy beaches.

A sharp turn to the left, up a steep hill, and we were beside one of three BOQs; I was spellbound by the awesome—yes, stupendous—panorama and the sight of one of the world's most beautiful bays.

Near the laundry shack on the base, about a hundred native women gathered around dawn every morning to collect and return laundry. Washerwomen would squat by the creek, lay garments over a boulder, lather them with soap and pound the fabric with a rock in a vigorous massage. After rinsing, they wring the clothes out by hand, then beat them against the rocks before spreading them to dry on the grass.

From our base at night we often saw fires burning in the hills. Almost every night in the outlying districts voodoo cults held *festas* (sessions), and it was eerie to hear the drums throbbing in the tropical darkness.

A familiar sight in the inland waters of Bahia Bay were natives sailing in dugout canoes called *pirogues*. These are sturdy craft, hewn out of huge tree trunks found in the Amazonian Basin. One afternoon my roommate, a physician, and I cruised in a Higgins boat to Mare Island, where there was a settlement, including a church and schoolhouse. As we were about to leave around dusk, our boat was grounded. There was nothing to do but leave it there until high tide, which was just before midnight. Two natives, wearing loincloths, took us back to Aratu in a *pirogue* for sixty milreis (three dollars). Since *pirogues* have no centerboard, there seems to be no reason for their not rolling over. One of the natives leaned far outboard to keep our *pirogue* from capsizing.

Equally picturesque are the *jangadas*, common along the Recife shores. Eleanor Roosevelt sent a model of a *jangada* to the President for his

Hyde Park collection of oddities. A *jangada* is a primitive boat adopted from the Indians (as is the *pirogue*), consisting of five to nine logs of light wood.

In Aratu, personnel also kept jungle pets. One was a woolly monkey christened Joe, another a four-foot boa constrictor, which Lieutenant "Raymond Ditmars" Finley, the squadron naturalist, kept coiled in a gallon mayonnaise jar. It was amusing to watch Joe scamper up into the rafters when the boa constrictor slithered around the deck. Joe, incidentally, enjoyed nibbling such delicacies as butterflies with a wing spread of six inches.

The enlisted men based at Aratu, Brazil, also a short jeep ride from El Salvador, killed a few deadly coral snakes and mounted a couple of large hairy tarantulas they caught snooping. These large tarantulas were the horrors. At Aratu I had the eerie sensation of having my leather shoe sole bitten by the teeth of a barracuda which became wedged between the planks of a boat pier. The fish, a good three feet long, had a savage gleam in its eyes, and its bite was powerful enough to be felt through leather soles.

Lt. Commander C. Fink Fischer, commanding a marine squadron at Aratu, had a strange experience one sunlit afternoon when a black buzzard crashed through the windshield of his giant plane as it dived for a practice bombing run. A passenger in the cockpit was splattered with blood. These black vultures are scavengers, and they are as common on the streets of Brazilian cities as pigeons are on Boston Common. Their larger cousins, the condors, which have wingspreads of up to twelve feet, are capable of wrecking planes in head-on collisions.

One incident involved a provost marshal named Commander Rich, a former police chief in Richmond, Virginia. He got into so much trouble because of his heavy drinking that he was sent home a couple of months after the run-in I had with him. I take the blame for the incident that took place at our favorite watering spot, the Palace Hotel in Bahia.

One night Lieutenant George Evans, our supply officer and a classmate of mine at Harvard, and I were having a postprandial brandy when Rich walked in. There was a familiar jingle we had often heard: "Commander Rich is a son of a bitch."

"There he is now," Evans said.

Evans, whom I had never met at Harvard, often visited Bobbie and me after the war, and we enjoyed his sense of humor. "Someone ought to tell that guy off," he said that night. By this time we were feeling quite convivial. In any case, I was too quick to oblige. I went to his table, sat down, and asked if he was Commander Rich.

"Yes, and so what?"

"Well, I understand you're a son of a bitch."

He was on his feet, snarling behind a pointed finger. "Arrest that man," he told his aide, who shrugged in embarrassment when I suggested that he arrest Rich because "he was a disgrace to the Navy." Although the aide talked him out of arresting me, Rich, in his stupor, sent a telegram to the Aratu base, addressed to no one in particular. The next morning I read it. "If Lieutenant John Cutler comes to Bahia he will be arrested on sight."

A few days later Captain Rosmore Lyon, commanding officer of Flight Air Wing Sixteen, brought Vice Admiral P. N. L. Bellinger to Aratu. After they inspected the personnel, Bellinger told me he would like to visit the Fratelli Vita plant. He seemed so friendly I told him about the confrontation at the Palace Hotel. He laughed it off and made no comment.

At this time I came close to being shipped out of Aratu. Word of the Palace Hotel affair got to Commander Lowell Williams, who summoned me to Recife and told me my next tour of duty would be at Fernando Noronha, the volcanic outcrop jutting out of the Atlantic about three hundred miles east of Recife.

Six miles long and almost two wide, Fernando Noronha was the site of a Brazilian penal colony because of its inaccessibility. Political prisoners and dangerous criminals confined there would bring their wives and were allowed to roam the island at will. It was so bleak at this outpost that military personnel stationed there during World War II were rotated in four-month intervals.

Convicts were assigned to kill rats that were swarming over the island, each required to kill a certain number every day. I had flown into Fernando once, when I learned there was little diversion there. In the same plane that flew me into Fernando was a USO troupe, including Frances Williams, a former star of George White's "Scandals." As we sat around a table in the Officers' Club, Frances recalled her stage experiences and the days when she roomed with Joan Crawford. There she was—a former celebrity on Broadway—sitting in a club perched on a rock on the ragged edge of nowhere.

Military personnel fished for tuna and barracuda, and dove-shooting was popular. At low tide it was easy to snare huge crabs and a kind of lobster called *langosto*. There were still plenty of rats—so many, in fact, that the boys had to use mosquito bars to keep them from falling on them from the rafters. Later a planeload of cats was flown in to get rid of some of them. At this time Commander Williams was living with Captain Lyon and Lt. Commander Jack Appleby in "Skunk Ranch." In the Navy Administration

Building in downtown Recife, known as City Hall, Vice Admiral Ingram was housed on the sixth floor, and Captain Lyon and Commander Williams one floor below. City Hall was also the home of the *South Atlantic News*, which had a circulation of six thousand.

Skunk Ranch was just across the street from Boa Viagem, a suburb of Recife. Next door to Skunk Ranch was the "Bat House," where Al McCoy, then physical director of the Fourth Fleet, lived with two other officers. Al invited me to stay with them while I was waiting to be flown to Fernando Noronha. There were dozens of bats in the attic, and in their nightly excursions they flew out of a hole in the window screen of my bedroom.

While living at the Bat House we occasionally saw an American soldier bring a mountain lion on a leash down to the beach. This monster, which was tame enough to be stroked, was about six feet long and looked ferocious. It was a sight when the soldier tugged at the leash in an effort to draw the reluctant puma into the surf.

It was time for another bold move. One night during cocktail hour, when I judged Commander Williams to be sufficiently relaxed, I suggested that Flight Air Wing Sixteen deserved to be written up, and that I'd like the job.

"Not a bad idea," he said. So instead of chasing rats on a penal colony on Fernando Noronha I became the official historian of Flight Air Wing Sixteen.

Chapter Nine
ROVING HISTORIAN

On July 9, 1943, the Administrative Command of Flight Air Wing Sixteen moved from Natal to Recife, which succeeded Natal as the headquarters of the Wing.

Before I arrived in Recife, late in 1943, Eleanor Roosevelt had stopped at the base after her tour of the Caribbean Command, Belem, and Natal. She had this message for the Fourth Fleet:

> The president, your commander-in-chief, asked me to come down to the area and gave me a message for all the officers and men of the armed service here. Many of you have been here as long as the men have been in the southwest Pacific and in other war areas. The president knows that you must be anxious to get home, and to be where the war seems more active, but he wants you to feel and to know that he watches what you are doing and what others are doing all over the world, day by day.

Motion picture stars and stage celebrities appeared from time to time at Brazilian bases. Among them were Joel McCrea, Joe E. Brown, Frederick March, and Ilona Massey. McCrea arrived in Recife after a tour of service facilities in Africa.

The most popular star was Ilona Massey, whose looks and voice had somehow escaped full exploitation by Hollywood producers, according to Walter Winchell. She toured the facilities in the South Atlantic area, including Aratu, when I was officer in charge of Hedron.

At Aratu, Ilona made the mistake of autographing a card containing the names of enlisted men. She was informed that her signature made her a member of the platoon and that it was her duty to fall out for reveille.

"Of course," she said. "I will be more than glad to attend such a gathering."

Next morning at six o'clock all hands were on deck to behold Ilona in all her blonde glory. After muster she joined the enlisted men for chow at the mess hall.

I wasn't the only officer who fell in love with Ilona.

Writing the *History of Flight Airwing Sixteen* was a dream assignment with some light moments. I mentioned one radio report that came in from a Navy flier: "Sighted sub. Am attacking. Dropped four bombs. All exploded. Dead whale."

I wrote of another Navy pilot who retrieved bombs dropped by a Ventura plane: "He hired an entire railroad and fifteen Brazilian railroad employees for ten dollars."

It was a narrow gauge railroad with flat cars propelled by poling.

As historian, I interviewed Navy fliers who helped eliminate Nazi U-boats as a major threat to shipping in the South Atlantic in the Navy's smashing victory as the Wing teamed with the surface power of the Fourth Fleet. Captain Rosmore Lyon's Air Wing added a glowing chapter to the history of naval aviation.

Occasionally I flew with the pilots on practice runs, and it was exciting to see them drop an emerald green slick on the ocean, then dive bomb the simulated submarine.

I also interviewed Lt. Commander Richard Craig, who was on night coverage on the convoy of fifty-six ships escorting Winston Churchill to his rendezvous with President Roosevelt in the North Atlantic. When Craig dropped to an altitude of five hundred feet through a cloud opening, he spotted the convoy just below him. He flew off in a hurry, for there was no time for recognition signals, and he might easily have been shot down.

Another flier I wrote up was Danny Deibler, who, on September 21, 1943, flew through all four seasons as he crossed and recrossed the equator.

One story I wrote was about Lieutenant Samuel Pryor, who was adrift on a lifecraft for seven days in the South Atlantic after he was forced to ditch his PBY. He and four members of his crew, barely surviving, were delirious when they stumbled ashore. During my interview with Pryor in Natal, he said they couldn't catch a single fish. To keep alive, they ate three sea gulls, gagging during the process. "They tasted like leather," Pryor said. They did, however, see plenty of fish, including sharks. The most impressive incident? One afternoon they saw a stingray stun into submission and devour an eight-inch fish that had risen out of water in an effort to escape.

I was still living at the Bat House with Al McCoy, Lieutenant Lester Berger, and Lieutenant Charles Smith, when on February 15, 1944, Flight Air Wing Sixteen marked its first annual anniversary with a gala party held next door at Skunk Ranch (or the Lion's Den). Music for the party was provided by the Southern Crusaders and liquor flowed freely as officers and guests danced to its rhythm. Vice Admiral Jonas Ingram appeared briefly to pay his respects to Captain Lyon. I noticed that Ingram drank only one scotch and soda, after asking Al McCoy to "make it light."

Chapter Ten
LIFE IN RIO DE JANEIRO

In the waning months of 1943 Vice Admiral Ingram established at each base a Naval Air Facility, which relieved the Hedron Detachments from all duties other than servicing and maintaining aircraft.

Hedron was a mobile unit, and it might be directed at any moment to move into another theater of war. Against that contingency, some permanent organization had to be set up to keep the bases operating. Moreover, an organization that was, like Hedron, primarily committed to the task of keeping airplanes flying, would obviously be able to improve the quality of its work if relieved of the details of berthing, messing, and maintaining the base itself, which included the construction of buildings and allocation of space in them.

I was editor of the *South Atlantic News* when Gene Tunney, the retired heavyweight boxing champion, came to Recife, Brazil, in the late spring of 1944. In a welcoming editorial I said Horatio Alger never wrote about a person like Gene, because nobody would believe the story. I knew a lot about Tunney because I had written about him in my syndicated biographical column. I mentioned, for example, that he had practiced running backward during his road training in preparation for his first fight against Jack Dempsey. Gene was a realist, and he knew he would have to retreat on the way to victory.

In any case, Gene Tunney came into our newspaper office, which was on the same floor where Vice Admiral Jonas Ingram, Commander of the South Atlantic Fourth Fleet, had his headquarters. Gene said he wanted to meet the editorial writer who knew so many little-known facts about him. Having been a boxing buff all my life, I was thrilled to meet "The Champ," as Admiral Ingram called him. The only other heavyweight champion I had met and talked to was Jack Sharkey.

I told Tunney: "I don't like you because you beat my idol, Harry Greb." Greb fought Tunney five times and was lucky to survive, but he won their first match.

I said, "Gene was probably the most underrated heavyweight champion we ever had, and he might have been our greatest."

"I fought a lot of tough punchers," Greb said, "but no one ever hurt me as badly as Gene did." The first time, when Gene was the light heavyweight champion, he weighed one hundred and seventy-four pounds to Greb's one hundred and sixty-two. Greb used elbows, butts, and illegal tactics the referee couldn't keep up with, and Tunney bled all through the fight. The referee kept asking if he wanted the fight stopped.

"For God's sake, no," Gene said. He was too proud and too courageous to quit. Tunney fought the Pittsburgh Windmill four more times, winning each time.

Tunney smiled when I mentioned Harry Greb, but I could tell he was interested in the fact that I knew a little about boxing.

Jonas Ingram, a former Annapolis football star, was easily the most colorful admiral in the U.S. Navy, and that includes Admiral Bill Halsey. One afternoon I walked into his office to ask Commodore Braine, his flag officer, if Ingram would let me profile him for a national magazine. (My article, "Boss of the Atlantic," appeared about a year later in *Liberty* magazine.) Braine said I came at the right time. A year or so earlier, he said, *Time* magazine had talked about featuring Ingram, but the admiral wasn't interested at that stage.

I spent many happy hours interviewing Ingram. I can still see him smoking his pipe, one leg slung over a corner of the desk. He never interrupted our sessions, even when bigwigs were waiting to see him.

One Friday afternoon, toward the end of the final interview, Ingram said. "Well, Brother Cutler, is there anything else you want?"

"Yes, I would like to go down to Rio de Janeiro to interview President Vargas and members of his cabinet."

"When would you like to go?"

"Monday," I said, knowing the buckety admiral was a man of quick decision.

Monday morning, I was the only passenger on the PBY *Mariner* seaplane that landed in the beautiful harbor of Rio de Janeiro. I'll never forget those snow-capped mountains above the azure water rimmed by the pure white Copacabana Beach. Sugarloaf Mountain, which Gene and I visited later via cable car, was on the left.

I reported to Commodore Harold Dodds, who was commanding officer of the Naval Mission in Brazil. Dodds impressed me immediately as being pompous and overly dignified. He reminded me of the definition of the life of a diplomat: "Protocol, alcohol, and Geritol." But he was cordial. He told me of my appointment at the U.S. Embassy that afternoon and said he would arrange all appointments with the ministers, who correspond to members of the U.S. President's cabinet.

As I was leaving his office, I was accosted by an attractive young lady named Jane Braga. I have never learned precisely how, but Jane Braga, who was the *Time–Life* correspondent stationed in Rio, wanted to talk to me, having heard that I was in Rio to interview President Getulio Vargas. Jane was an American who had been divorced from a Brazilian executive. Jane knew why I had been sent to Rio, apparently because she checked with the Naval Mission in Rio every day. When I asked her if she had ever interviewed Gene Tunney, who I knew was in Rio at the time, she told me he would be attending U.S. Ambassador Jefferson Caffrey's cocktail party that afternoon. When she told me Tunney was staying at the Copacabana Hotel, I called him up. By this time it was mid-afternoon. He invited me over for a drink and said later we would go to the Embassy together. Was I delighted! Jane Braga, Gene Tunney, and now Ambassador Jefferson Caffrey, all in one day!

Ambassador Caffrey was a gracious host who seemed interested in my assignment. I remember one thing he said: "Vargas has enemies in high places." Gene took me to dinner that night, and for the next thirty days we had breakfast, lunch, and dinner together. Never once did he let me pick up the tab, and because of this lovable guy who looked you straight in the eye, I met celebrities I never would otherwise have met.

One day Tunney and I took the Cog Railway up to the Corcovado, which commands a beautiful view from its ten-yard square pinnacle. Sugarloaf is the peak of 1,296 feet of solid granite. You reach the top by an aerial railway. Infrequently passengers are left dangling over the gorge when the railway gets out of commission. One Naval officer told me he once had to wait for more than two hours while repairmen took their siesta. According to legend, Sugarloaf was considered unclimbable until an American sailor climbed it and placed the Stars and Stripes on its apex.

A tour of duty in Rio is a far cry from life in a tent at Belem or Recife in the early days.

There was the dinner party at the Copacabana Hotel with John "Shipwreck" Kelley and his glamorous wife, Brenda Frazier, the debutante of debutantes, who told me how she hated Walter Winchell. On my left was a countess, on my right Shipwreck Kelley, who spent several minutes, as Tunney had predicted, explaining why he wasn't in uniform. An old football injury to his knee, he said. (At that time he owned a professional football team in New York—the Giants, if memory serves.) After the war I learned that Kelley was working for the CIA. But that countess . . . the most beautiful woman I have ever seen, with a personality to match.

One morning at the Copacabana Gene ordered five scrambled eggs. In his musing he casually remarked that he could have licked "Gentleman Jim" Corbett. When I said the only time he could have touched Corbett would have been when they shook hands at the beginning of the fight, Gene shook his head, hands folded as he leaned on his elbows.

"I could box, too, remember," he said. "And I could hit a lot harder than Corbett."

In his biography of Jack Dempsey, Nat Fleischer wrote under the heading "Rating the Heavyweights":

> Who among the large field [of heavyweight champions] possessed the best ring cleverness?
> Of the answers I've received to that query, Gene Tunney comes in first.
> But Corbett, with his science, stamina, and speed, is a close second.

Gene got annoyed with me just before the Brenda Frazier dinner, which featured champagne before, during, and after dinner. That afternoon I had sat for a Brazilian artist, who did a pencil sketch for the non-Picasso price of twenty-five dollars, and he insisted on completing it, which made me late for dinner. It was the only time Gene got angry with me. He phoned me.

"Look, if you don't come right down I'll come up there and drag you down. You're keeping a lot of important people waiting." I went right down.

Gene could be absolutely serious when you suspected he had to be kidding. One day he told me (he never asked, he told) we were going to have a picnic lunch at the Copacabana Beach.

"I'll have the hotel make the chicken sandwiches, and we'll take along a bottle of Madeira. Ask Jane Braga to bring along an interesting friend."

Then he added, "I'll bring along some gloves so we can have a little workout." He wasn't smiling.

Things didn't work out the way Gene had planned. He forgot the boxing gloves, fortunately, and an unexpected assignment had taken Jane Braga to Buenos Aires. So instead of having a couple of fascinating correspondents to talk to, Jane, who had a macabre sense of humor, arranged for us to take along two vapid secretaries with a remarkably limited conversational range. Gene solved the problem by completely ignoring the girls, who were obviously overwhelmed to meet a celebrity. It wasn't so much that Gene was stuffy or that he considered himself a heavy intellect.

He simply didn't like small talk. He did, however, let the girls enjoy their lunch while we jogged up the beach and played *petaca*.

During the first two weeks in Rio I completed all my interviews with members of the cabinet, including Foreign Minister Oswaldo Aranha; the minister of war; and the minister of the navy. Never will I forget the look of rage on the face of Commodore Dodds, who arranged all the interviews. While shaking hands with the somber minister of the navy, I made a terrible faux pas. I told him I would remember him to Admiral Ingram. In an elevator after the interview, Dodds fumed. "You never never say such things to a Brazilian dignitary." And I never again did.

I had to wait two weeks before getting to see President Vargas at the Catanete Palace. But what a delightful two weeks! Gene and I visited museums and hospitals and dined with a few fascinating corporation executives. One afternoon in a hospital a burly British sailor jokingly told Gene he thought he could "take" him. "Who will you get to help you?" Gene said. It was fun all the way, including the night Gene addressed the military personnel at the air base. The crowd roared when Gene started his speech: "Japan has given us a long count . . ."

At Harvard the Kittredge course on Shakespeare I had taken made things easy for me because Gene really liked to talk about the bard. He told me how furious he had made Jack Sharkey when he compared the Boston fighter to the lumbering Ajax in *As You Like It*.

"Poor Jack didn't have the faintest idea who Ajax was," Gene grinned.

Finally the appointment came through. At dinner that night I told Tunney about my date with Vargas the next day.

"Sorry," he said, "but you'll have to break it. Tomorrow we're going to visit Madame Chiang Kai-shek on an island in the harbor. She's here on vacation."

I couldn't believe it. I couldn't believe I was going to miss the opportunity of meeting the wife of Chiang Kai-shek, and I couldn't believe that Gene was serious.

"Listen, Gene," I said, "a Navy lieutenant—even a full Navy lieutenant—doesn't break dates with the president of a Republic of forty-one million people."

"Now you listen to me," Gene said. "I paid $250 to charter this boat and we're going out to that island." I finally convinced him that I couldn't go.

But neither Brazilian presidents nor Chinese premiers fazed Gene Tunney, nor did superior military rank.

One morning in Recife, we were on an elevator with an Army brigadier general who had wanted to get off on the third floor. Gene ordered the operator to go up to the sixth floor, where we got off. The general almost turned purple.

Commodore Dodds assigned various Naval officers to drive me to appointments with Brazilian ministers. One morning the chauffeur was Commander Lowell Williams. On the way he said: "Cutler, how in hell did you wangle this assignment?"

The next morning a Brazilian Army officer picked me up at Victory House, where I was staying, and drove me to the Catanete Palace. The Army officer had asked me whether Americans considered Vargas a dictator, and of course, I didn't fall for the bait.

In an inner sanctum was the smiling little dictator.

By this time, my Portuguese was fairly good, and I addressed President Vargas in his language.

He smiled, "Where did you learn to speak such beautiful Portuguese, Lieutenant Cutler?"

Then, in English, I told him about the profile on Admiral Ingram. I asked Vargas if he would be willing to assess Ingram's role in the war against Nazis.

The answer came in beautiful English. "I have already told President Franklin Delano Roosevelt of my opinion of Admiral Ingram." Then, as if noting my embarrassment, he added, "Lieutenant Cutler, I hope you can visit Sao Paulo before you leave Brazil. It will remind you of your own Chicago." I wondered if he had ever been to Chicago. End of interview. End of my Rio de Janeiro holiday.

Not quite. Commodore Dodds had told me he had heard from Admiral Ingram, and I was ordered to fly back to Recife at once, but, Gene Tunney insisted I could wait until he left the next day. One more day wouldn't make any difference, he said. I again reminded him that I was a lieutenant. And lieutenants—even full ones—don't counter orders of admirals. I thought I had won another battle with the champ.

When I walked into Commodore Dodds's office, this pompous official, who wore a pince-nez, actually seemed to be chuckling. "There has been a slight delay," he said, and he really was masking a smile. "Commander Tunney wants you to remain in Rio one more day." When I went into the inner office for the travel request, the officer in charge was grinning. "Sorry we had to dump you off the plane, Lieutenant, but we had to ship some Nazi prisoners up to Recife."

In my *History of Flight Air Wing Sixteen*, I had already written about the German and Italian prisoners of war who were temporarily kept in a barbed wire enclosure in a prison camp at the Ibura airport. I had written that the four hundred prisoners were willing workers, helping with carpentry projects, and preparing food for cooking in the Marine mess. They whittled out plaques, model planes, and other wooden articles. A few spoke English. One had worked in the Brooklyn Navy Yard for twenty years; another had a wife in New York State. A bearded Nazi said, when I addressed them in broken German, "That's okay, Lieutenant. We understand English." A fourth had been a greenskeeper on a New Jersey golf course before joining Hitler's Merchant Marine.

The commander who told me I had to be dumped off the plane because some Nazi prisoners of war had to be shipped down to Recife sounded plausible. But I found out later that Commander Callahan was one of Gene Tunney's pals.

A few days before this incident in Commodore Dodds's office, I had received orders from the Bureau of Personnel to report to a writing unit at the Navy Department in Washington, D.C. I had read about this elite group of writers in *Coronet* and had applied, noting that I had had two syndicated columns and had written magazine articles, as well as several hundred features for various newspapers.

Chapter Eleven
MEANWHILE, BACK IN DUXBURY . . .

Mothers-in-law can be difficult, but Bobbie can adjust to almost any situation, and she and my mother, Margaret, got along very well. During my thirteen months of Naval service in Brazil, my mother often visited Bobbie in Duxbury. Her greatest joy in life was taking care of the children. The twins, Meg and David, were about a month old when I left for Norfolk, Virginia, before flying to Belem, Brazil, and Robert was about a year and a half. So there were three babies for my mother to look after. Babies were her specialty, since she not only had had five of her own but had also worked for several years as a pediatric nurse in Boston after my father's financial difficulties. His first jolt came when the grocery store in Magnolia, of which he was co-owner, failed. Later he had lost what little money he had in the stock market crash of 1929. After that, he worked for various fruit markets in Boston and Brookline until supermarkets drove them out of existence in the mid-fifties.

My mother was vigorous in those days. She loved every part of baby care. She also wanted to help with the cooking, but Bobbie liked being boss in her kitchen. Bobbie told me later that my mother kept asking her why she had to cook everything "so fancy." Bobbie liked to try out new recipes, and she still does.

My sister, Ann, and her husband, Lee Starratt, occasionally brought my father down to Duxbury on a Sunday for lunch, and they would drive him back in the afternoon.

I never knew exactly what Lee Starratt did, but I remember Bobbie telling me that her Aunt Amie had given him work around her large estate in Canton. At the time, help of any kind was hard to find, and Lee apparently was an expert handyman. He and Ann lived in Dedham, where my mother often visited them. But I know she much preferred visiting Bobbie in Duxbury.

My young brother Jimmy and his girlfriend came down once, before he went into the Air Force, and Bobbie took them to the small beach near our house for a swim. Jimmy died in action early in World War II.

Other Air Force personnel could see his plane going down. In any case,

65

nothing was heard about him again. Bobbie wrote to me about this in Brazil and it was hard to take, as I had practically raised Jimmy and my brother Harry. Both brothers were several years younger than the other children.

My father died of cancer at Massachusetts General Hospital in 1960 at the age of eighty-two. I was with him when he died. His last words were "Take me home." I watched the machine that records breathing come slowly to a halt, and I knew he was gone. I was shaken and left the hospital to head for the nearest bar for a tranquilizer.

Funeral services were held at St. Cecelia's Church in Boston, although my father was not a churchgoer.

After a cataract operation, my mother came to Duxbury to stay with Bobbie and recuperate, taking the bedroom next to the kitchen on the first floor. She stayed for about a week. Of course, she always came for Thanksgiving and Christmas when Bobbie invited her—always a bit hesitantly, because she did not want to be in the way. But Bobbie insisted that she come, and she did, until her last days.

In 1959, my mother had a stroke and could no longer stay alone at Fidelis Way in Brighton, where she and my father had lived in a small apartment for several years—in only a living room, bedroom, and a kitchen. She had a small yard in front where she planted flowers, which she loved, but neighborhood kids tore them up, leaving a mess. After that she had to be content with houseplants, which overflowed in her apartment. A few weeks later, she was moved to a nursing home in West Roxbury. She tried to appear cheerful, but I remember the day when Bobbie, Ricky, our youngest child, and I went to see her. When we left she looked sad, knowing her days were numbered and that she would never see her beloved little grandson again. Ricky was five years old at the time.

One thing I will never forget. She left me a special gift—the five hundred dollars I had given her to repay the money she had given me so I could enroll at Harvard.

She had little to leave, and I think my sister received the bulk of her estate. Ann took all the furniture, which Bobbie and I did not need. But I shall always think of her as the most unselfish and loving of mothers, always doing for others and never thinking of herself. Bobbie's mother summed it up. "She had an inner strength," she said.

Ann and Lee had a comfortable house in Dedham with a large yard in back. When we first came down from Dartmouth, at the beginning of World War II, Bobbie, little Robert, and I stayed with her for a few days. While we were in Olathe, Kansas, Ann and Lee were divorced, and two years later

Ann married Thomas O'Connell. They had two sons, Thomas Jr. and Keith. After the war we visited them occasionally in Westwood, and my mother loved to go there.

When Tom and Ann went for a vacation in Scottsdale, Arizona, they fell in love with the place and bought a house. Tom gave up his job in the circulation department of the *Wall Street Journal*. Most of their neighbors came from the Midwest, and Keith married a young woman from Iowa. Young Tom, who married a woman with three children said, "I love her so much, I'll take the children, too." They had a daughter named Kelley who had the same bright red hair that my mother had had as a child.

One spring, my Harvard class of 1932 had a reunion at the Camelback Inn in Scottsdale, and Bobbie and I drove there in our Pontiac convertible. At the inn we greeted classmates, took bus tours to Jerome, with its abandoned copper mine, and other places, but we still had time to spend with Ann and her family. I remember one delicious dinner when Tom cooked a roast beef over mesquite on the grill.

The next time we went to Scottsdale was not so pleasant, for Ann had cancer of the spine, and we knew her days were numbered. But she was as cheerful as ever and happy to see us. My old friend from childhood, Ethel Beatty, was there, helping out and taking Ann for her chemotherapy. Ann spent most of the time in her reclining chair, but she was happy to see us. Bobbie, Robert, and I had flown out and stayed in a nearby hotel, which had a kitchenette, and we cooked our breakfast in our room. Ann's neighbors were wonderful, stopping in daily to see if they could do anything for her. We left knowing we would never see Ann again. When she had a temporary remission, she planned a trip to California to see Tom Jr. and his family, but as she was about to board the plane, she suddenly felt sick and was unable to go. She died a few months later, on July 4, 1975. We didn't go to her funeral, but we were glad we could be with her when she could enjoy seeing us.

Chapter Twelve
THE BIG LEAGUE

During the five-thousand-mile flight from Rio to Washington, D.C., I took a turn down memory lane, recalling some of the amusing and rewarding experiences I had had in Brazil. There was one recurring thought I first heard expressed by James Michael Curley when I was writing his autobiography: "Never be afraid to make the bold move." He said it with conviction. After serving in the Army and Navy, I think this is especially true in the military. You get further if you make things happen, rather than wait for them to happen.

I flew all the way to Miami via Natal, Brazil, and I was so numb with fatigue I could have slept standing up. At the airport in Miami, a flight officer, mistaking my torpor for good manners, told me he was fed up with officers demanding flights north. Since I was so polite, he said, he was going to put me on a plane later that night. All the way back to the airport in Washington I squirmed in the bucket seat. It was all I could do to keep from flopping on the metal floor of the plane. But that flight was a prelude to more excitement.

Meanwhile, I had notified Bobbie when I was returning. In her letters, which kept me informed about how things were going at home, Bobbie had often mentioned a couple named Bob and Barbara Mullowney, who took her to the Winsor House, a historic tavern in Duxbury, for dinner every Saturday. Let's hear a word from Bobbie:

> It was about eleven one night in late August of 1944. I knew that John would be coming back to the States soon, after his thirteen-month stay in Brazil, but I didn't know just when. The phone rang. "I'm in Washington, D.C.," John said, "and will be in New York in about an hour or so. Can you come down and meet me? I'll get a room at the Commodore Hotel, which is near Grand Central."
>
> How was I to get to New York on such short notice? I called South Station. No trains to Providence. There was a train leaving Providence at 1 A.M., but how would I get there? I had no car. I had come home moments earlier after dining at the Winsor House with Bob and Barbara Mullowney.
>
> I called Bob. "You've got to drive me to Providence to catch a train.

John will be in New York tonight." Not a moment's hesitation. "We'll be over in five minutes." And they were. We set off, me with a hastily packed bag. Ella Woodbury, who was living with me (she cooked, cleaned, and helped with the children) was told I was leaving for a few days. Off we went in the Mullowneys' ancient Ford station wagon, bouncing along Route 44. Bob drove fast, swerving around curves. As we approached Seekonk, the engine started sputtering. "Damn," said Bob. "Out of gas." Fortunately we were near a police station. Bob went in to see if he could borrow some gas. "No, but we will call an all-night station to bring you some." But alas, that would take time, and I had only a few minutes to catch the last train. I called for a taxi and got to the railroad station just as the train was pulling out. In despair, I wept. Here I hadn't seen my husband for a long dreary thirteen months and he had been missing the development of our three babies, who were now walking and talking. What was I to do? The Providence Biltmore is just across the street from the station, so I picked up my bag and trudged to the front desk and explained my predicament to the night clerk. It was then about 3 A.M. The clerk said, "We always save a room for people like you." I fell into bed and next morning I took the first train out and was sitting in the Commodore coffee shop, having John paged, when he appeared. That night we walked down the street and stopped in the Stork Club. While we were sitting at the bar looking around for celebrities, someone put a hand on my shoulder. It was Dick Mullowney, brother of Bob. He also had been considerate of lonesome war wives in Duxbury and on New Year's Eve had given us all corsages for the gala at the Winsor House. "Come inside and I'll buy you a cover charge." Now we could have dinner and see the famous floor show. Sherman Billingsley, the owner, came over to our table and ordered a bottle of champagne for us.

Next morning we went back to Duxbury for a week to get ready to move to Washington. We packed children, clothes, rented our Washington Street house and set off by train for D.C.

The apartment just off Connecticut Avenue near the zoo proved too small, so we rented a house in nearby Takoma Park, Maryland, where we were surrounded by Seventh Day Adventists. The house was filthy. Cockroaches roamed the kitchen and filth and dust covered everything. The furnace was queer; boiling water gushed out of a pipe outside and when you turned on the water in the tub, it was scalding. Finally, we let the furnace go out and heated the house with the gas kitchen stove. One day, I was glancing through the Sunday *Washington Post* and saw an ad for houses for sale in Falls Church, Virginia. We bundled the children into the car, an aged Buick sedan John had brought home one day, and set out. Just off Route 50, we turned off into the development. Going into the model house, we saw the small living room, two bedrooms, and tiny kitchen. We said we would take a house. Two hundred dollars down and sixty dollars a month. We picked out a house on the map and were told we could move in within two weeks.

We furnished the house with Sears, Roebuck early American, plus a few junk shop items. It was comfortable—a brick Cape-type house. All the trees had been bulldozed as builders do, and a small tree was planted in front of every door. The front yard was mud, and in back the drainage was so poor a regular stream passed by the kitchen door. The day before Christmas, a small fir tree floated down the stream and I grabbed it. There was our Christmas tree. Food was scarce. Meat was nonexistent, except for chickens which arrived with feathers and innards. I spent hours mixing that little yellow tablet into the sickish white oleo, and laundry was done in the bathtub. Those stiff khaki Navy uniforms had to soak all night. Sheets and children's diapers all went into the tub (no Pampers then). Baths had to wait. The furnace had to be fed its diet of coal, sooting up everything. But it was a pleasant year. We had many Navy friends and some of the neighbors were friendly. Finally, our old and good friends, Professor and Mrs. Carl Kinsley, who had retired in the Sleepy Hollow section—a lovely area with tennis courts, gardens, and substantial houses—invited me to use their washing machine. I would go over, children in tow, with bags of dirty clothes, lug them home wet and hang them in the backyard, or in the house if it was raining. I grew to know her cellar. Later, after the war, police caught a well-known criminal who had been living for weeks in the cellar. The felon was once a carpenter who worked on their house, so he knew the cellar well. He would creep in in the dark of the night, then would go into the kitchen to raid the refrigerator. During the day he would sleep. Both the Kinsleys were a bit deaf, so they heard nothing and both were too absentminded to notice that food was missing. When police finally tracked the criminal to their door, the Kinsleys were horrified.

I was first assigned to the historical unit directed by John Jennings, the historical novelist who wrote *The Shadow and the Glory*, *Next to Valour*, *Gentleman Ranker* and, later, *Salem Frigate*. Directly across the hall were the writers *Coronet* magazine had mentioned, including Jesse Stuart, Robert Lewis Taylor (who wrote profiles for the *New Yorker*), Hannibal Coons, and Donald Kehoe, both magazine writers.

Robert Lewis Taylor was a practical joker par excellence. One day he complained to a corporation president who manufactured jelly beans that he was disappointed to find so few black jelly beans when he bought a bag. The manufacturer, not realizing he was being taken in, sent him a ten-pound bag of black jelly beans. Another day, a secretary from another Navy office came in to interview Taylor about a new Navy airplane. Taylor asked her to sit down and gravely told her about a revolutionary type of plane that would have flapping wings. "We got the idea from birds, of course." The young lady took it all down, visibly impressed.

Roark Bradford, author of *Old Man Adam an' His Chillun* (on which Marc Connelly based his musical *Green Pastures*), had just left the unit, and Robert Lewis Taylor was soon to leave for special writing assignments in New York. Also in the unit were five advertising executives, who handled public relations.

Kehoe, an authority on unidentified flying objects, later wrote a book on that subject. My favorite was Jesse Stuart, a Kentucky author who wrote novels and poetry. In the Navy, he seemed ludicrously out of place in an enlisted man's uniform. I got to know Jesse well, and after the war when he spoke at a symposium in Symphony Hall in Boston, Bobbie and I entertained him at lunch. Another speaker at Symphony Hall was Walter Karig, author of *Zotz!*, who was head of the book and magazine department at the Navy Department during my year in Washington.

I moved into the "elite" office months later.

My first assignment in Washington was to write a secret document titled *History of Antisubmarine Warfare in the South Atlantic*. This involved using top secret battle reports from both the British Admiralty and our own battle reports. One morning I went down to the office of Rear Admiral Fletcher Low, who was in charge of U.S. Submarine Warfare. I waited in a small antechamber while a Navy captain went in to see Low. I am sure that the ensuing conversation in muffled but audible tones was not intended for a lieutenant's ears. Admiral Low told the captain that the Nazi high command had offered to use German submarines against the Japanese fleet! No mention of this was ever made in the media.

Low shook his head when I asked about the top secret documents. "Neither you nor anyone else will ever see them. They will be locked in a safe for the next generation." Those were his exact words.

I tried again in another part of the Navy Department, where historical documents were kept. This time, when I gave my credentials, I had no trouble getting all the top secret data needed. (Later, after V–J Day, I saw Lieutenant John Hersey in this historical section. Was he getting material for his book on Hiroshima?)

Most of the information in the top secret reports obviously cannot be divulged, but there were unclassified tidbits that are of interest. Some survivors of U-boats sunk in the South Atlantic in 1943 were sure the Nazis would lose the war. Others were confident of ultimate victory. One prisoner aired his resentment against officers who smoked coronas and sipped Hennessey brandy. I recall one sad incident.

The USS *Saucy* arrived on the scene five hours after one of the Flight Air Wing Sixteen fliers sank a U-boat. While picking up the twenty-eight survivors, the crew of the *Saucy* fired on sharks that were trailing some of the men who were still in the water. A German prisoner who had been rescued, thinking the shots were aimed at his comrades, jumped overboard and drowned. There were some inconsequential items. When the U-591 was stationed at Bergen, Norway, in 1942, the crew lived in barracks about a half hour's walk from the harbor. Some of the men preferred to stay in the barracks rather than go into town for a drink. "Ocean water tastes better than Norwegian beer," one said.

My favorite character was a Nazi submarine commander named Herr Guggenberger, who told his captors he "certainly would like to meet" the pilots of the plane who "so fearlessly and bravely" sank his submarine. He had been commander of the U-81 when it sank the HMS *Ark Royal.*

After completing a brief history of antisubmarine warfare, in which I incorporated material from my interviews with Flight Air Wing Sixteen pilots, I was shifted to writing administrative history, a boring assignment. The Tenth Fleet had an officer doing a story on the Atlantic operations, so it seemed a duplication of effort. I worked with Lieutenant (jg) Clifford Lord, who had been director of the New York State Historical Society at Cooperstown, after a few years of teaching history at Columbia University.

During this period I saw a lot of the historical novelist John Jennings. One day Jennings and I had lunch on the top floor of the Department of the Interior. Another day we lunched at the Cosmos Club. In Brazil, after reading one of John's novels, I marveled at the dialogue, which had the authentic ring of life during Revolutionary days. At the Cosmos Club, John told me how he was able to reproduce dialogue so convincingly. He said he read contemporary plays.

That article I had read in *Coronet* magazine didn't prepare me for the dull routine in the historical section. The only amusing incident I recall came one morning when a Chicago sportswriter, who was in the unit, teased me about a sentence I had written in a report: "All hands were swept off their feet."

Another Chicago reporter was John "can-you-lend-me-a-buck" Riley, who wrote service reports for "hometown" newspapers. He was one of the hard-boiled scribes of the *Front Page* tradition. He told us he handled murder stories. He would get on the phone and say, "Is this the widow Morelli?"

"This is Mrs. Angela Morelli. I am not a widow."

"That's what you think," Riley would say. "Your husband was shot and killed just before midnight."

No, John never returned those bucks.

Then came another lucky break. I heard two officers in the corridor just outside our office talking about the difficulties Vice Admiral Aubrey Fitch had in finding a speech writer. Fitch was Deputy Chief of Naval Operations (for Air). "So far," one said, "Commander Burke has tried seven writers, and he still isn't satisfied." Burke was Fitch's flag lieutenant.

I went out into the corridor and apologized for overhearing their exchange, adding that I had written speeches for Major-General Karl Truesdell while in the Army, and would like a shot at doing the same for Fitch.

At this time Commander Arleigh Burke, later to become Chief of Naval Operations, was known as "Thirty-one Knot Burke," because of his exploits in the South Pacific, where he sank several Japanese subs in the "Slot." From April 1 to July 25, 1943, Vice Admiral Marc Mitscher, as Commander Air, Solomon Islands, coordinated units of the Army Air Corps, Navy and Marine Corps aviation and contingents of the Royal New Zealand Air Forces, and he molded these forces into a potent offensive weapon against the Japanese, destroying more than five hundred Japanese aircraft and sinking more than twenty vessels. Arleigh Burke, the most widely publicized hero in that campaign, was brought back to Washington to stimulate morale.

Arleigh Burke took me to lunch at the Mayflower Hotel, and over a martini, he said, "I have never spoken to even one governor, and now I have to speak to all six New England governors." He was to be the keynote speaker in the Imperial Ballroom of the Hotel Statler in Boston.

I was lucky. Any writer could dream up something exciting and glamorous about a man like "Thirty-one Knot Burke." It was the first time I had ever done anything in jumbo type. It wasn't the last.

In between speeches I had various writing assignments. I wrote the 1944 Naval Aviation Manual for the signature of Ernest King, Chief of Naval Operations, and two speeches for the Rear Admiral who headed the Bureau of Ordnance. One speech was for Fitch's wife, who was to address a Red Cross rally. When I gave a speech I had written for Undersecretary Artemus Gates to his flag lieutenant, it took an hour to assure him there was nothing wrong with the word "churning." He thought the word was too slangy. I also profiled the great photographer Lt. Commander Edward Steichen, who was in charge of the DCNO camera unit.

Meanwhile, Bobbie and I had fun. Here is an excerpt from a letter I wrote Bobbie's Aunt Amie on October 28, 1944:

> You would be interested in Miss Kay Halle, who was a guest at our house last week with Professor Michael Choukas of Dartmouth, now with the Offices of Strategic Services. That afternoon Miss Halle had entertained John Marquand and his wife, and she has often been a guest at the White House. She runs a kind of salon in Washington, where we met people in high places.

Bobbie and I got to know Kay well, and found her fascinating. She came from Cleveland, where her family owned the Halle department store. It was in the living room of her Cleveland home, she said, that those two Yale sophomores, Briton Hadden and Henry Luce, dreamed up the idea of *Time* magazine.

My best friend in the unit was Lieutenant Clarke Mattimore. Every afternoon around quarter of five we would go into the lavatory to freshen up, and usually we saw Rear Admiral Richard Byrd standing in front of a mirror shaving. "Good afternoon, gentlemen," he always said.

One day he was missing. "I wonder where the old bastard is?" Clarke said.

"Maybe he shaved this morning," I said. "Anyway, the big hero isn't here."

Came a voice, broken by a chuckle, from a cubicle, "Oh, yes, I am."

We didn't stay to bid the admiral a good evening. Thereafter Clarke and I used a different lavatory, but I'll bet Byrd missed us. I never got the chance to tell him I had featured him in a "Who Is It?" I recalled something he wrote in his diary when he was twelve: "I have decided to be the first man to reach the North Pole." He was the first man to fly over the North Pole and he was also the first man ever to fly over the South Pole. I remembered also that he took two refrigerators to the South Pole. There were, of course, more heroic things he would like to have been reminded of.

Admiral Byrd wasn't the only celebrity I saw roaming the corridors of the Navy Department. One day I saw Lt. Commander Robert Montgomery talking to Navy Secretary James Forrestal in the hall. Another day I saw Lt.

Commander Douglas Fairbanks Jr. leaving his office with his beautiful wife, and I often passed Chief of Naval Operations Ernest King in the corridor. He never smiled or nodded a greeting. Stern character!

In mid-December of 1944 I joined a group on the shakedown cruise of the USS *Bennington*. Included were Edward Miller, editor in chief of *Liberty* magazine, Robert Littell, a senior editor of *Reader's Digest*, and an editor of *Life* magazine. The *Bennington* was the first of a new class of large aircraft carriers. During the trip, Miller, who bought my profile of Jonas Ingram ("Boss of the Atlantic"), told me one unpublicized virtue of his little magazine. "You can read it in the can," he said.

As the Bennington slowly cruised through the Panama Canal I squatted by the railing on the starboard side and saw that as we entered the Gatun Locks, there was literally only about a foot of clearance.

In Cristobal in the Canal Zone, I spent most of the money I had on a dozen pairs of silk stockings—six pairs for Bobbie, the others for an officer in the Navy Department. On the flight back to Washington, Miller and I had just bid three no trump in a bridge game against Littell and the *Life* editor while we flew over Haiti, low enough to clearly see Christophe's Palace. (We made our bid redoubled.)

We deplaned at the Washington airport in predawn darkness. The editors got tired of waiting for a ride and one by one drifted off. I couldn't leave. I had two dollars in my pocket, and there were no buses at that hour. Suddenly a black chauffeur appeared. I told him the editors had left and asked if he could drive me to Falls Church. On the way, sitting with him in the front seat, I asked who owned the Cadillac limousine.

"Secretary Gates, sir," he said. I stiffened. I was glad I hadn't told him my name. If I ask him to let me out so I can walk the rest of the way home, he may get suspicious, I thought. When he dropped me off, I didn't dare offer him a two dollar tip. Drivers for undersecretaries of the Navy have pride, I figured.

It was still dark at 3:00 A.M. when I rapped at the door of our house. Bobbie, in her nightgown, opened the door and promptly fainted. When she revived she said that a couple of nights before, as she was preparing for bed, she was terrified when a man peered through the bathroom window.

Two weeks later I returned from a martini luncheon at the Mayflower with Mattimore. An officer in our unit, with a worried look, said there was a call for me from the office of the judge advocate general. "Are you in any trouble?"

Just as I expected. I told the officer of the post-midnight ride home in that sleek black Cadillac. He shook his head in silent sympathy. Well, I figured, it was about time I was court-martialed.

I told a Wave in the judge advocate general's office that someone wanted to see me. "Oh, yes, Lieutenant Cutler. Come this way."

I went into the den of the prosecutor. When I saw him I remembered the package I had dropped on a table in our living room in Falls Church one dark morning.

"Cutler," he said, "where are those silk stockings you promised me?"

In September of 1943 the editor of *Leatherneck*, the official U.S. Marine magazine, asked me to write an article titled, "Would You Be Afraid in Combat?" In my files I found enough material to write the piece, but until then I had had no firsthand combat experience. On the *Makin Island*, around three o'clock in the morning when we were cruising off Iwo Jima, I had a definite feeling of fear. Japanese planes were heading our way, and they kept getting closer. We smeared our faces with grease in the event of a sinking. I remember thinking what a terrible swimmer I was, and how awful it would be to flounder around in the dark, cold Pacific on a flimsy lifesaver. A minute to go. None of the men on the deck said a word. Forty-five seconds. By this time I was scared stiff. Thirty seconds and finally fifteen seconds. This was it. I said a silent prayer. Then it happened. Our Combat Air Patrol (CAP) "splashed" the enemy planes. I really enjoyed breakfast that morning.

Oddly enough, when I stood on the bridge of the flagship *El Dorado*, just a few feet away from Lt. General Simon Bolivar Buckner and Vice Admiral Kelly Turner in the midst of the raging action off Okinawa, I felt more excited than scared.

In his book, *Before the Colors Fade*, published by Houghton Mifflin Company in 1964, Fred Ayer Jr. wrote:

> It has been written that George Patton was fearless. Such a statement is an obvious absurdity since no man is fearless. Uncle George often said this to me: "Any man who tells you he has never been scared in battle is either a damned liar or completely insane."

In the spring of 1945, Lt. Commander Andrew Hewitt and I flew to the Pacific with Class II Priority, which meant we could travel at will. On the way we stopped in San Francisco, where we spent the night at the Pacific Union Club before flying the following day to Honolulu. During the twenty-two hour trip in a Clipper we sat with Dr. Richard Lahey, founder of the Lahey Clinic in Boston. The next stop was Guam. When we landed in Guam, a yeoman was waiting in a jeep. I was about to throw my bag into the jeep when I heard a familiar voice. "John Henry Cutler." It was Gene Tunney, and with him was a distinguished-looking person with whom Gene had been traveling.

"He's got a lot more on the ball than Thornton Wilder," Gene told me. He had also traveled with Wilder earlier in the war. The gentleman was the author John Marquand and we were delighted when Gene brought Marquand over to our room in the BOQ later that day. We had a few drinks during which I committed another unpardonable sin. I told Marquand he reminded me of his character the late George Apley. This may explain why he greeted me so coldly that evening at chow.

At the table with Marquand were Rear-Admiral "Bing" Miller, head of public relations at the Navy Department in Washington, and Paul Smith, the arrogant and obnoxious editor of the *San Francisco Chronicle*, who later succeeded Walter Davenport as editor of *Collier's*. Tunney, who was expected, had not arrived. Smith made a disparaging remark about Gene, and Miller added a comment that irked me. Clearly they didn't really know Tunney. When I defended Gene, in a tone that was honed by the afternoon's I. W. Harper, Marquand was visibly surprised. A young lieutenant contradicting an admiral. In any case, Smith shut up, and when Tunney joined us, all was serene.

After chow under a tent, Marquand asked Tunney to accompany him to Miller's party, and I tried to get Gene to go to a movie that was about to be shown. Marquand grabbed him by one hand, and I pulled on the other. Marquand won.

A few months later, John Marquand had a story in *Harper's* magazine titled "Luncheon in Hawaii." He was partially alluding to that "Supper in Guam." The brash young lieutenant barges into the admiral's party. "Sorry to be late, Admiral," he says, "I'll have a double martini." Some of the dialogue was so familiar.

In Guam Vice Admiral Chester Nimitz's flag lieutenant arranged for us to catch up with the USS *Randolph*, flagship of the big carrier fleet.

Those days of waiting in Guam were suspenseful. Correspondents and military personnel gathered every night in the Officers' Club wondering what was to happen next. One night my old Boston friend Jim Britt, who used to broadcast the Boston Braves baseball games, introduced me to Robert Sherwood, the playwright, whom Britt was escorting around the Pacific war zone. The night before we left on varying assignments I chatted with Ernie Pyle, whom everyone admired, and spent the rest of the evening at a table talking to John Lardner, who was doing a regular column at the time for *Newsweek*.

Next morning I said another goodbye to Gene Tunney and boarded the USS *Indianapolis*, a cruiser which later sank in the Pacific. Its commanding officer was Captain Charles McVay III, who was later court-martialed because of the sinking. In Saipan, he tried to bar my way at the head of the ladder, but said, "All right, goddam it, come aboard." The ship was so overcrowded we were shoved into a small cabin with a couple of wire service correspondents. We left the cruiser at Tinian and boarded a destroyer which went off course to transfer us by breeches buoy to the USS *Randolph*, the flagship of the carrier fleet. As we went from the tiny destroyer to the huge carrier while standing in the "coal bag," several hundred enlisted men and officers were leaning over the side shouting a welcome. If they thought we were bringing special orders, they were wrong. I, at the time, had no more idea of what was up than they did. Only the ship's captain knew where we were going.

We soon found out. From the captain's bridge I witnessed the first mass air raids of Tokyo. All the fliers I lunched with didn't return for supper. An alarming number of them were shot down, including Commander Charles Crommelin who, with his four brothers, had all graduated from the Naval Academy at Annapolis. I was standing on the bridge one afternoon when he waved to me from the cockpit of his fighter plane which was numbered zero. It was the last time I saw this squadron commander.

Every day we heard Tokyo Rose gleefully telling us what suckers we were—asking what our wives and girlfriends were doing back home.

Tokyo Rose was a Nisei—an American-born Japanese. Between 1943 and 1944, GIs in the Pacific tuned in to a fifteen-minute radio show of news and heard her flirtatious, silky voice. Tokyo Rose's intention was to undermine the men's fighting spirit. "Hello," she would say, "you fighting orphans in the Pacific. How's tricks?" Tokyo Rose went to jail for ten years at the Reformatory for Women at Alderson, West Virginia. President Ford pardoned her in January 1977.

In my report to Vice Admiral Aubrey Fitch, I described the mass air raid on Tokyo:

> Shortly after nine o'clock on the evening of 15 February 1945, the Hellcat, Avenger, and Helldiver pilots who on the following morning were to batter the hangars, aircraft factories, and shore installations in the Tokyo

area, were sitting in the wardroom of the USS *Randolph* smoking and chatting while awaiting a scheduled announcement by the late Commander Charles Crommelin, USN, at that time Air Group Commander of "Crommelin's Thunderbirds."

Most of the men in that wardroom were green pilots, but they had been with "Fighting Twelve" long enough to know that Commander Crommelin was one of the five brothers on active duty and that all five had graduated from the Naval Academy. The scuttlebutt was that their skipper had the distinction of being the second oldest Annapolis aviator on active combat duty and that he had almost 4,500 hours logged. They knew he had once made a perfect carrier landing after his body had been nicked in two hundred places by flying Plexiglas when a bomb exploded in the cockpit of his Hellcat. Many of them had seen this sequence in the carrier epic "The Fighting Lady." What those green pilots did not know was that their skipper would barely escape death during the 16–17 February raid on Tokyo, only to meet his gallant death during a later Pacific action in support of the operations on Okinawa.

USS *Randolph* pilots also knew that momentous action impended. Word had been passed that Ernie Pyle was on the medium carrier serving in the same task group. Nobody, except the Air Combat Intelligence officers, the skipper and the exec knew for sure, however, and everybody was burning with curiosity.

A sudden hush descended on all hands as Commander Crommelin adjusted the microphone. He looked solemn there, arms characteristically akimbo.

"Tomorrow, gentlemen," he began, "we hit Tokyo." In the deep silence that followed you could have heard a rose petal drop. Then a spontaneous burst of applause brought a smile to the Air Group Commander's face. It was as though he had announced a beer picnic for the following morning.

The USS *Randolph*, beginning her first war cruise exactly four months and one day after being commissioned, had raced from San Francisco to join Vice Admiral Marc Mitscher's fast carrier task force.

"We will keep planes over the target all day," the Air Group Commander said, "and night fighters from other carriers will keep the bastards up all night. Then we'll hit them again the day after that."

"Geez!" I heard one young pilot exclaim later that night. "I actually caught myself clapping. I must have been nuts!"

The next morning the first Hellcat roared down the flight deck. The plane's number was zero, its pilot was Commander Crommelin. It was 6:45 A.M. At brief intervals fifteen more fighter planes of the first sweep were launched, and the steady procession continued through that morning and early afternoon. A bomber strike was launched, too, and a few Hellcats took off on photographic missions.

The targets for the day were Japanese planes and aircraft facilities in the

79

area northwest of Tokyo. The purpose was to batter Japanese factories and to cripple Japan's air arm in support of the amphibious assault our forces were to make on Iwo Jima three days later. The secondary mission was to make a photographic reconnaissance of the Tokyo environs.

On February 16, "Crommelin's Thunderbirds" shot down thirty-eight Nip planes, damaged eleven more. Thirty-three more were destroyed on the ground, and an additional seventeen were damaged. Several hangars and other shore installations were either burned or battered. One fighter pilot told of flying in at tree level, taking careful aim, and scoring a direct hit on a hangar door with a rocket bomb.

"Hell," he grinned, "I couldn't miss."

During the action Mitscher's fast carrier task force shot down 332 enemy planes, wrecked another 177 on the ground. "Crommelin's Thunderbirds," making their initial strike against Tokyo twenty-seven days after leaving San Francisco, downed forty-seven Japanese planes and destroyed forty-two on the ground to compile one of the best records of any of the numerous carriers in the task force, and only lack of suitable targets kept their score from mounting higher. . . .

After that dramatic experience I boarded the baby carrier flagship, the USS *Makin Island*, which provided close air support during the Battle of Iwo Jima. Later I wrote an article on the captain, Vice Admiral Calvin Durgin, titled "King of the Baby Flattops."

Chapter Thirteen
IWO JIMA AND OKINAWA

One night Rear Admiral Durgin invited me to a filet mignon dinner in his cabin and there I met his flag officer, Thomas Gates, a Philadelphia banker, who later became Secretary of Defense. It was past midnight when Gates and I stood on the bridge watching the first night landings of fighter planes on the deck of a baby flattop, the USS *Carney*; it was exciting. It was a risky venture that became common later. I had seen at least three fighter planes crash on the flight deck of the USS *Randolph*. None of the fliers was killed, but one was horribly burned. In every case the planes were pushed over the side, since there was no time to salvage the valuable equipment.

In the *Reader's Digest Illustrated History of World War II*, there is a graphic description of the last gasp of Japan titled, "Into the Inferno of Iwo Jima." The subhead reads, "By capturing Iwo Jima, the Americans would be one step nearer Japan's home islands and would remove a menace to U.S. bombers attacking Japanese cities."

When the first American Marines scrambled ashore onto Iwo Jima, the story begins, "just after they stormed into a hell they had not bargained for. For one thing, they could scarcely see their objectives; the tiny eight-square mile surf-lashed island, shaped like a pork chop, was shrouded in smoke and dust from a massive three-day naval barrage that has preceded the assault. As the Marines leaped from their landing craft, they sank shin-deep in the ash and cinders of the beaches."

The *Makin Island* on February 20, 1945, joined the largest fleet that had been used in the Pacific operation until then. The fleet included 450 vessels of the U.S. Fifth Fleet gathered offshore. The battle of Iwo Jima was the bloodiest and most heroic operation in the history of the U.S. Marine Corps.

After the successful invasion of Iwo Jima, there was a welcome day of relaxation on the island of Mog Mog in Ulithi. Everyone, including Admiral Durgin, made a stop at the free bar, and even when fellow officers tossed me into the Pacific, I felt no pain. On Mog Mog I saw Jack Dempsey, but I didn't get a chance to speak to him.

On the way to what proved to be the climactic battle of the war

(Okinawa), I went ashore in an amphibious duck, a kind of boat-jeep, on Kerama Rettu, a tiny island at the foot of the Japanese archipelago. I was rebuked by a Marine corporal for picking up a delicate Japanese porcelain teapot which did not break until it reached our living room in Duxbury. It was the day after our Marines had taken the island, and the corporal was warning me about land mines. I didn't mind being rebuked. Two Japanese— an officer and an enlisted man—were the sole occupants of a small portable jail with bars. When I tried to interview them, the Japanese officer, a Betty pilot, looked stonily past me, but the enlisted man was almost cordial. He told me word had drifted in about the massive destruction caused by the mass air raids on Tokyo.

My third and final assignment was to observe the action at the battle of Okinawa. With a Marine colonel I was catapulted off the deck of the *Makin Island* and landed on Okinawa, where a jeep was waiting. On the way to command headquarters (a Japanese funeral vault), the driver, a Navy enlisted man, abruptly braked to a stop and crawled under the jeep. I followed suit and looked up to see a kamikaze pilot spraying shot all over the barren field. From the command post I went in a Higgins boat to the flagship, the *El Dorado*. Then came absolutely the most exciting experience of a long life. I stood on the bridge watching and listening to the two men who commanded the largest military battle force up to that point—battleships, cruisers, destroyers, and all sorts of landing craft. The battle directors were Vice Admiral Kelly Turner and General Buckner, who was killed a few days later by a sniper's bullet.

Simon Bolivar Buckner headed the force that recaptured the Aleutian Islands in 1943. In June 1944 he had been chosen to lead the U.S. Tenth Army in the assault on Okinawa. His tactics in the closing stages of the three-month Okinawa campaign were criticized for being over-cautious. He was killed only three days before Japanese resistance on Okinawa ended. He was cut down by shrapnel from a shell and was buried there.

Okinawa, about sixty miles long, is 330 miles southwest of Japan. Lieutenant General Buckner led an invasion force of 172,000 soldiers and Marines, whose assignment was to storm the last bastion before mainland Japan.

The Japanese had 100,000 men led by Lt. General Mitsuru Ushijima. The Japanese also had almost two thousand kamikaze pilots (suicide bombers who had vowed to give their lives in the attempt to blast the U.S. invasion fleet out of the water). According to the *Reader's Digest Illustrated History of World War II*, "The kamikazes, packed with as much as two tons of explosives, would swarm in like hornets out of the misty haze to the north, then scream down on the American ships. The only way to stop them was for the Combat Air Patrol (CAP) of Marine Corsair fighters to shoot them down before their final dive, or for shipboard guns to blow them apart with a large calibre shell."

The huge armada of American warships and troop carriers had assembled off Okinawa on April 1, 1945. By June 22 Okinawa had fallen. Japan's casualties totaled 131,000 dead, including 42,000 civilians. In addition, approximately 11,000 Japanese were taken prisoner. American land forces suffered 15,500 killed and 51,000 wounded.

On April 7, Japan had ordered a coordinated attack called Operation Ten-ichi ("Heaven 1"). On that day seven hundred aircraft, half of them suicide bombers, launched a devastating attack on the American armada. Of these, the Japanese lost 335, but they sank three destroyers, a tank landing ship, and two ammunition ships, as well as damaging some twenty-four other vessels.

I heard the call "Abandon ship" as one U.S. destroyer sank.

From the bridge on the *El Dorado*, a kamikaze plane came so near our ship I could see the closed eyes of the suicide pilot as his plane splashed into the sea less than a hundred feet away.

After the artificial fog descended and the guns became silent, I had chow, went into the library, and spent the evening reading a book on the history of boxing.

Next morning Turner's barge boat took me to an AKA cargo transport which was about to take off. I had to climb the Jacob's ladder (a rope ladder draped over the side). It dropped me at a tiny island, Asor, where Naval personnel were having a farewell party for the rear admiral who was leaving for another assignment.

I sat at the bar talking to Franklin Delano Roosevelt Jr., who was commanding officer of a destroyer, and Walter Davenport, editor of *Collier's* magazine. The next stop was Guam.

During my first stop in Guam, I had been invited one night to have chow with a Marine company of about two hundred men. I talked to a corporal, who told me his men were headed for combat duty (Iwo Jima, as it turned out). The day I landed in Guam on the way back to San Francisco, I ran into this same corporal—a striking coincidence. He was unshaven, dirty, wearing a tattered uniform. He waved a weary arm at the few men around him. "These are the only guys left. All the others were killed on Iwo Jima." By this time I had a good idea of what war was like.

During the hitchhiking from Okinawa to San Francisco, I had no time to get my clothes laundered. I remember I threw dirty socks and underwear over the side while on the transport ship. I also remember seeing the porpoises in ballet formation. Somewhere my hat disappeared, and when I deplaned in San Francisco (after hearing of the death of FDR as our plane approached for a landing on Johnson Island) I was out of uniform and didn't have a dollar in my pocket. And I needed a shave. I got another jeep and we drove up to the naval building in San Francisco. It was locked for the night. I rang the bell and took the elevator up to a floor where a Naval lieutenant was officer of the day. I told him I had been ordered to report back to Washington immediately, and asked for a travel request. He said the office was closed. I would have to wait until the next morning. I said I couldn't wait, and finally persuaded him to give me the address of the Navy lieutenant who was in charge of travel requests. It was a twelve-mile drive to an apartment house. The Navy lieutenant got out of an elevator. A lovely looking Wave! She would scarcely speak to me on the way back to the Navy building. In the office she said one of her assistants handled travel requests, but she finally found one and started typing. Suddenly she laughed.

"This is the funniest thing that has ever happened to me," she said. I gave her one of the shell bracelets I had bought in Honolulu and thanked her for being such a good sport. "But I really have to get home," I said. "I am out of uniform, and I need a shave." She burst out laughing.

One poignant memory I associate with the flight home. The war had already taken the life of my younger brother, Jimmy, who was shot down over the North Sea while co-piloting a Flying Fortress.

During my last year teaching at Dartmouth College, Jimmy lived with me and at my expense attended Clark School, a private preparatory school a few miles from Hanover. He played end on the football team. He was quick to enlist in the U.S. Air Force after Pearl Harbor.

Then came the second tragedy. On the way to Cleveland, Ohio, where our plane stopped to refuel, I had a premonition for the first time in my life. I remember how panicky I felt when I called Bobbie in Falls Church.

"Something bad has happened," I said. "What is it?" She told me my other young brother, Henry, had just been killed in a strafing raid by low-flying Nazi planes in France. Harry, as we called him, had been an infantry man in North Africa, Sicily, Italy, and France. I cried. I pictured him lying fatally wounded in the jeep he was driving before he died the next morning. To the end of her days, my mother, who became a Gold Star Mother, never got over the death of her two younger sons.

Years later, the names of Harry and Jimmy were among hundreds inscribed in a hall of flags aboard the USS *Massachusetts* which, having been mothballed, is now berthed at Fall River, Massachusetts. The hall honors all Massachusetts veterans who were killed in World War II, and I learned of it from my grandson Benjamin, who toured the battleship in 1985 as part of a Cub Scout outing.

When I returned to my desk at the Navy Department I learned that Vice Admiral Jonas Ingram was irked by some of the things I had written about him in "Boss of the Atlantic" in *Liberty* magazine. A Commander Green, who was stationed in Norfolk, Virginia, with the admiral, had come up to our "D" unit to complain about the article. When I reread it I could guess why. I wrote that the only South American statesman whose name Ingram could pronounce correctly was Benjamin Cohen of Chile, and repeated a remark he had made after inspecting a barracks: "This place looks like a Brazilian whorehouse." I wondered whether the admiral took offense at another anecdote. At a reception in Rio de Janeiro he yelled across the room to Commander Edward Lanigan: "Hey, Lanigan, stop chasing that skirt and come over and have lunch with me."

Lanigan came over. "That skirt," he said, "was Senhora Getulio Vargas." President Vargas wasn't at the party.

Soon after my return from the Pacific, Vice Admiral Aubrey Fitch was transferred to the Naval Academy, where he became superintendent. His successor was one of the great war heroes, Vice Admiral Marc Mitscher. Fitch's flag lieutenant took me down to see Mitscher's counterpart, and told him about the work I had done for Fitch. Captain Read, of the Dillon & Read investment firm in New York, wasn't impressed. He needed no literary help, he said.

Two or three weeks later, Captain Read called me into his office. Mitscher, he said, was to speak to thirty thousand employees of Pratt & Whitney, and he wanted me to write a speech. I asked what the theme was.

"He wants to thank the firm for its production of war planes," Read said. "Pratt & Whitney was the first to convert to military airplanes."

In my first draft I had Mitscher open his speech with these words: "I want to congratulate all you workers for seeing that Pratt & Whitney was not caught with its plants down."

Captain Read read it and shook his head. "Admiral Mitscher doesn't talk that way, Cutler. You'll have to change the opening."

"Well, would you please let the admiral read it, and if he objects, I'll come up with something else."

The day after the speech the *New York Herald Tribune* had a headline on the front page: MITSCHER SAYS PRATT & WHITNEY NOT CAUGHT WITH PLANTS DOWN. At that time, comedian Fred Allen had a radio program called "Allen's Alley." One Sunday night he mentioned the phrase, and *Time* magazine also did. In any case, Read kept me on the job.

One hot July day in 1945, I worked overtime. The last bus had gone, and while I was waiting outside the Navy Department for a taxi, a car stopped and the driver offered me a lift. There was casual conversation until Duxbury was mentioned.

"I'm a bit interested in that place, you see," the driver said. The accent was as genteel as it was English. "My people came from the same ancestral home in England as the Myles Standish who lived in Duxbury, Massachusetts. The name of the home was Duxbury Hall."

I asked if he was related to our Myles Standish.

"Oh, yes. We are descended from the same family. And it just so happens that my name, too, is Myles Standish."

During the ensuing conversation it was clear that he considered the bluff soldier who came over on the *Mayflower* one of the less illustrious members of the clan.

Then came V–J Day. Captain Parrish (with whom I corresponded after the war) had recently succeeded Rear-Admiral Holloway as head of the DCNO writing unit, and I remember how flattered and delighted I was when he called me into his office on the very day the Japanese surrendered.

"Secretary Sullivan just phoned and asked me to send him my two best writers." He smiled. "You and Hannibal Coons are going to write the DCNO story of the war against Japan."

When we walked into Assistant Navy Secretary John L. Sullivan's office, I was awed, but Hannibal, a magazine writer who reminded me of Alexander Woolcott, was chewing gum when we sank onto the black leather sofa. (He was later to write for the television shows *Dennis the Menace* and *The Addams Family.*)

"I want you gentlemen to write a quick history of Naval aviation's role in the war against Japan before the Army takes credit for our victory."

You won't believe what Hannibal said. "And I suppose you want the history by next Tuesday, Mr. Secretary?"

"I don't give a damn about that, but I want you to hurry," Sullivan said. When I asked if we could take a load of battle reports to my place in Falls Church and skip regular duty, he readily agreed to let us take a week off to write the story.

Hannibal stayed with us in our small house in Falls Church, Virginia, and much to Bobbie's disgust spent the day in his underwear, with his pendulous paunch drooping over his shorts. In one week we completed the hundred-page treatise. I wrote during the morning and Hannibal tapped his typewriter late into the night.

Rear-Admiral "Bing" Miller gave us Letters of Commendation for *The History of Naval Aviation in the War Against Japan.* That capped a rewarding Navy career. Captain Parrish gave me a "4.0," the highest rating.

In the final weeks I had earned the rank of lieutenant commander, but when the Navy gave us the option of accepting three hundred dollars in severance pay, I took it. In those days, that amount of money went a long way, especially if you were about to take a fling at free-lancing.

And that is how it came to pass that I got to the switch first and wrote a piece for *Collier's*: "Why I Quit College Teaching."

Chapter Fourteen
HOME AFTER THE WAR

Sometime in 1943, when I was serving with the U.S. Navy in Brazil, Bobbie casually mentioned in a letter that her great-aunt Miss May Sumner, who lived in Scituate, had bought us a house. It was especially reassuring to an aspiring free-lance writer to move into a comfortable home that had no mortgage.

I was well aware of the hazards and pitfalls of free-lancing, but since I was not starting out from scratch, life was not as precarious as it might otherwise have been. It was, in a way, exciting because of the unpredictable ups and downs.

The *Collier's* article was an encouraging beginning, and the weekly features published in the *Boston Sunday Post* took care of the grocery bills. One morning I wrote and sent to the *Toronto Star Weekly* three features, and the editor bought two. One was on Fernando Noronha, written from personal experience.

During the interval between my release from the Navy and the launching of the *Duxbury Clipper* in May 1950, I also sold long and short pieces to the *American Weekly*, the *Boston Globe*, *Argosy*, *American* magazine, and *Norte* (a South American publication). *Esquire* magazine paid me four hundred dollars for a profile of Bill Cunningham, who at the time was the leading sportswriter in New England. It was titled "Bill Cunningham's Eight-Day Week." In the "kicker," an editor noted that "Boston's candidate for Westminster Abbey or limbo is a tough scribe to tangle with." It was fun to get to know Bill, and I really thought I had it made when I gave him the first draft. He looked up after reading the first few paragraphs and said, "This is terrific." Even today I can quote the first brief paragraph, but I make no claim to its being "terrific."

> Bill Cunningham is a Boston institution, loved and hated as an institution usually is! Magna vox of the *Boston Herald*, syndicated columnist, emcee, lecturer, and radio analyst on a coast-to-coast hookup, he writes each month the equivalent of a novel and caramba, how the man writes! He has the most racy, buckety, slam-bang vocabulary in journalism.

As I look back on those fledgling years, I can see I was myself a bit racy and buckety. Caramba, indeed!

By this time I had my first agent, a lovely young writer named Julie Tatham, who lived in New York. Later when I started writing books and more magazine pieces, Carl Brandt was my agent. After he died, my choice was either Harold Ober or Paul Reynolds. When Reynolds read the manuscript of *Put It On the Front Page, Please!*, he agreed to represent me, thanks to the good offices of the late Sumner Putnam (brother of Eliot, who was headmaster of Noble & Greenough School). Sumner was publisher of Ives Washburn, Inc., New York. I was so delighted to be with Paul Reynolds I wrote letters to him and Sumner, expressing my pleasure. The letters crossed! Reynolds got the Putnam letter, and vice versa. Paul told me later that he deleted a similar incident from a short story by one of his writers, since it seemed too contrived. There was another mix-up later during a luncheon at the Century Club. We were halfway through the meal when Paul discovered that he was eating my crabmeat salad while I was enjoying his filet of sole. When I lunched with Paul Reynolds I was always too excited to notice such details. It was a great privilege to be associated with an agent of his stature.

Julie Tatham had done a lot to put me in orbit, and she didn't even fire me when I tried to sell a magazine article on the history of cranberries. There was one fun assignment. *Pic* magazine had asked her to write a brief humorous piece titled, "The Trouble With Men Is . . ." The editor wanted a writer to debate her, and she gave me the chance. The title of my piece was "Women Are Wonderful But . . ." Naturally, Julie won the debate, since I had only the next to the last word.

At this time (August 1947) I was a part-time lecturer at the Boston University College of Liberal Arts, where I taught Romance languages. I was elated one night when, after a day of teaching at the university, Julie called from New York to say she had sold two of my articles that day. One was the *Esquire* piece on Cunningham, the other the piece for *Pic*.

Now let's have a few words from Bobbie:

September of 1945 found us settled in the house on Washington Street, where I had been living during the thirteen months that John had been in Brazil. It was spacious but lacked character. Having lived in an early-nineteenth-century house down the street since I had moved to Duxbury, and having been surrounded by similar houses, this one just wasn't Duxbury to me.

The year before, I had looked at the Cape owned by Elisha Mowry, diagonally across the street. He had bought it in the early 1920s and used to summer in it. But never having been heated and with no chance of getting a furnace in war time, the big house seemed more sensible.

One Sunday in October when leaves were still on the elms and the maples were just turning scarlet, Mr. Mowry ("The Bear"), came to our house. "Someone is coming down this morning to buy my house," he said. "I know you have always wanted it, so this is your last chance." What were we to do? He left, and we thought long and hard. We went over after lunch and looked around. What work it needed! An awkward chimney was in the middle of the kitchen. Ceilings which were falling down had been covered up with beaverboard. But it did have charm and charisma. Old floorboards, H & L hinges on Christian doors, four fireplaces—one with the longest mantle (twelve feet) I have ever seen—delicate carving in the woodwork and a delightful screened porch which invited the eastern and western breezes. There was a small workshop in back, just outside the kitchen door. We didn't then know that sills would have to be replaced, fireplaces rebuilt, dampers put in, a new kitchen and baths installed, not to mention painting and papering. We fell for it.

"Here come the people," said the Bear.

We went over and hid behind a privet hedge in the backyard. We had arranged to do this to think things over, and Bear was to look out a second-floor window for a signal. We signaled "Yes." And so it was ours.

During the first year at 281 Washington Street, John was busy writing. It was hard and disappointing work. Of course, a wife must read everything and give help, criticism, and encouragement. Manuscripts carefully typed and mailed would often come back with a big "NO." What would we eat that week? Every day I would rush across the street to see what the morning mail had brought. Was there a check? The *Boston Sunday Post* provided at least one twenty-dollar check per week, and as often as not a couple more. Once there were six. But twenty dollars would buy food for a week if we shopped carefully. Powdered milk by the gallon had to be stirred up and iced. "I heard that you had funny milk," said one of my children's friends while supping in our kitchen. Funny, but good for you. Of course, there were some manuscript acceptances from a variety of magazines, and how we would celebrate when those checks came in! . . .

John was selling more and more magazine articles and lecturing three days a week at Boston University, going up on the train from Kingston, sitting with the bridge crowd, who would put in a wild bid just as the train pulled into the station. John also went up on Wednesday evening to give a course on Brazilian history and I would wait till 10 P.M. for him to come home. Never will I forget the excitement when his agent called at nine to say that she had sold two stories of his. What joy!

Then came famine. *Liberty* magazine, which had accepted my piece on the possible unionization of major league baseball, sent a consolation check for $250 when the movement suddenly collapsed. The organizer was Robert Murphy, a Harvard classmate and friend. There was a similar situation a short time later. I had written an article titled "Overweights Anonymous," and *Reader's Digest* had provisionally accepted it. One afternoon Paul Palmer, a senior editor, called to ask me to explain why overweight women might express their frustration by having a chocolate marshmallow fudge sundae—the gooier the better. I mentioned something a psychiatrist had told me about a subconscious return to trouble-free fetal days. This may be one reason why the magazine rejected the piece and sent me another consolation check for $250, but was that welcome!

My agent submitted the piece to *Coronet* after the *Digest* turned it down. It wasn't a bad story, since it was full of first-hand information gleaned when I followed the progress of a pilot study on group therapy for overweight persons at the Pratt Diagnostic Clinic, in Boston. *Coronet* kept "Overweights Anonymous" for two months before turning it down, and when that magazine later ran a piece that was similar, I was thoroughly disgusted. Then came the coup de grace.

I submitted an article on fashions in clothes to *Esquire*. *Esquire* was thoughtful enough to send three interoffice memos along with a courteous rejection slip.

"An interesting idea," the first memo read.

"Could be," said the second.

The final terse comment was from Arnold Gingrich, the editor in chief: "No. Obviously too much what our readers expect."

Hanover, New Hampshire, is a delightful residential community, especially if you are an outdoor sports enthusiast, which I am not. One drawback was that college teachers moved in the narrow orbit of an intellectual enclave. They were a gossipy bunch. If you weren't on the Dartmouth faculty, it was hard to crash society. Thus, for me at least, Duxbury had far more to offer than Hanover. A seashore community full of fascinating residents is more alluring than a mountain town full of Dartmouth personnel.

We liked Duxbury because it was a woodsy community with deer walks. It had red-winged blackbirds swaying on swamp reeds in the marshlands, whistling their wild call to nature. Duxbury had red foxes, blue herons, and brown thrashers. It had stately umbrella elms lacily, if starkly, silhouetted against a winter sky. The sea surges into its inlets and guzzles, and washes onto the wind-scarred dunes. The terrain is only inches above arrowheads and shell mounds. Yes, there was something historic and majestic—something cozy and friendly and intimate—about Duxbury.

The change of scene was rewarding in many respects, but it was also risky. Magazine writing was tough and competitive, and since many periodicals were beginning to fold, the market was even more limited.

At this time Walter Karig was head of the book and magazine department of the U.S. Navy in Washington, and when he wrote me a year or so after I was released from active duty and invited me to return to the Navy with the rank of commander, I was tempted. My assignment, he said, would be to travel around the country writing articles for the Navy. An agonizing decision turned into a reluctant refusal, and I have never regretted this.

Came the summer of 1947. Aware that I was floundering at this point, Bobbie's mother, Cid Ricketts Sumner, suggested I attend the famed Breadloaf Writers Conference in Middlebury, Vermont. Cid, who had already made a name for herself as a novelist, had been at the Breadloaf conference several times, and she was sure I would enjoy the general ambience.

When Cid invited me to be her guest at Breadloaf, I had been trying to write short stories—all of them bombs. Nevertheless, I had the gall to take my most recent clinker to the conference to find out at first hand whether I was a potential John O'Hara. I also took along a book manuscript I had been working on titled *The Village Green*. A novelist at Breadloaf told me the manuscript contained only one good chapter. My short story was so amateurish A. B. Guthrie, who wrote *The Big Sky*, sparing me harsh criticism, simply said, "Now, John, after all . . ."

In 1947 I wrote what was intended to be a short story. The name of the heroine was Curry, and the "plot" centered on her recipe for jambalaya. One evening during highball sips, I was sitting on the porch at Breadloaf with a group that included Paul Camey, who had published short stories before becoming a press agent for Twentieth Century Fox, and Monroe Stearns, then a teacher of English at the Berkshire School, in Sheffield, Massachusetts. Later he became trade editor of Prentice-Hall and Bobbs Merrill, in New York. He asked me to read aloud "my masterpiece."

"I would rather listen," I said. "You read it, Paul."

Camey didn't read the whole story. He and Monroe laughed through the first part of it, and by the time Camey was nearing the climax, Monroe's laughter was almost convulsive. He really stirred my bile. I got so mad, in fact, that I finally quoted from Ecclesiastes: "For as the crackling of thorns under a pot, so is the laughter of the fool."

Either Monroe didn't hear me or he didn't care, and finally, when he almost fell off his chair into his highball, I blew my top. "You know," I said, "I've got a good mind to punch you in the nose."

"The story," Monroe said, "has flavor. Curry provides it for the sauce."

Monroe and I renewed our acquaintance several years later when he called from New York to ask whether I was interested in ghosting the autobiography of James Michael Curley.

I was indeed.

Those two weeks at Breadloaf were stimulating. There was I, a cub writer, rubbing elbows with the great and the near great. I recall what Robert Frost said when I told him I had given up college teaching to try free-lancing: "Ah, then you've burned your bridges behind you." There were pleasant evenings when Frost stood behind a lectern and read some of his poems, including "Birches" and "Mending Wall."

One afternoon we played softball on Robert Frost's farm in Ripton, Vermont, with old white-hair and blue twinkly eyes himself watching from the sidelines. Everyone in the lineup except me was a well-known writer. John Ciardi was the catcher on our side; Guthrie played centerfield; and Theodore Morrison, the director of Breadloaf, played shortstop for the opponents. I almost beaned him on a peg to Ciardi at home plate.

John Ciardi, a leading American poet who later became editor of the *Saturday Review of Literature*, was one of my favorite authors. After dinner the first night at the conference I was sitting with him and Anya Seton, having a few postprandial drinks. Miss Seton, who was the daughter of Ernest Thompson Seton, the writer, illustrator, and naturalist, was best known for *Devil Water*, *The Winthrop Woman*, *Green Darkness*, and *The Hearth and Eagle*. When the bar closed, Anya pulled a pint of rye out of her pocketbook and passed it around. During this conversation Ciardi said he wanted to edit an anthology of poetry so he could leave Edgar Allan Poe out of it.

Bernard DeVoto—old sourpuss himself—told us about the torment John Marquand went through when writing a novel. He would lose weight, bite children, wear out eighteen pant seats, or threaten to commit suicide. DeVoto permitted himself a certain amount of poetic license.

The air hung heavy with literary allusions and admonitions:

Show them, don't tell them. A short story is a segment cut off from life, but it stands for the whole. Plausibility is the morality of fiction. Reminisce to give your story a special aroma or flavor. Then there is the fly-on-the-wall treatment: Effects in fiction come from excitation of feeling. You don't go out and find a novel behind a rosebush.

John Ciardi, a showman, told us he could write a sonnet on anything, reminding me of Guy de Maupassant, who boasted that he could write a short story on any topic. (When challenged to write on a piece of string, Maupassant wrote a masterpiece—"La Ficelle.")

Another night during one of our informal discussions John Ciardi casually mentioned that there were no rhymes for certain English words. Among them were twelfth, orange, and coccyx. Whereupon Monroe Stearns pulled out a pencil and started scribbling. He came up with the following:

"It was by the old village clock six
When I fell and fractured my coccyx."

Ciardi grinned. "A poem is never finished," he said. "It is abandoned in despair." Monroe abandoned his, but he proved something.

In one lecture on poetry Ciardi asked us to give him the title of a mythical sonnet, then dashed off the fourteen lines in less than five minutes. Another time, DeVoto read an opening paragraph of a novelist noted for the compression of his prose. The novelist had a character "leaning into a heavy wind." When I noted that a wind had to be heavy if someone was leaning into it, DeVoto simply leered. He gave an amusing lecture on the "oh, ho! he whinnied school," referring to writers who have their characters averring, asseverating, expostulating, or ejaculating. During this lecture Ted Morrison interrupted to say it had just been discovered that the author of the *Iliad* and *Odyssey* was not Homer, after all. It was another writer with the same name.

There was one embarrassing moment for me. One of the "pains" at the conference was a brash young Robert Mendes, whose manuscript was published as a novel titled *Spit and the Stars*. One evening Mendes was "sporting with some Amaryllis in the shade" while the professional writers cocktailing on their porch were watching him. William Lederer, the author of *The Ugly American*, mistook Mendes for me, and the next day he came up to me to "congratulate" me on my "conquest." I rose and turned to the lovely lady I was sitting with.

"This is Cid Ricketts Sumner, Bill," I said. "She is my mother-in-law."

Margaret Coit turned out to be the big surprise of the conference. She often joined Monroe Stearns, Paul Camey, and me during evening cocktails, and told us of the thousand-page manuscript she had in her "suitcase." She was vivacious and charming, but incredibly naive, we thought. One morning when DeVoto was scheduled to criticize her manuscript during the formal session, Margaret asked me to sit beside her. She was so nervous she was literally shaking, and she grasped my hand so tightly I thought she would tear it off. She almost exploded when DeVoto said some harsh things about her manuscript, which was later published as the Pulitzer Prize-winning biography of John Calhoun. Margaret, who came to Duxbury to visit us a few years later, also wrote a widely acclaimed biography of Bernard Baruch, the great financier.

Time raced by at Breadloaf. Bobbie drove up from Duxbury to join us on the final day in August, and the following morning Mrs. Sumner, Bobbie, and I returned to Duxbury, after dropping off John Ciardi in Harvard Square.

In the *Fifteenth Anniversary Report* of the Harvard Club of 1932, my career was reviewed up to 1947. The report begins with my marriage to Roberta Rand Sumner on April 6, 1941, in New Hampshire. "Children: Robert Burnley, born January 15, 1942; David Sumner, born July 4, 1943; Margaret Avery, born July 4, 1943; Abigail Rand, born April 1, 1947." (Our son John Ricketts was born in 1954.) Note that Bobbie and our twins were born on July Fourth.

Neal O'Hara, who summered in Duxbury, wrote a daily "Take It From Me" stint for the *Boston Traveler*. I was pleased when he invited me to join his staff of guest columnists while he was on vacation. After all, his "guesters" included comedian Fred Allen and novelist John Marquand, along with the mayor of Boston and the governor of the Commonwealth. It was good advertising, too, to have O'Hara refer to "the erudite editor of the *Duxbury Clipper*." He knew well, however, that the little erudition I had did not include a practical knowledge of newspapering, and made several constructive suggestions. He was the first victim of one of his bits of advice.

In 1948 his guest columnists were Governor Robert Bradford of Massachusetts, Fred Allen, the editor of the *Gardner News*, and me. I was thrilled when I read a letter to the editor in the old *Boston Traveler*: "You had several VIPs writing your column last week, but the best by far was the editor of the *Duxbury Clipper*."

Then came a break in the routine.

Neal pointed out that a popular department in any newspaper is a reader's forum in which Mr. Enraged Taxpayer or Mrs. Outraged Citizen sends in sticks of literary dynamite. This, he said, often enlivened proceedings and aroused reader interest.

"The *Clipper*," we wrote in the tenth issue, "would welcome such contributions (i.e., comments on controversial issues). Its columns are open to the three sides every question has: your side, his side, and the correct side."

At this point the cat lay down with the pepper. Neal O'Hara found he was the No. 1 selection for target practice.

In guest columns I had written for him he had given me wide latitude, never objecting when I referred to him as "the poor man's Mark Twain" who "invariably arises at the crack of noon." Figuring turnabout was fair play, I invited Neal to take over my "Just Between Us" column in an August issue when the tourist season was at full tide. This was a "think aloud" feature I wrote as a filler.

"Annually," he opened, "when I ask the editor of the *Duxbury Clipper* to do a guest column for me in the *Boston Traveler*, I make this assertion: 'The space is yours; say in it what you please. It will not be blue-penciled.' So, what could be more gentlemanly and equitable than for your editor to grant me the same privilege?"

Then, instead of blasting away at my inept skippering of the *Clipper*, he handed the hot end of the poker to his favorite "dislikes," including Drew Pearson: "As courageous columnist, he pulled his neck in like a Duxbury clam when he allowed the very little man in the White House [Truman] to call him an SOB." Neal accused Eleanor Roosevelt of being "the first and only First Lady of the Land who commercialized her position," and pinked FDR with a few verbal quills.

Although I did not approve of Neal's comments, I did not revise them out. Then, wham! In the next issue, one of Duxbury's leading liberals, an energetic woman in her mid-eighties, let fly at O'Hara and me.

> Your readers are very much shocked and offended by O'Hara's article and also painfully surprised that you printed it. Isn't it too late—or out of date—to bring up the coarse and ill-bred comments on Mr. Roosevelt five years after the end of the 'Roosevelt hate era'? I had hoped that if the *Clipper* had any political comments to make they would be characterized by a lack of partisan bias.

Hector Holmes (brother of the Reverend John Haynes Holmes), a brilliant lawyer who lectured on patent law at Harvard Law School, also came fighting out of his corner:

> I found Mr. O'Hara's column mildly amusing [O'Hara had a national reputation as a humorist], but hardly edifying or consonant with the tone and character of your altogether charming paper. Mr. O'Hara is so gifted and can write so well it is too bad he didn't give your readers something they all could enjoy.

After the exhilaration of the Breadloaf Writers Conference, I settled down to the humdrum routine of peddling Sunday newspaper features, with part-time teaching at the Boston University College of Liberal Arts.

Beginning writers grasp at straws. I remember how thrilled I was in 1940 when *Reader's Digest* picked up a squib, "She has a nice sense of rumor," I had written for a *Boston Transcript* "Who Is it?" Twenty years later *Reader's Digest* included that squib in an anniversary issue that reprinted the best "picturesque speech" items of the preceding twenty years. Again I was credited with this pun, but a later anniversary issue included "she has a nice sense of rumor" ascribed to "anonymous."

In early 1949 Julie Tatham, the New York literary agent and writer, had signed a contract with a publisher in Racine, Wisconsin, to write a series of adventure books for girls. She suggested that I write similar books for boys aged eleven to fourteen.

Never having written any successful fiction, I asked Julie just how one went about writing books for boys. She gave me a formula. Start each chapter by getting into the thoughts of your hero. Then get him into exciting action that leads to a predicament at the end of the chapter. Open the following chapter by getting your plucky hero out of danger, then more thought, more action, and another predicament.

And so it came to pass that I put "my hero" Tom Stetson through the wringer. It was an amiable Baptist minister with whom I had chatted for several hours on a plane trip from Brazil who enabled me to write three adventure books.

Leo B. Halliwell, a Baptist minister, had witnessed strange jungle incidents that no other white man had ever beheld. For the previous eighteen years he had lived among head-hunters and Indian tribes deep in the lush Amazonian back country where primitive folk lived and died unmolested by civilization. During all the time he had been patrolling the inland waters in his only home—a motorboat—Halliwell's only companion had been his wife.

During the trip Halliwell held me spellbound with his unending stories of ministering to Indian tribes in the jungle of Brazil. In some cases he was the first white man ever to come into contact with savage tribes, some of whom were cannibals. Back in Duxbury after the war, I had written perhaps a dozen feature stories for the *Boston Sunday Post* based on stories the minister had told me, along with some independent research. Those *Post* stories gave me all the necessary background I needed for the adventures of my jungle hero.

One day a tribesman came to Halliwell with two bottles, which he wanted to put in a refrigerator. He had tasted ice water and wanted to take some to his father. It did not occur to him that the water would become warm in transit. Another night the missionary was playing his radio when an Indian woman suddenly looked puzzled. Mrs. Halliwell explained that a woman in New York was singing, whereupon the woman slapped herself on the chest, indicating that the singer must have a good pair of lungs. Their naiveté was astonishing.

In January of 1943, Halliwell visited a hut which had enough water to permit a canoe easy access. Tables were placed on a platform, and the Amazon lapped the missionary's feet as he sat on the platform. While there he saw a snake stick its head out of a well and gobble up a toad that was sitting on the platform.

In his travels Halliwell had been bitten by a saw-toothed piranha, and had been shocked by an electric eel known as an *uraque*. This eel can stun a cow, and often does when cows come down to the river to drink, causing them to drown.

Once, while watching some natives hoisting cattle for loading, Halliwell saw a boy kicked into the river by a cow. As he fell he cut himself, and the smell of his blood attracted piranhas, which reduced him to a skeleton in a matter of minutes.

Although Halliwell, whom I interviewed above the clouds while flying over Brazil, had penetrated into wild settlements never before explored by white man, he said, Catholic missionaries and others had converted many of the Indians.

The first book was *Tom Stetson and the Giant Jungle Ants*. Its sequel was *On the Trail of the Lost Tribe*, followed by *Tom Stetson and the Blue Devil*. Tom was a resourceful youngster who once made a lantern by cupping fireflies in a plant, and he helped block the advance of a tribe of wicked Indians by using honey to lure millions of *tocandeiras*, destructive ants up to an inch long. In those jungle books roamed all the animals I had seen in the Belem zoo. I often wished I had kept the address of that unknown, white-haired, bespectacled Baptist minister who made a long airplane flight too short. I think he would have liked the Stetson books.

Those three jungle books bridged the gap between newspaper and magazine free-lancing and the launching of the *Duxbury Clipper*, in May of 1950. Following an arrangement with the Racine, Wisconsin publisher, I would write the first chapter, outline the rest of the book (usually around fifty thousand words) and receive a check for five hundred dollars. When I sent in the remaining chapters (which never followed my outline) I received a second check for five hundred dollars. The first two books, written in 1949, took about a month each to write. By the time I started the last book, I was too busy with newspaper features and college teaching to find enough time to complete the book.

When I got a curt letter from the publisher saying I was past the deadline, I locked myself in my study and banged out the text in thirty-five hours. After rewriting one page, I sent off the manuscript and waited for chilling orders to repair the damage. Instead, I got a nice note from an editor saying it was by far the best of the three books.

My real writing career was not to begin until 1956, but in the intervening decade there was mounting excitement of publishing a newspaper for a growing town. In his syndicated column, Neal O'Hara asked why a town more than three hundred years old had to wait so long before having its own newspaper.

Chapter Fifteen
SPEAKING OF MOTHERS-IN-LAW

My mother-in-law, Cid Ricketts Sumner, encouraged my writing career from the day I met her in 1941. The first boost was her invitation to spend two weeks at the Breadloaf Writers Conference in 1947, and she gave me unfailing support. She was a successful author. Her early books included the *Tammy* series, three of which were made into movies, starring Debbie Reynolds and Sandra Dee.

In the early 1950s I profiled Cid in the *Clipper:*

Bertha Ricketts was calm even as a baby, and to such a degree that her family called her "Placid" before shortening it to "Cid." Tall and gracious, with luminous hazel eyes and a smile that lights up her face, she is beautiful and consistently charming. She is a happy combination of logic and fair-mindedness, but I think of her primarily as a person of warm and deep understanding.

She insists she is lazy, then dashes off the first draft of a novel in four weeks or paints all the woodwork in the house. She says she can't cook, but her spoon bread, shrimp gumbo, and chicken jambalaya are very disturbing to a person who is dieting. When she tells you she never made a career of being a mother, don't be fooled! There are four strong arguments to the contrary named Roberta, Prudence, James ("Jacques" was born in Brussels), and Frederick.

Cid was born and raised in Mississippi, but has lived more than half her life in New York and Massachusetts. Her mother was a music school teacher, her father a professor of mathematics at Millsaps College. She was tutored at home until she went to high school, and after graduating from Millsaps she received a master's degree in English and psychology from Columbia. To earn enough money to continue her studies for a Ph.D. she taught English for two years in a Jackson high school. She returned to Columbia for a year before switching to the Cornell University Medical School, then left to marry one of her professors.

At various times she has studied piano and harp and has painted watercolors, but writing has always been her first love. The voluminous diaries she kept from the age of eleven to twenty show the introspection and humor, the strong flight of imagination and turn of phrase that are today so characteristic of her writing. I know, because I peeked.

At the age of eighteen she sold a poem to *Smart Set*. She thought she had arrived until a Tennessee magazine, after accepting three of her poems, went bankrupt. "I never received the two dollars promised," she said. She tried short stories next. She would write thirty-nine (the number required in a correspondence course), and if she failed to sell any it would be farewell to literature. She sold the thirty-sixth! She sold others later, but it was as a novelist that she rose to her full stature. There is no need of my telling you about her brilliant descriptions or the imagery and sweep of her prose. You'll know if you've read *Tammy*.

Quality, a novel Cid Ricketts Sumner had written in 1946, was made into a movie called *Pinky*, in 1949. I remember the day Cid called me to say Twentieth Century Fox had offered her $10,000 for the film rights to *Quality*. When she asked if she should accept the offer, I asked what Carl Brandt advised.

Brandt, her agent, had advised her to accept the offer because it was unlikely "that Hollywood would cross the color line." A few weeks later we read in the *New York Times* that Twentieth Century Fox had paid $125,000 for the book, and later we learned that it was to be filmed as *Pinky*. It would be the longest film that had been produced in Hollywood since *Gone With the Wind*.

Cid said she was surprised to read in *Ebony* magazine that *Pinky* would be issued in twenty-seven languages. "When I wrote *Quality*, I had no idea that the book would cause such a splash," she said. The book sold fairly well after it appeared as a condensed novel in the *Ladies' Home Journal*.

Hollywood's attitude toward controversial issues had changed. *Gentleman's Agreement*, which treated anti-Semitism, was a case in point. Shortly thereafter Hollywood became interested in the Negro question. *Home of the Brave* and *Last Boundaries* had already been shown on the screen, and *Pinky* was to appear in the following weeks. Elia Kazan, who did *Gentleman's Agreement*, also directed *Pinky*.

Mrs. Sumner said she had had some correspondence with Elia Kazan in connection with a nightgown worn by Ethel Barrymore in the motion picture. Barrymore was cast as Miss Em, an aristocratic southern lady who befriends Pinky and who leaves her a legacy. "When I saw a notice in one of those Hollywood columns that Miss Barrymore was going to wear a $450 nightgown in her role as an impoverished southern gentlewoman, I wrote Mr. Kazan and told him: 'For heaven's sake take that nightgown off Miss

Barrymore. Miss Em never heard tell of a nightie that cost $450, and even if she had, she wouldn't have been caught dead in it. I have a very suitable plain cotton nightgown. Shall I send it?' "

There was no need to send it. In his air-mail letter, Kazan said he had gone to the head of the wardrobe department and asked for a description of Miss Barrymore's nightgown. He quoted the description given him—"white, plain cotton gown with a ruffle of embroidery at neck and wrist." He added, in effect, that the $450 business was probably the work of the publicity department. At this point, I asked Cid why she hadn't called her novel *Pinky* instead of *Quality*.

"Simply because 'quality' was the heart of the matter," she said. "When I wrote *Quality* I felt, as I still feel, that there was no snap, legislative cure for the Negro problem; there was only the long, slow, hard way of improving the quality of each individual—black and white—by education and mutual understanding. My novel was not a problem of whether blacks and whites should intermarry—a theme which Hollywood seems to be emphasizing—but rather it dealt with the struggle one colored girl had to make a satisfactory life for herself in a perplexing environment."

Pinky, the gripping film account of a girl who "passes" was warmly reviewed by *Ebony* magazine.

I asked Cid where she got the idea for *Quality*.

"I heard about a Negro girl who was sent North to be educated. Her grandmother sent her, and it was this grandmother who gave me the idea for Aunt Dicey. When she returned to Mississippi she committed suicide. She was unable to adjust herself to her environment after being North. In *Quality* I was trying to figure out some way such a girl could make a good life for herself. Pinky, you see, went North, too, but when she came back, instead of feeling sorry for herself, she devoted herself to making her people happy. The house that Miss Em left her she turned into a hospital for her kind."

Bobbie's Aunty May, her great aunt, was a true New Englander in every way. She lived frugally but was generous beyond belief. She lived year-round in Scituate in her former summer home.

When I first met her I was a bit ill at ease, for I had never known anyone quite so formidable. One afternoon Bobbie and I were sitting with Aunt Amie and Aunty May in a Beacon Hill tearoom. By this time I could tell that both ladies were Proper Bostonians, but if there is any doubt of it, a remark made by Aunty May clinched it.

"Oh, dear, I just can't seem to think of the name of that investment house in Boston. Not Kidder Peabody—what's the name of the other one?"

As far as Aunty May was concerned, the only two investment houses in Boston were Kidder Peabody and Lee Higginson. Her old-fashioned ways did not jibe with our style of living. She was dead set against liquor, perhaps because her older brother had liked the hard stuff and had married at the age of seventy-five to a younger woman and spent his days golfing and cocktailing. She did not speak to him for eleven years until, on his death bed, she finally forgave him.

If she went out to a restaurant, and she loved going out for lunch, her chauffeur would stop at the door. The doorman would come over to welcome her, and I remember once when she said, "Do you serve liquor here?" "Yes, ma'am," said the doorman.

Aunty May said in a haughty voice, "Drive on, Lloyd."

Bobbie and her family despised Lloyd, because he took advantage of her. After he divorced his wife, a colorless woman, Aunty May supported the wife in fine style. She donated heavily to charities, as I found out years later when she asked me to balance her checkbook. Twenty thousand dollars here, fifteen thousand dollars there, and so on. Yet, when she died, and we were going over her possessions, we saw that her silver was only plated. She had her hats redecorated every fall, rather than buy new ones. As the Boston Dowager said, "We have our hats."

But she was generous to her nephews and nieces. When I went to Brazil, Bobbie and I had enough money saved to put a down payment on a house—a small house, of course. Duxbury had few houses with heat in those days, and one Bobbie found with heat was for sale for ninety-five hundred dollars. She could make a down payment and have a mortgage which we could easily swing with my Navy salary and money from my syndicated columns. When her aunt heard of this, she said, "Why not let me have the mortgage and you can pay me with no interest?" This Bobbie did, but after the first payment, as Bobbie wrote me when I was in Brazil, Aunty May said to her, "I can't bear to have you paying me money." She erased the debt, and we owned the house clear. She told Bobbie that she would have to do the same for the other children when the time came. She had already bought Bobbie a second-hand Ford convertible, which I foolishly sold to my sister when I went into the Navy and we needed the money. There Bobbie was in Duxbury with three babies and no car. She had to depend on friends or walk to get her groceries. But I was far away in Brazil and did not realize the hardships she faced. Of course, Aunty May and her housekeeper (Lloyd had long left for a defense industry job) would take her out shopping when Bobbie asked.

When our children were born, Aunty May would arrive, checkbook in hand and ask for a private audience with me. "How much did it cost? Tell me exactly, how much did you have to spend?" And she would write a check for several hundred dollars, for which we were so grateful in those meager days. In fact, whenever any major expense came up, she was there to help us out. She also helped out Bobbie's brothers and sister when they needed a car or a house.

At Thanksgiving, she would always provide the turkey, thinking that was the major purchase. One Thanksgiving, we were so broke, we could not find money for vegetables, cranberry sauce, and all the fixings.

Bobbie had to scurry about and find some antiques to sell to a Plymouth dealer. She came home with $13.95, and as she entered the door she called out to me, "John I have some money, now we can have a real Thanksgiving dinner." Bobbie's mother always came to these affairs, along with Aunty May and Aunt Amie (Bobbie's father's sister, who lived in Canton). We would sit in the living room of our Cape, enjoying lemonade and cheese, and one at a time, Bobbie's mother, Bobbie, or I would go out to the kitchen to baste the turkey. Hidden on a shelf in a cupboard would be our cocktails, old-fashioneds, probably, and we would take a large sip. Those turkeys were basted more than most turkeys.

Aunt Amie was against liquor in those days, too, although later she became reconciled to modern habits and even served cocktails at her own house in Canton where she lived alone in the house her father had built in the 1880s—a large Victorian house with high ceilings, filled with gorgeous antiques, many of which we have today in our house.

I remember, once when she was visiting us in Falls Church, Virginia, when I was stationed in the Navy Department just across the Potomac, Bobbie and I were sipping our cocktails from a kitchen cupboard. Aunt Amie said, "It seems to me that things are getting more spirited around here." She probably knew what was going on. Of course, she was of a different generation than Aunty May and more modern in her ways. She was generous, too, in helping out with our children's education. She said about our son David's private school, "I can hardly wait to pay for David's tuition." She was so happy when our daughter Meg was accepted by the Winsor School (the headmistress, Valerie Knapp, lived at the College Club in

Boston, where Aunt Amie spent winter months) that she happily paid all the bills for that school. What a help it was, because our income did not provide for private school tuition. Aunt Amie agreed it was important for our children to get the best education possible.

Chapter Sixteen
THE FIRST BLOW

By 1957, our eldest son Robert was in the fourth form at Groton. David and Meg, our twins, were at Derby Academy in Hingham, Massachusetts, while Gail was in a Duxbury school and Ricky was in nursery school. Robert and David had both been Little League all-stars for three years, and both showed promise in baseball and football. Along with Meg, they were regulars on the Duxbury Yacht Club junior tennis team, with a few championships to their credit.

In 1958 Robert, his girl, and another prep school couple attended the Groton-St. Mark's annual dance at The Plaza Hotel in New York. Bobbie and the two girls spent the night at the Hotel Mansfield on West Forty-fourth Street, across from the Harvard Club of New York, where Robert and I stayed. The next morning I arranged for a visit to Gene Tunney's office near the Biltmore Hotel. Tunney had a plush office with antique furnishings, carpeting you could sink into, and walls lined with books. The boys—Robert and his friend Hank Alexandre—were excited about meeting the famous world boxing champion who had retired undefeated. Even the two young ladies had heard about "Gentleman Gene." Bobbie remembers the occasion:

> We all sat down after the introduction. Tunney got up from his wide mahogany desk, went over to the book-lined wall and pulled down a slim volume. "I must read you this poem," he said. I, who prided myself on my knowledge of poetry, had never heard of the author—someone obscure. Tunney read the young people several poems and never mentioned the famous "long count" which the boys were so eager to hear about first-hand.

The following year Gene Tunney came to Boston to have his annual check-up at the New England Baptist Hospital. When he called and invited me to drop in, I took my sixteen-year-old daughter Meg in to meet him. I had to explain to Meg who he was. I also took a book on boxing, which we had given to David. Tunney signed it, "To David—always lead with your left, and keep your chin up."

One thing I remember of the conversation was Gene's comment on

"Jumping Joe" Dugan, who a few years earlier had played third base for the New York Yankees. "He was an awful bore," Tunney said.

Up until this time everything had gone well. Our children were all getting along with their peers and causing us no headaches. Then came the first blow.

Robert, who had been born in 1942 in Hanover, New Hampshire, while I was teaching at Dartmouth, was a blue-eyed, blond baby with the features of my mother. Bobbie and I were happy to have a normal child who showed athletic promise and got good marks all during his school years. After sending him for seven years to Duxbury schools, which were under par at the time, we decided to send him to boarding school. But which one? The rector of our Episcopal church told us he was sending his son, Richard, to the Groton School, and since Robert was his best friend, he suggested that Robert also apply. Robert was accepted and received a scholarship of $1,250 a year.

There were tears in his eyes as we left him at Groton. He was only twelve years old—too young to leave home, we discovered later. Parents were not allowed to visit the boys for six weeks, presumably to let them get adjusted to being away from home. Robert's first report was disastrous—all Ds and Fs. He had not been prepared for Groton, unlike most of the other students, who had attended private schools before entering Groton. His classmates teased him about having attended public school. Robert soon adjusted, however, and before long he was on the honor roll and was competing in sports. By the time he was in the sixth form, the graduating class, he had been on the football, baseball, and tennis teams and was captain of the basketball team. Jake Congalton, the basketball coach, said, "Robert was really inspirational in all our games."

Admitted to Harvard in his junior year, I felt he should also apply to some other college, but his guidance director said, "No. Harvard is enough."

Robert spent five years at Groton. Our whole family attended commencement exercises in June 1959, and to be sure we could take in all the commencement exercises, we spent one night at the Groton Inn.

In his last year at Groton, Robert had scored ninety-eight percent on his physics exam at midyear, but he flunked the final in June. The Reverend John Crocker, the headmaster, told us Robert had "rested on his oars." He passed the course with a C because his average grades were high. Mr. Crocker got in touch with Harvard, and it was decided that his admission should be postponed for a year.

Here was a dilemma. I felt that since American boys were being drafted at the time, Robert should get his military service over with. I, of course, was upset and disappointed that he wasn't going to my alma mater, but I was comforted by the thought that he would go after his military service. Robert enlisted in the U.S. Army and was sent to Fort Dix, in New Jersey, for basic training, then to Albuquerque, New Mexico, for advanced training. His next assignment was Korea, where the U.S. Army was engaged in mopping-up operations after the Korean conflict. Robert wrote us often and seemed to be getting along well, making friends and enjoying the company of pretty Korean girls. Robert had always been popular with girls.

While at Groton, Robert had played tennis at the Duxbury Yacht Club during summers. He was winning one tournament easily against his arch rival, Gerry Millar, in a battle for the club championship, until Bobbie and I went up to watch the match. Then he lost every remaining game along with the club championship. Bobbie and I were puzzled. Did we upset him that much? What was the reason? And why had he flunked that physics course at Groton?

One weekend we went up to the Holderness School in New Hampshire, where David was in the ninth grade. (Later David became captain of the baseball team, captain of the football team, and captain of the junior varsity hockey team.) Robert came by train to join us at Holderness, having just completed basic training at Fort Dix. He seemed perfectly normal at that time.

He had been in Korea for nearly a year when we got a disjointed letter from him. I remember it was during the summer, because David was reading the letter aloud to us on our porch.

"Something is wrong with Robert," I said. "Either that or he was drunk when he wrote this letter."

It did not occur to me at that point that Robert was showing signs of mental illness. Bobbie and I wondered what was happening to him. A beautiful Norwegian exchange student, whom Robert had been dating, had returned to Norway and had written Robert a "Dear John" letter.

In Korea Robert had been in an accident when a jeep he was riding in went off an embankment. His leg was broken and his face lacerated, we heard. We did not know how badly injured he was. I immediately wrote his commanding officer to ask if anything was the matter with our son. By return mail, he said nothing was wrong. A week later, however, he wrote that something indeed was wrong, and he told us that Robert would be shipped to the Walter Reed Hospital in Bethesda, Maryland. He arrived at the hospital wearing pajamas, a bathrobe, and slippers.

108

Bobbie and I rushed down to the Walter Reed Hospital to see him. We expected him to be badly scarred, but he was still his handsome self, with only a few, hardly noticeable facial scars. A conference with a psychiatrist there did not calm our fears. Robert was to be medically discharged from the Army and sent home. From our hotel, we called an old Navy friend, Dr. Alan Grinsted, a psychiatrist, to consult with him. He did not make us feel any better when he said Robert might never recover and that schizophrenia was a terrible disease with no cure available. Bobbie cried, and we returned to Duxbury.

After a month or so, we were called to Maryland to bring Robert home. On the way back we stopped at the Taft Hotel in New Haven, Connecticut, and I asked for a second-floor room, thinking Robert might try to jump out a higher window. He remained silent and didn't finish eating the sandwich we had had sent up to the room. At home, we consulted Dr. George Starr, a good friend, who gave Bobbie the name of a psychiatrist, whom she called.

"What is your son doing right now?" he asked. Bobbie said, "He appears to be reading, but I don't think he is taking anything in." The psychiatrist said, "If he is entitled to Army treatment he will get just as good care in a veterans' hospital as anywhere else."

We took Robert to Army headquarters in Boston, where I ran into an old Harvard classmate, Edward Ronan, who was in charge. Ronan had a dossier on Robert. After glancing at it for a moment, he looked up and said, "Wow. IQ 160."

After consulting an associate, Ronan gave Robert "complete disability" and arranged for him to be admitted to the Veterans Administration Medical Center in Brockton, Massachusetts.

It was so sad for Bobbie and me to see him there, the youngest patient among so many old, unkempt-looking men. Every Sunday we went to see him, and occasionally he was allowed to come home for a weekend. Not really knowing what I meant, I said to Robert, "Don't give away any family secrets." Was this the reason Robert would never talk to the staff about what bothered him? I don't know, but at any rate he did not talk much to them. Bobbie went to see the social worker often. We were both sad at what had happened to this brilliant, handsome boy who was so young. One day he said to Bobbie, "Bring me lots of books. I will be here a long time." He was there for about ten years but came home often, once to join us on a ski trip to New Hampshire, another time to go with us to Bermuda.

Finally, in 1979, the hospital officials said he should be discharged. He lived at home for many years then, taking trips to Italy, Austria, Greece,

Romania, and Bermuda with us. He seemed to enjoy it all. But we realized he would never attain his potential. The years went by. The other children grew and graduated from prep school. Our youngest, Ricky, was growing up fast. It was such a pleasure, living the life all over again that we had lived with Robert and David. Like his two brothers, Ricky was the best pitcher on the Little League team, got high grades in school, and was popular with his peers.

Robert is now home for good. He helps around the house, doing dishes, washing, helping Bobbie with the gardening, sweeping, and so on. He earnestly wants to help and to be liked. He was a skillful and enthusiastic tennis player, so we built a tennis court. But he has given that up. He enjoys swimming in our pool every day in the summer, takes care of our little French poodle, and seems glad to be at home.

Will some new treatment help him? We are investigating, and if a new therapy is available, we will give Robert a chance to try it. The best possible thing that could happen would be to give Robert back his old self and, in his remaining years, give him something to live for. He is now forty-nine.

Chapter Seventeen
LAUNCHING THE *CLIPPER*

It all began at the bridge table one Sunday night late in April 1950. I was trying to make a redoubled bid while my lovely wife, Bobbie, was playing her usual loquacious game of dummy. With four young children to fend for, I was proceeding cautiously. The stakes, after all, were a fortieth of a cent a point, and I was no Harold Vanderbilt. That is, I couldn't play bridge as well as Harold.

Debbie Nelson was nodding briskly about something. "You are absolutely right, Bobbie. Absolutely! Nobody in this town ever knows anything that goes on. Tonight, for instance, there was another of those cozy ninety-nine cent ham and bean suppers at The First Parish Church, and George and I didn't know a blooming thing about it."

A few minutes later Bobbie said, "Debbie and I think you ought to start a little newspaper so we'll know about church suppers, PTA meetings, and all that kind of thing."

By 1950, Duxbury, which has been called everything from "America's first summer resort" to "the last outpost of Americanism," was becoming a year-round bedroom community, but recreation was still its chief industry.

From 1800 until 1850, thanks to its position as the leading shipbuilding center in New England, Duxbury prospered. During the romantic days of sailing ships, its seafarers built their square houses and furnished them with treasures brought from East India and the Orient in ships owned by Ezra Weston, a dominant personality still remembered as "King Caesar." Ship captains built the square colonials, while first mates were content with the simpler Cape Cods. According to Daniel Webster, who shopped for rum and other bare essentials of nineteenth-century living in Duxbury, Weston was the largest shipowner and shipbuilder in America. His vessels traded all over the world, and in his own right he was a legendary character. There was a secret passageway that led from his wharf down under the sparsoak to the cellar of his former residence, a square colonial on King Caesar Road. Behind this residence were quarters for the shipyard workers, and the ancient bell which once summoned them to meals still hangs in its belfry.

Duxbury's days of despair came during the latter half of the nineteenth century when sailing vessels gave way to the faster clippers and steamships. The shallowing of Duxbury harbor also contributed to the industrial gloom, and the town went broke. The bank where Daniel Webster occasionally cashed a check failed, and residents moved to greener pastures. Duxbury was too poor to afford fancy Victorian architecture with its clutter of turrets, balconies, scrollwork, and gingerbread trim, thus its colonial architecture, classic in its simplicity, was preserved simply because there was no money for improvements. Today, standing behind white picket fences and lilac hedges, the renovated white Cape Cods and square colonials give the town a unique flavor that is not lost on tourists from almost every state in the Union.

Duxbury was still a ghost town when the railroad was built in the 1890s, a step toward sophistication that gave rise to the story of the tourist who asked why John and Priscilla Alden constructed their homestead so close to the railroad tracks. Soon Duxbury's inns and hotels were attracting summer visitors from points as remote as California and Alaska. By 1915, water mains were installed and the town's windmills were reduced to landmarks, ending another picturesque phase. More and more people from the hinterlands were drawn to this charming rural hamlet with its sandy beaches lapped by ocean water. Along with its pine-clad hills, tree-shaded ponds, and deer walks under majestic trees that protect its narrow, winding streets from sun glare, Duxbury had a history that went back to the Pilgrims.

By 1950, most of the colonials along Washington Street, the "Main Street" of the town, had been restored (some by descendants of the original settlers, others by outlanders like Bobbie and me), and the street itself had become a tourist attraction. It takes more than a tourist attraction, however, to support a weekly newspaper.

Even the main stem had few business establishments, and although there were pockets of commercial enterprises scattered around town, including a blacksmith's shop in the section called Island Creek, most of Duxbury's twenty-five square miles consisted of ponds, cranberry bogs, and woodland, with only a few sparsely settled sections. If Bobbie and I had carefully canvassed the advertising potential, we might have considered a more promising venture—opening an antiques shop, for instance. Why not? We knew as much about antiques as we did about operating a weekly newspaper, and how can trafficking in old pewter, cobbler's benches, and trestle tables get you in trouble?

Soon after Bobbie decided she wanted a newspaper in the family, she found, while looking for something more literary, one of those how-to-do-it manuals in a bank in nearby Plymouth. This brochure, titled "Establishing and Operating a Weekly Newspaper," was issued by bureaucrats at the United States Department of Commerce who must have gathered their data from professors of journalism. I did not read this guide to more worrisome living until 1959. If I had, the *Clipper* would still be in dry dock, for it would certainly have convinced me that Duxbury was not ready for a newspaper; also that John Henry Cutler was not ready for a newspaper. I would not have hesitated before leaping, but, rather, would have frozen in my tracks.

For one thing, the government brochure warned of the hazards of operating a weekly in a resort area. "Unless you can be assured of making sufficient money during the boom period to carry you through the lean months, you should avoid most resort towns," said the bureaucrats. Duxbury, a small resort area, was certainly not quite the boom town that was Bar Harbor or Saratoga Springs or Newport.

"Are you an editor, reporter, feature writer, circulation manager, businessman, advertising expert, promotion man?" There is at least a slight implication in the brochure that if you are not all of these things, you had better not try to launch a weekly. Then this note of reassurance: "But even if you are a crack Washington correspondent or a respected metropolitan city editor, you may lack the knowledge of the business and mechanical side of publishing which the weekly editor must have."

It was fortunate, too, that Bobbie's mother, Cid Ricketts Sumner, had not yet written her capsule account of Duxbury for "New England Journeys," a special edition of *Ford Times*, published in 1954. When Cid brought Duxbury into focus in her article, "Washington Street, Duxbury," the community did not loom as a teeming metropolis with a long line of eager advertisers clamoring for space in a weekly gazette:

> It is a quiet village street two miles long, but the very essence of New England is here—history, romance, simple beauty, marvelously preserved, first by chance, now by careful design. For it was to Duxbury, Massachusetts, in about 1622 that the first settlers came from Plymouth to build summer homes and to cultivate their lands, returning in winter to the safety of the stockade.

After describing the colonial architecture that was so accidentally but happily preserved, Cid wrote:

> There is only one traffic light in Duxbury, on State Highway 3A. Turn there toward the sea, round the curve and you will see the Liberty pole, so

named in Revolutionary times. On your right is Blue Fish River where from 1764 to 1857 there was a quarter-mile-long wharf. The townsmen were kept busy during these times, shipping mackerel and cod. Here were launched many of the finest of the sailing vessels built by Ezra Weston . . . and his sons. The first house on the left contains the Historical Society collection, open to visitors; on the other corner is one known as the Cable Office, because when the first Atlantic cable was laid, coming in on Duxbury Beach, messages were received here.

Crossing Blue Fish River one has a fine view of the marshes, the bay, and a glimpse of the outer dunes that form it. Among the stores near the post office is one over which still hangs the old sign—"Sweetser's General Store—English and West Indian Goods." Set back of the colonial with an anchor on the lawn are the world-famous Clapp Marine Biological Laboratories, open to visitors. Beyond the Congregational Church (1840) is the historic Winsor House, now run as an inn by a descendant of an early sea captain and shipbuilder of that name. One room is a replica of an English "pub" with rare prints and old muskets.

Move slowly under the arching elms. If you are held up by traffic don't honk. Lean out the window and listen—two cars have probably just stopped for conversation or to take in the family dog. It's that sort of village. Look down the short lanes that lead to the water. Many were made by ox teams hauling lumber for the shipbuilding. Now in summer one sees white sails on the blue water.

Just beyond Surplus Street (formerly Poverty Lane) are some of the loveliest of the old houses. Farther along, set back from the road, is a large gray house once the home of Fanny Davenport, the actress. In her old carriage house is a bookshop, a good place to rest and browse.

At the flagpole in South Duxbury one may turn back toward State Highway 3A, passing the graveyard where Myles Standish is buried, or go on by the Country Way to Plymouth.

And that's how it happened. Bobbie was right. It was time for another bold move, the kind that turns the drabness of life into adventure. And the time to launch a little newspaper was in May, just before summer boom time.

Nineteen days later Volume One, No. 1 of the *Duxbury Clipper* was mailed to Duxbury residents. Within a week Bobbie and I heard that two other persons were about to launch a weekly newspaper. One was Sumner Hinckley, who had already accepted money for subscriptions. The other was the Unitarian minister who used ununitarian language when he saw our sheet dated May 11, 1950.

"I'd like to go down there and punch John Cutler on the jaw," he said.

When Bobbie and I launched the *Clipper* in 1950, we were handicapped because we didn't know much about town activities. For that reason I initiated annual *Clipper* meetings which were always held on Sundays before the annual town meeting. Sessions started at two o'clock and ended around five with an informal cocktail hour.

At first I invited only six or seven of the town's leading citizens, including Percy Walker, the town's only realtor, who was known as "Mr. Duxbury." Over the years these *Clipper* meetings expanded to include the chairman and/or vice chairman of the board of selectmen, the planning board, and the finance committee, and several other town officials, including the police chief and the fire chief. Every board and committee in town had at least one representative and some, like the finance committee, had three or four members present in my living room. These meetings not only helped with *Clipper* editorializing but also proved to be valuable for various boards—especially the finance committee.

Later, as Duxbury's population increased to more than fifteen thousand, it became too cumbersome and complicated to warrant these annual *Clipper* meetings.

Soon we were *Clipper*ing through the crosschops of Duxbury life, and since neither Bobbie nor I knew much about bookkeeping, we didn't have a precise notion of how much money we were losing or how long we could afford to lose it. The first edition contained six pages. By the spring of 1978, when we were no longer losing money, a *Clipper* of forty pages was about par for the course.

Bobbie and I thoroughly enjoyed operating this unpretentious little sheet, despite the occupational hazards. Some fellow parishioners invariably stir up a mad if your editorial is good, and if it is very good, there are those who hate you for life. And, oh, those slips that show: I once had a Sunday School teacher receiving a "panty" (instead of "pantry") shower, and, while editorializing on the needs of the town, I wrote: "What Duxbury needs is more pubic [i.e., public] facilities."

Ah, that merry procession of little boo-boos:

We meant "gifts," but it came out: "Unable to attend the baby shower, but sending fifths were . . ."

Handlebar moustache became "handlebag moustache," one trim never previously conceived. "Old Pogy" became "Old Fogy," but since it was in reference to a fish factory, and not an elder of the community, it did no harm. "A favorite tipple" became "a favorite nipple," and we are still blushing.

At the end of our first year, a South Shore publisher offered to buy the *Clipper* for a thousand dollars. Today we wouldn't sell it for a million.

In *The Duxbury Book* (1637–1987), published on the 350th anniversary of Duxbury, our son David wrote:

> The *Duxbury Clipper*, conceived over a bridge game, and for many years produced in our dining room, is still young as newspapers go. Yet, into its third decade, it has left an indelible mark on Duxbury, and perhaps because of that, has become among the most successful community weeklies in New England.
>
> A "ma-and-pa" operation from the start, the *Clipper* was founded by my parents, John and Bobbie Cutler. Their combined knowledge of newspapers equaled that of a journalism student about to start his freshman year; now after thirty-six years at the helm, they are walking encyclopedias of what a weekly should be.
>
> In May 1950, when the *Clipper* was born, Duxbury had a year-round population of three thousand, the summer crowd, and a paucity of business. It did not seem a propitious time for so bold an adventure, and in launching their market surveys, the budding publishers heard many a discouraging word.
>
> "You're out of your mind," suggested their good friend Arthur "Beanie" Beane when asked for an assessment. And the late Percy Walker equated the idea with the old Duxbury Railroad which, as he recalled, didn't last long.
>
> There was also the government brochure, a piece of gobbledygook from the bureaucracy, which suggested that with at least ten thousand (my parents had four hundred dollars), some previous experience, and a great deal of hard work, one could achieve a "modicum" of success in publishing a weekly. Horrified by the advice, my mother stashed the document behind a bookcase, where it remained until the *Clipper* was safely afloat.
>
> And just who were these upstarts who launched an institution? My mother, a housewife, presided over a brood of four, later five. She could sing, and act, and paint, and grow most anything. She was a whiz cook, but a newspaperwoman she was not. She was, however, wonderfully versatile, and could fix almost anything—two resources which proved most valuable.
>
> My father, a Harvard Ph.D., was a skilled writer who had freelanced for several national magazines. He knew his way around Boston's newspaper row, having written for the *Boston Globe*, the *Boston Herald*, and the now-defunct *Boston Post* and the *Boston Evening Transcript*; but he was not a professional journalist. No editor ever drilled him in the rudiments of a news *lead* and he was not comfortable with the five "w's" of journalism—the who, what, where, when and why. He had never written a *hard* news story,

and he knew zero about production. He once referred to a blanket—a cylinder cover on a press—as a bedspread. Neither he nor my mother knew anything about advertising.

But they would learn, and the good merchants of Duxbury proved to be willing teachers. One, Jacob Schiff, who owned a shoestore, said he would advertise occasionally if the paper came out on Thursday, which is why Thursday became Clipper Day in Duxbury. Jack Kent Sr., who owned the marine appliance store, later Bayside Marine, was lukewarm when my father made his pitch.

"I don't know, John," he said. "After all, most of the boys down on the waterfront know we're here."

My father pointed out the reminder factor, noting that church bells ring every Sunday to remind parishioners of the services. People needed reminding, he said. There is no record of how Jack took that, but he bought an ad, and he and his son, Jack Kent Jr., have been aboard the *Clipper* ever since.

It was a modest beginning as the *Clipper* set sail. With six pages in the first issue, it would slowly grow to eight, and I remember the sparkle in my father's eyes when he announced, "we have to go to ten this week." In 1986, the *Clipper* averaged forty pages, often hit forty-eight, and occasionally topped fifty-two. Six pages were barely enough for the local sports.

The first issue was printed by kindly Tom Porter, who had a small press in his garage off Elm Street. It was he who gave the *Clipper* its name, my parents having toyed with such ideas as *The Alden Journal*, or *The Standish Times*, or anything, really, that didn't include the word *Gazette*.

As the years wore on, the printers would change. Most weekly newspapers are put out by commercial printers, and that was the case with the *Clipper* until 1976, when the family took a major plunge and bought a press of its own, a Goss Community, capable of printing 18,000 copies an hour. At least three times since that purchase, the publishers have enjoyed the privilege of shouting "Stop the Press," to change or add a major news story.

With the addition of the press, the *Clipper* is now a totally vertical operation at its office on South Station Street, and the offices are larger than in the early days, especially at our Washington Street home. To the children, it seemed most natural to clear away the 4-H news or the high school sports report when it was time for dinner, despite the fact that an occasional classified was found under the couch or behind the refrigerator. We all thought the dining room was the hub of Duxbury.

It was in that room that my parents learned the important lessons of weekly publishing. The credo evolved quickly: be provincial, keep it local; write about the schools, and town hall, and Duxbury Bay; and leave the national stories to the national press. The *Clipper* always has and always will be for and about Duxbury.

The *Clipper* survived the early days, the spaghetti days as we called them, for several reasons. There were the publishers, of course, whom I still admire greatly for their strength, their intelligence, their tenacity, and their quickness to learn. But there were other reasons as well, and atop the list was (and is) Duxbury. It is a special place that inspired loyalty and love, and my parents understood, from the beginning, I think, that the *Clipper* would succeed because of Duxbury. Duxbury is an interesting place, filled with interesting people. Someone is always off to Nepal, or home from the Orient.

From the beginning, Duxbury residents wrote for the *Clipper*. In the early days, there were "Homespun Yarns" by Grace Anthony, and "Turns of a Bookworm" by Margaret Metcalf of Westwinds. There were wonderful contributions from Alison Arnold, Dr. Alice Bigelow, Gershom Bradford, and my grandmother, Cid Ricketts Sumner. There were (and are) "Postscripts" by Jack Post, historical pieces by Dorothy Wentworth, an occasional political column by David A. Mittell, Jr., and for too short a time, hilarious reports on the Frostbiters by Dr. Lansing Bennett.

Classifieds and letters to the editor are important in measuring the impact of a weekly, and the *Clipper* does well on both counts. Over the years, the *Clipper* has published far more letters (Sounding Off) than most papers of comparable size. That is a tribute to the readers, and to the editorial stands of the paper.

The *Clipper* prospered as Duxbury grew from a cozy, well-kept secret to a Boston bedroom. Advertising increased from meager, to modest, to healthy. After a while, the help-wanted sign went up, as my parents tired of working sixty-hour weeks. Among the editorial assistants were Jo-Ann Collins, Peggy Dunn, and Rita Luckey. Later came Sidney Arnold, Ruth Berg, and Suzanne Miller; then Judi Barrett, Maddie Merrifield, Paula Maxwell, news editor; and Priscilla Sangster, managing editor.

After thirty-six years, Mr. and Mrs. "Clipper" are still in charge, and very much a part of what my mother calls the hectic Mondays and frantic Tuesdays. Some things, like deadlines, never change. By now, running a weekly seems a most natural enterprise, and as one who was at least present at the creation, I confess to a deep affection for "the local rag." The *Clipper* is as much a part of Duxbury as the Powder Point Bridge. For thirty-six years it has served as our "first rough draft" of history. It will do the same for many years to come.

Priscilla is still managing editor, but there have been other staff changes. Paula Maxwell is our news editor, and Joanne Lee Stewart, our production manager. Our able staff also includes Doreen Dowd, Beverly Perry, and Victoria Eccelston, and several new columnists: Maureen Brown, a former fact-checker for the *New Yorker* and the *Atlantic Monthly*; Barbara

Fitzpatrick, who has written for *Boston* magazine; Patricia Cook, who writes a cooking column, which she formerly wrote for the *Christian Science Monitor*; Jane Bradley, who has written for several publications, including the *Boston Globe*; the Reverend Robert Merry, who delights the public with his nostalgic pieces; Bob Hale, formerly president of the American Book Sellers Association and author of *The Elm at the Edge of the Earth*; Judith Montminy, who has covered Duxbury school activities and also writes weekly features for the *Boston Sunday Globe*; Leo Egan, formerly known in New England as the "Voice of Sports"; Patti Ryan, social notes editor; Katy Randall, our cartoonist; and three photographers, Deni Johnson, Fran Nichols, and Chris Bernstein.

Ever since the *Clipper* was launched, I have liked to personalize the news to make it friendly and folksy. Here is an example:

Snug Harbor on-the-wharf is an oasis of convenience. Down in Snug Harbor you can meet a pretty girl, buy her a ring in the jewelry store, have the notice of the engagement published in the local newspaper, buy wedding invitations and mail them, walk diagonally across the street and get married, come back and buy clothes for your wedding trip, have the Duxbury Travel Service plan the cruise and return, buy a home from a realtor, and later buy toys for the children. You can discuss philosophy with Stuart Huckins, town affairs in the back room of the fish market with Carl Santheson, watch the Duxbury Yacht Club races in the summer and the Frostbiters in the winter, shop for groceries while your car is getting greased, have a prescription filled, rent an apartment, buy a boat or birdseed, catch eels, dig clams, and gossip with the neighbors.

In the summer of 1953, when Harold Stassen, then National Security Director, came to Plymouth to dedicate a replica of the first fort and meeting house, Bobbie sat beside him at luncheon. He was interested in her explanation of how we started the *Clipper* on a capital investment of four hundred dollars.

"We honestly don't have the vaguest idea, Mr. Stassen," she said.

He asked that a copy of the paper be sent to him in Washington, D.C. "Send a note with it beginning—'Continuing our conversation about the *Duxbury Clipper*, we are sending you a copy at your request.' Then my assistants will see that I get it." He smiled. "I want to show some of my colleagues in Washington a sample of private enterprise in New England."

In November of 1959, the *Voice of America* crew came to Duxbury to broadcast a Thanksgiving message. After recording "turkey talk" at a local turkey farm, the production team came to the town offices, where Bobbie briefly told the story of John Alden and Priscilla. Other broadcasters were Isabelle Freeman, Maurice Shirley (the town treasurer), and J. Alvin Borgeson. Tapes were sent to some foreign countries, and some broadcasts were beamed from Washington, D.C. According to the producer, who sent Bobbie a tape recording, Duxbury voices were heard in thirty-seven languages, including six Russian dialects.

Duxbury also made the April 1960 cover of the *Saturday Evening Post*, when two local school children were pictured in various stages of work and lassitude.

Twice we appeared on a South Shore *Starring the Editors* program, along with three other weekly editors in the area. In our discussion of municipal affairs, the relationship of the press with town officials came up both times, and all agreed that selectmen can on occasion be difficult to deal with. A reporter for a metropolitan daily who was in the audience gave wider currency to our views.

One Duxbury resident received a postcard from Curacao, Netherlands West Indies. It was addressed *Duxbury Clipper*, and nothing more.

In 1961, when Marlene Schmidt, Miss Universe of that year, was piped aboard the seaplane tender *Duxbury Bay* at Miami, Florida, Captain L. R. Geis of the tender sent our town Christmas greetings.

"Your name," he wrote, "was given to me by Lt. Commander Donald Harvey. We would like to know more about Duxbury, about the bay, its history, its present situation, and its future."

If Captain Geis wanted to know these things, it's lucky he didn't ask Rollene Saal, a columnist for the *Miami News*. In her April 30, 1964, column she wrote:

CAPE COD, Mass. – Duxbury must surely be the first resort town in the United States. This tiny, scenic village on the Massachusetts South Shore was incorporated in 1637, just seventeen years after the Pilgrims landed on the Big Rock.

What probably happened was that as soon as the Pilgrims made a little money they grew dissatisfied with the small-town life of Plymouth.

So, following the lead of Captain Myles Standish and the somber Elder William Brewster, a select few moved across the bay.

Duxbury is still fairly select, formal and sedate. No bongo-playing on the beach; no twisting along the seashore, which is fine with the residents, most of whom are Boston bankers.

Bobbie has always been interested in theater and acting. She had her first experience in the drama club at Cornell. When I first met her she was taking a course in radio drama at Emerson College in Boston and had spent the previous three summers doing summer stock.

When the Duxbury Playhouse first started in Duxbury in the old GAR Hall, she was one of the first to join the group and had the lead in many plays—often in an ingenue role. I had seen her in *The Women* in the role of Crystal, and I remember that in the bathtub scene she looked as glamorous as any movie star. Another role I recall was that of Tondaleo, a native girl who tempts a white man. She was exceptional in that role and looked even more glamorous than usual.

The Duxbury Playhouse finally found a home in a large barn at the end of Bay Road, and there she acted in several plays. I remember one was a play her mother and the director Al Moritz collaborated on. It was based on one of Cid's *Tammy* novels. Bobbie and other members of the cast fought hard to keep the playhouse going, but the venture failed and the barn was torn down.

When Lawrence Dunn came to Duxbury to head the mathematics department at Duxbury High School, he asked Bobbie to assemble local residents (in our house) who were interested in the theater. This developed into the Duxbury Bay Players, a group that is still flourishing, staging musicals and plays three times a year. During the past few years, *Clipper* work has kept Bobbie from participating, but during early years she acted in several productions. I remember her excellent performance in *Barefoot in the Park* as the mother and in *The Chalk Garden*. She had the leading role in *Come Back, Little Sheba*, for which she got exit applause from an enthusiastic audience. Marjorie Bush-Brown, the sister of James Conant, president of Harvard, told me she did a better job than Shirley Booth, whom she had seen in the same role on Broadway. Bobbie had a major role in Arthur Miller's *All My Sons*, and she had the leading role in *Our Town*. Our son David has followed in his mother's footsteps, playing leading roles in his prep school days at the Holderness School, where he won a drama prize at graduation.

121

Chapter Eighteen
THE PURPLE SHAMROCK

One morning in the spring of 1956, my old friend Monroe Stearns called me from New York, where he had become trade editor of Prentice-Hall, Inc., to ask whether I was interested in writing the autobiography of the fabulous, if roguish, James Michael Curley, a five-time Mayor of Boston who had also served as Governor of Massachusetts for one term. Elated, I agreed to meet Monroe the following morning in the lobby of the Statler Hotel in Boston. We took a taxi to the office of Curley's lawyer, Samuel Nesson, and after a preliminary discussion of ground rules, we all went to lunch with Curley and his son, the Reverend Francis Curley, S.J. Noticing that Curley had only one old-fashioned before luncheon, I got rid of the notion that the most charismatic person I had ever met was a heavy drinker.

"Tell John about the mayoral campaign when you hired college students to act as Baptist ministers to embarrass your opponent," Father Francis said. My attention was immediately riveted on Curley, and I was deeply disappointed when, with a dreamy look of mock innocence, he professed ignorance of any such incident. Later, after intensive sleuthing and a dozen interviews, I tracked down the story, and it was worth all the trouble it took.

In previous mayoral campaigns, Curley had faced Protestant opponents, whom he used for target practice. In his brashness, he poked so much fun at the "Black Baptists," as he called them, that his opponents, fearful of being painted into a ridiculous corner, were afraid to appear on the same platform with him. In 1921, however, Curley faced a former fire chief of impeccable repute named John R. Murphy. Murphy was favored to win the contest, because he would not only cut into Curley's solid Roman Catholic supporters, but would also profit from various scandals in which Curley had been involved. But Curley was nothing daunted, and in his usual resourceful fashion he used some artful tactics.

One night, while addressing a Catholic audience in Roxbury, Curley paused dramatically. "Where was James M. Curley last Friday night?" he asked. "He was conducting a political meeting in Duxbury. And where was John R. Murphy last Friday night? He was eating steak at the Copley Plaza." At the time, of course, Catholics were not permitted to eat meat on Fridays.

While Murphy with mounting frustration tried to counter the charge, Curley henchmen embarrassed him further by launching what proved to be a devastating, if dirty, campaign. Masquerading as Catholic priests and carrying prayer books, they walked around Charlestown, Murphy's home territory, and elsewhere, telling shocked groups what a disgrace it was that Murphy, having renounced his Catholic faith, had joined a Masonic order. It was also rumored that he intended to divorce his good wife and marry a sixteen-year-old girl. Even the topers of Charlestown's sleaziest barrooms were shocked and embittered. I thought of those Chicago kids who wept when their idol, "Shoeless" Joe Jackson, was kicked out of organized baseball because of the part he had played in the Black Sox scandal. "Say it ain't so, Joe," they wailed. "Say it ain't so."

Meanwhile, another Curley group, some of them alleged to be Boston College students, posed as righteous members of the Hawes Baptist Club and went around neighborhoods in South Boston urging staunch Irish Catholics to vote for Murphy. They knocked on doors after midnight, waking furious, sleepy-eyed residents. Such a proposal, of course, was the kiss of death in Dear Old Southie, the citadel of the sons and daughters of Cork and Galway. And when Murphy appealed to William Cardinal O'Connell, urging him on the Sunday before election to have pastors of the city parishes counter the rumors that were making the rounds faster than Murphy's denials, a Brighton priest named Murphy read the cardinal's letter to his congregation, and ended with these remarks:

> I was born a Murphy and all my life I have been proud of the Murphys, but there is one Murphy I am not proud of. And remember, now, I am not talking politics.

That wasn't all. The next story was even harder to track down. One Sunday morning in my living room, while I was interviewing Wilton Waugh, a former political editor of the *Boston Post,* I got the details, and I felt as though I had just raised a Spanish galleon loaded with gold. Waugh told me of a Hingham resident known in his day as the "Black Pope" because of his affiliation with the Ku Klux Klan. Curley paid the man two thousand dollars to persuade his friend, the Reverend A. Z. Conrad, the Congregational minister of the Park Street Church, to attack Curley in his sermon the Sunday before election.

"Conrad was always good copy, and I often covered his sermons,"

Waugh said. I asked what the "A. Z." stood for. Waugh said he didn't have the vaguest idea, and neither did anyone else.

It was another mystery to be solved. Early in the 1970s, Bobbie and I met Lester Allen at a cocktail party in Duxbury. He was editor of the *Boston Sunday Post* when it ceased publication.

"John, I finally found out what that A. Z. stood for—'Arcturus Zodiac.' " A political mystery was solved. Conrad's father, it turned out, had been an astrology buff.

Wilton Waugh told me that morning that because of Conrad's fiery and eloquent denunciations, the corner of Park and Tremont streets, where the church was located, came to be known as "Brimstone Corner."

Curley's strategy worked. On the appointed Sunday, the Reverend Conrad blasted Curley, warning his parishioners not to vote for the blackguard unless they were in favor of hell and damnation. Even as Wilton Waugh was explaining the hilarious incident, I wondered how many Congregationalists would have voted for Curley in the first place, considering the charges that had been made against him by the Boston Finance Committee and members of the Good Government Association, whom Curley called "GooGoos."

Curley's strategy, of course, was to keep his fellow Roman Catholics from voting for John R. Murphy.

I was grateful to Father Francis for clueing me in on a few of the Celtic capers that highlighted that 1921 campaign.

After the luncheon at Joseph's, Sam Nesson drove us to the famous "house with the shamrock shutters" on the Jamaicaway. On the way, Father Curley gave his version of his father's political success: "He was never afraid to make the bold move."

In Curley's library the walls were lined with books, including many classics and the plays of Shakespeare. Sam Nesson, who, I soon learned, gave the word exaggeration a bad name, motioned toward the books.

"Curley knows every word in every book," he said. The scotch he had had at Joseph's was affecting him, I thought. In my subsequent research I learned that James Michael, early in his career, had referred to the Bard of Avon, as "John Shakespeare."

Father Francis took me down into the spacious cellar and showed me wall bookcases full of thick bound volumes of newspaper and magazine clippings. They were scattered all over the place, even in a cello case—and there were more than six hundred in all. As a fledgling biographer, I asked

Monroe Stearns when we returned to the living room whether I should go through all the clippings.

"Suit yourself," he said. I spent three weeks going through them, mining a nugget now and then. Despite the tediousness and almost unbearable repetition, the clippings gave the chronological flow I needed and spared me from spending long hours going through files in newspaper libraries.

I had grown up in Boston and had heard all the legends about Curley. I don't remember the event, but my mother told me I was a youngster when Mayor Curley dug the first shovelful for a subway that ran from Kenmore Square to St. Mary's Street in Brookline. Curley, she said, took off his top hat and let it drop over my ears.

One afternoon I thought I had hit paydirt. Legend had Curley robbing the city blind (more about this later when we come to my biography of John F. Fitzgerald). There were the usual stories of stashing money in Swiss banks. On this afternoon of research, I pulled three or four bound volumes from the cellar wall bookcase and noticed a few canvas money bags. I picked one up and read, "The First National Bank of Boston." I felt furtive, as if I was part of a conspiracy. I could picture the headlines: "Curley Cache Finally Discovered." But what about the book I was supposed to write?

No problem. The bags were empty.

One morning I was riffling through the clippings when a gnome of a man came in. He asked me whether he would disturb me if he started taking down the photographs on the wall in preparation for the move that the Curleys were soon to make to another section of Jamaica Plain. He said he worked at City Hall.

"I take it you are on vacation?" I said.

"Hell, no! But it's more fun working for the governor than pushing a broom at City Hall." As I learned later while writing *Honey Fitz: Three Steps to the White House*, it was common practice for Hibernian politicians to divert City Hall workers from municipal projects to more personal chores. Years later, while sitting in the modest living room of a former state senator's home, I saw two men painting the kitchen and dining room. Mike Ward, who had also been a member of the Boston School Committee, casually mentioned that the men were supposed to be painting a school in Dorchester. There was plenty of time for that, he said, since school didn't open until September.

Another morning in the shamrock-shuttered house, the gnome came up to the table where I was working and handed me a ten-dollar bill. "The

125

boss gave me two bills, one for you," he said. During the following weeks I learned that it was common practice for Curley to hand out ten-dollar bills. When I was invited upstairs for lunch, and gave Mrs. Curley the money, I detected a bit of irritation that suggested that she knew of her husband's generous habit and definitely did not approve of it. She led me into the kitchen and I sat down at the table with the little guy. Suddenly the governor came into the kitchen and motioned for me to follow him into his library. A minute later, he brought me a tray of scrambled eggs, toast, and coffee.

I was puzzled by the lack of interchange between husband and wife, until it finally dawned on me that Curley had his own way of reproving a person. It also dawned on me that Mrs. Curley took a dim view of writers—especially of biographers, apparently because of *The Purple Shamrock*, a solid biography of Curley that had been written by Joseph Dinneen, a reporter for the *Boston Globe*. Joe was hard on His Honor.

Mrs. Curley's frosty attitude changed one morning in the library when I handed Curley the few chapters I had written about him. As he read the manuscript, he kept passing pages to his wife. I sat there, tense, discouraged by Curley's impassive look. A long moment of silence was broken when Curley called to his cook in the kitchen.

"Bridget," he said, "if anyone calls, tell them I'm not available." I was even more reassured a few minutes later when Mrs. Curley glanced up from the page she was reading and smiled. My God, I thought, she is smiling.

"I had no idea the book was going to be like this," she said.

Was I pleased? Is a donkey in a field of clover pleased?

Curley didn't have very much to say, but when his wife cut into the conversation, he nodded toward a window. "Squirrels," he said. "Those squirrels . . ." I saw no squirrels. It was simply Curley's way of cutting a person off.

The months I spent with James Michael Curley while researching the book were consistently rewarding. They were also, to say the least, eye opening. Curley, in his confessional mood, which had been induced after he saw how the public had accepted his Robin Hood roguery, as fictionalized in Edwin O'Connor's *The Last Hurrah*, would casually tell me things the press and Boston Finance Committee had been probing in vain for years. One of the comments was, "Oh well, there was always another source of money."

Curley was amazingly compliant when I asked him to arrange an interview with principals in his story. One Saturday afternoon, at my request, he invited Judge Daniel Gillen to join us in his library. Since Gillen had grown up with Curley in Roxbury, I knew that if I could get them reminiscing, anecdotes would flow. I can still see Curley sitting in the black leather chair he had had in his office at the State House. Judge Gillen, who guarded Curley's interests with all the devotion of a St. Bernard protecting his pups, looked apprehensive when I told of my conversation with Thomas O'Connor, who had built the Dutch Colonial home on the Jamaicaway.

The Boston Finance Committee had been investigating the financial aspects of this house for years. Known as the house with the shamrock shutters because of the distinctive markings on its white blinds, it had also sarcastically been called the "demonstration house," implying that contractors had donated materials for building the house "to impress me with the superlative quality of their wares," as Curley put it. One inquiry had to do with the floor covering laid in the "mansion," as the press called it. The Finance Commission, Curley told me, thought it more than a coincidence that he hired the same firm that had installed the carpeting in City Hall. Former Mayor John F. Fitzgerald joined the critics: "A few years ago, Curley was working as a corporation inspector for three dollars a day. The year before he was elected mayor he paid nothing except a poll tax. Now he has a beautiful home on the Jamaicaway, with furnishings from the home of Henry H. Rogers, who died worth one hundred million dollars."

Thomas O'Connor, who was ninety-four when I called to interview him, had built the house. In the autobiography I had Curley say, "Thomas O'Connor built my house, and I don't remember that he ever complained that I owed him any money."

But I knew there was more to it than that. The Finance Committee had a valid point when it asked how anyone receiving only seventy-five hundred dollars as a Congressman (which Curley was paid at the time the house was built) and ten thousand dollars as mayor could afford such a palatial residence. With these facts in mind, on that Saturday afternoon, as Curley and I sipped a tall drink, I told the governor that Mr. O'Connor refused to be interviewed.

"Oh, too bad," Curley said, doing his best to look mournful.

"But he did answer two questions I had for him."

The mournful look became vulpine. Curley waited for me to continue.

"First, I asked O'Connor whether he had built this house.

" 'That I did,' O'Connor said."

Curley was eyeing me more closely.

"And did Mayor Curley pay you for building the house, Mr. O'Connor?"

" 'That he did,' O'Connor said."

I leaned toward Curley and our eyes met. "Now, Governor, what I want to know is this: Did you pay him?"

It was Curley's turn to lean toward me. Without saying a word, he gave me the most eloquent wink I have ever seen. What the Boston Finance Committee would have given for that wink.

During this exchange Judge Gillen remained stonyfaced.

During the summer of 1956, I used to pick up Curley at his summer home in Scituate, drive him to the local post office, where he collected his mail, then proceed to the Jamaicaway house. One morning I met for the first time—but not for the last—a character I'll call Tim, the prototype of a character in *The Last Hurrah*. Tim was an arrogant loafer, who always sat on the floor with his hat on. I marveled at Curley's patience when this ignoramus argued with him. Curley not only did not throw him out of the house, but would invariably hand him a ten-dollar bill, saying, "How did you know I had it?" This was a routine ritual. Tim never gave me a single anecdote of the dozens he promised, never took off his hat, never stopped ranting, and never rose to leave until he got his money.

Meanwhile, the telephone would keep ringing, and some tearful widow whose son was about to be thrown out of a hospital would tell her story between sobs. People came to the door to beg for help. Nobody who got in touch with this generous man ever left his company the poorer, despite the fact that when Curley died several months later, he left an estate worth less than twelve thousand dollars.

There were many sidelights I couldn't put in a book that was supposed to have been written by Curley. We were having lunch one day in the China House. The cocktails and Chinese food were delicious. The chef must have had special orders from the headwaiter. On the way out I asked why there had been no bill. Curley explained.

"Years ago, when I was mayor, I had occasion to lower the assessment," he gravely said. I don't ever remember him laughing or even smiling.

As we walked down the street, Curley took my arm as always, as if I were the senior citizen. A truck driver yelled, "How are you, Jim?"

"They call me everything," Curley said. But I never heard anyone else call him by his first name.

One morning I told Curley I wanted to visit the neighborhood where he was born. He directed me to an alley in Roxbury and pointed to a three-decker shanty. A young woman flew down the alley, trailed by her

128

husband, who was unshaven, shirtless, and coatless. But he was wearing the top of his underwear. I don't know about the bottom.

"Oh, Governor Curley," the woman shouted. "You've come back to your birthplace."

This was the kind of local color I was looking for. In a brief interview, she told me Curley as a boy used to sell liquor bottles and other items to her father. "The Governor called him Jakie the Junkie," she said. She sounded proud. "My father had the first junk license in Roxbury."

As I backed out of the alley, Curley softly said. "You're not going to put that business about liquor bottles in the book?"

I assured him I was. He asked me to stop after I backed onto the street.

"Your charming wife," he said. "Does she partake of the elixir of sociability?" Curley had never met Bobbie.

He disappeared into a package store and came out with a bottle of pink champagne for charming Bobbie.

The several months I spent with James Michael Curley in the twilight of his life were rewarding, exciting, and at times shocking. Curley was a dozen different men, depending on whose interests he was serving, including his own. In an era when you could usually rent a Hibernian politician if you couldn't buy him, James Michael was the political kingpin of Massachusetts and undoubtedly the most unpredictable and colorful politician in American history. One political enemy said of him, "I suppose that fellow is the damnedest single human being I ever met." Often flamboyant and obnoxious, he was mayor off and on for sixteen years, spent four terms in Congress and two in jail. He failed in his bid for the U.S. Senate, but served for two Depression years as governor. At his death he lay in state for two days in the State House Hall of Flags, only the fourth person in the history of Massachusetts to receive this honor.

In the "Forewarning" of his autobiography, I put these words in his mouth:

> Over the years I have been called Sympathy Jim, jailbird, convict, brigand, buccaneer, spellbinder and highbinder, a ruthless monster, the Irish Mussolini, the Ambassador to South Boston, and the Kingfish of Massachusetts.

And there were other descriptions: old ham, actor, political Barnum, low-brow mayor of a high-brow city, and a combination of Santa Claus, Robin Hood, a Chinese warlord, and John Barrymore. Producer Jack

Warner called him "the greatest actor I have ever seen." To political adversaries he was cunning, conniving, contriving, cold-blooded, venal, devious, and vicious. His archenemy, Daniel Coakley, over the radio branded him a "bully, bravo thug—a moral and physical coward, a blackleg, and jailbird."

His gall was unrivaled in the political arena. In return for his support in the 1932 election, President Franklin D. Roosevelt offered him the post of Ambassador to Poland, noting that it was a sensitive assignment. "If it is such a goddam interesting place," Curley cut in, "why don't you resign the Presidency and take it yourself?" One wag said that if Curley had taken the job he would have paved the Polish Corridor.

A gifted tribune of the people, he had, as John Gunther said, "a gift of gab almost unrivaled in America." Curley could purr like a kitten, snarl like a wildcat. He could at will change a jeering assembly into a cheering audience, making them laugh or cry while winking at a crony in the wings. One minute he called an audience in Marshfield "swine"; the next minute they were applauding. Curley the urbane could be Curley the crude. He could charm intellectuals in the afternoon and call hecklers at a political rally in the evening "a bunch of pickpockets and crapshooters." It had taken him years to refine the shantytown inflection of his youth into a rich, fluid intonation, which he could modulate from a musical whisper to a booming cadence. He had grown up in Roxbury, where a hooligan once yelled, "Look at Lazy Jack Nolan up there on the platform, all dressed up in his brand new jockstrap." Early in his career, Curley gave raucous assemblies tit for tat:

"Does any one of you bums want to step up here and make something of it?"

The Curley I got to know was the same witty orator who ridiculed a heckler who shouted at a rally, "Curley, you bum, I wouldn't vote for you if you were Saint Peter."

"If I were Saint Peter," Curley said, "you wouldn't be in my precinct."

At another rally a woman down front, after listening to the praise heaped on Curley by a chairman, sneered, "If he's that perfect, they ought to make him pope." Curley rose and bowed. "And if they do make me pope, madam, the first thing I will do is make you an archbishop."

This was the Curley I got to know—a man who differed mostly from himself, a man who said, "In politics you always have to think ahead of the mob."

I could understand the reasons for his downfall, just as I knew why he was once revered by his followers. The New Deal made ward politicians obsolete. Social Security, unemployment insurance, and the psychiatric social workers had usurped the functions of ward bosses, who earned votes by getting people jobs, bailing them out of jail, and putting coal in their cellars and turkeys in their Christmas baskets. Curley was a master at these things. He would walk through the market in Faneuil Hall at Thanksgiving, and if he saw a shawled woman looking wistfully at a turkey, would hand the grocer a ten-dollar bill and tell him to wrap it up for her.

There was another factor. Radio and television put an end to political rallies, once the poor man's entertainment. In his "iron mike" and raccoon coat, Curley could no longer charm streetcorner crowds with his tailgate oratory. As early as 1930 his rowdyism was beginning to lose him votes.

During the first interviews with Curley, it was hard for me to pin him down. He seemed to glory in the names his opponents called him, but he stubbornly refused to admit that he was the last of the bosses. When I insisted he was, he would stubbornly shake his head and deny it. He said over and over, in different ways, that he preferred to be remembered as the benefactor of the downtrodden Irish. His proudest monument, he said, was hung in the main reception hall of Boston City Hospital. Over his oil portrait is a plaque inscribed: "The Honorable James M. Curley, Mayor of the Poor." "It is as the friend and defender of the poor, the alien and the persecuted that I hope to be remembered—as the 'Mayor of the Poor.' " Those were his words, and he meant them.

His son, Francis, the only one of his nine children who survives, thinks his father deserves a more conspicuous monument, citing such landmarks as the Tobin Memorial Bridge, the Fitzgerald Highway, and the John Hynes Memorial Auditorium. In City Hospital shortly before his death, Curley quipped: "There are enough roosts for pigeons in the city." If there were to be a statue there would be problems. Should Curley look sober, mirthful, ironic, serious, irreverent, glowering? Curley was too multifaceted to classify simply. There were too many Curleys.

I'd Do It Again! covered Curley's life until his complete retirement from politics in 1957.

In his unsuccessful campaign against Henry Cabot Lodge for the U.S. Senate in 1936, Curley invaded Beverly Cove, his opponent's hometown. After his ringing speech, Curley sat down and whispered to a dignitary on the stage: "That ought to hold the sons of bitches."

Two years later, Curley opposed another Brahmin, Leverett Saltonstall, in a contest for governor. When the *Boston Transcript* noted that

Saltonstall (whom Curley dubbed Stopandstall) had a Back Bay name and a South Boston face, Curley told a rally:

"Saltonstall may have a South Boston face, but he doesn't dare show it over there."

Next day Saltonstall spent hours in Southie chatting with policemen, storekeepers, barflies, and passersby. "If I have a South Boston face, I'm proud of it, and you can be sure of one thing—it's the same face before and after the election. I'm not two-faced."

When I asked Curley about the incident, he flatly denied the story simply because it made him appear politically inept. For once he had failed to "keep ahead of the mob." There were times when I thought that with Curley, lying wasn't a vice—it was merely a manner of speaking.

I was interested in Curley's version of his relationship with William Cardinal O'Connell, aware of the feud between them because His Eminence, whom Curley privately called "Crimson Willie," took a dim view of the Mayor's buffoonery and, at times, vulgarity. (In my interview with former Governor Paul Dever, who served as attorney general under Curley, I heard a sample of Curley's vulgarity. "Curley called me into his office at the State House, put his foot up on the radiator, and said, 'Listen, you little pisspot, what do you want?'" Dever also told me about Frank Daley, one of the Mayor's "bag men," who used to accept "contributions" from certain contractors at a designated location under the watchful eye of Curley from a window in City Hall.

When Dever was governor, Curley came into his office with a young man who was looking for a job. Curley said he had known the youth for a long time, and that he could vouch for his character and ability.

"I'll see what I can do," Dever said. "What's his name?"

Curley turned to the young man. "What did you say your name was, son?"

Both O'Connell and Curley were sons of Irish immigrants, and after being reared in poverty, both had risen to the highest positions the city could offer. The cardinal was reserved, proper; Curley, outgoing, boisterous. They clashed partly because the cardinal liked and catered to the Brahmins, whom Curley disliked and attacked.

In private, Curley would boast that he once warned O'Connell "to mind his own business." He told me of one session he had had with the prelate. "I told him a word in politics meant as much as a word in religion." (Earlier, Curley told me that "politics and holiness are not always synonymous.") Actually, during that session at the cardinal's residence, O'Connell gave

Curley a tongue lashing, adding: "Don't you ever again put your foot inside this door on a political mission." Paul Dever told me this.

When Curley died, O'Connell's successor, Archbishop Richard Cushing, flew from Washington, D.C., ostensibly to deliver the eulogy at the Requiem Mass at Holy Cross Cathedral. Suspended by a wire from the dome of the church, Cardinal O'Connell's red hat swayed over the coffin. When Cushing's prayer ended, the congregation waited for Cushing to speak. He sat down. There was no eulogy.

Curley had two separate personalities. He was a devoted family man whose home life was never touched by scandal, but he was also a consummate politician. Father Francis shocked me that first day at the house on the Jamaicaway when he mentioned his father's reaction at his son Paul's unexpected death, during the 1945 mayoral campaign. Thinking of the sympathy vote, a grieving but tearless Curley said, "Well, that assures my victory."

Curley, like Rose Kennedy, was stoic in the face of tragedy. Five years after Paul's death, Mary and Leo Curley died of cerebral hemorrhages on the same day. James Jr. had died earlier, leaving only George and Francis by the time I knew the governor. One morning in his study, he looked up from the manuscript in which I wrote of these deaths. "Yes, I have known tragedy," he said softly.

An illuminating example of the paradoxical fusions in his character occurred minutes before he died in City Hospital in 1958. He had just been moved from the operating table across bumpy floors when he looked up at George. "I wish to announce the first plan in my platform for reelection as mayor of Boston will be to have the goddam floors in City Hospital smoothed out." He winked at his son to show he knew the close of his last campaign was near. Twenty-eight minutes later he was dead.

During his final days he told Francis:

"All my life I've followed the biblical injunction—'cast your bread upon the waters.' I've done that all my life, and you know what happened? The damned ducks ate it all up."

Curley was so fabulous, stories about him are endless. In quest of votes he would walk through the Boston City Hospital with a kind word or quip for every patient. On Sunday mornings he wore a special pair of squeaky shoes to draw attention to himself as he walked down to a pew in the front of the church. He would visit museums and galleries for further exposure. One favorite spot was the famed Vose Galleries, then located in Copley Square opposite Trinity Church. For a few years Curley had a big black

Lincoln, which his chauffeur would park on a crosswalk, perpendicular to the sidewalk, blocking half the street. Curley enjoyed sitting and chatting with Robert Vose, father of Robert Vose Jr., current president of the galleries (now located on Newbury Street). Mr. Vose's private office, which was close to the elevator on the second floor, had an opaque glass panel in the door. The chauffeur used to rap on the glass with a large diamond ring, then open the door to announce Curley, who had no qualms about interrupting whatever Mr. Vose was doing.

One afternoon Robert Vose Jr. was showing Curley around the exhibition floor. Curley paused before a large painting of the Battle of Bunker Hill and asked who had painted it. When Vose told him it was by Dennis Malone Carter, Curley nodded. "That's a good Irish name. We must buy the painting for the city, provided there's enough in it for me."

"I have always thought he said that specifically for the three or four persons standing close to us," Robert Vose Jr. said. "He did buy the picture, and it now hangs in Faneuil Hall, but he didn't take a nickel for himself."

To me, Curley was fundamentally a Robin Hood who gave what he took. I remember a little story Joseph Scolponetti told me. At one stage Curley was so broke, he borrowed two hundred dollars from Scolponetti, who had been his corporation counsel. Scolponetti was with Curley one day when a dowdy woman approached them on the street with the usual tale of woe. Curley reached in his pocket and handed her the two hundred dollars.

It was from this episode that Curley took the title of his own book, *I'd Do It Again!*

George Curley celebrated the acceptance of the manuscript one evening in his apartment on Marlboro Street in Boston. Nesson, who had been in New York that day conferring with Stearns, came in late with the news that the book would be titled *I'd Do It Again!* All of us, including the governor, agreed it was the perfect title. One guest, who was a former mayor of San Francisco, said of celebrities he had met in his time: "I have known the great and the nearly great, and the more I knew them, the more nearly great were the great and the more nearly, nearly great were the nearly great."

On his way out that night Curley turned to George: "Do you need any money?" George shook his head.

When Prentice-Hall scheduled a press conference in Parlor A of the Statler, the publisher's public relations director warned me to stay in the background. The reception was for the author, and the author was Curley. Although he had not written a line of the book, there were days when he thought he had. Shortly before he died, he told a reporter it had taken him "only three months" to write his autobiography. Curley was lucid most of the time, but there were moments when his mind wandered.

For example, he told me more than once of his efforts to persuade President Roosevelt "to widen the Mississippi River." I wasn't surprised, therefore, to read this remark, but I was astounded several years later to read in J. J. Smith's column in the *Boston Herald*, that Francis, now an unfrocked priest who had left a teaching post at Holy Cross College and was living on welfare in the South End of Boston, said his father "had written" every word in the autobiography. This was the same Francis who had urged his father to give me leads—the same Francis who had shown me the nearly seven hundred bound volumes in the Curley home, the same person who had arranged various interviews. (Those bound volumes are now stored in a library at Holy Cross College.)

To settle the matter of authorship, Prentice-Hall prepared an affidavit stating that I am the sole author of *I'd Do It Again!* (This affidavit is now in a special collection under my name in the Mugar Library Special Collections at Boston University.)

While waiting for the Parlor A door to open, Bobbie and I were chatting with Mike Ward, an old political "pro," and a *Boston Globe* reporter whom I had interviewed. He had apparently leaked the information that I was the ghostwriter, because a few minutes later other reporters asked me some embarrassing questions. I asked them to keep my name out of their stories, and they all did.

At this point, Curley walked over, grabbed my arm, and marched me into Parlor A, introducing me as "the young man who wrote all those fine paragraphs." That summer Bobbie and I, with press passes, often sat in the second row at the Cohasset Music Circus directly behind Curley and his friends. During one intermission, he introduced me to his guest, using almost the same words, including "all those fine paragraphs."

The way the *Globe* acquired second serial rights reflects the enormous interest in the Curley legend in Massachusetts.

Long before the manuscript was completed, Robert Choate, then publisher of the *Boston Herald*, told me he was interested in second serial rights. I learned what happened later when Lawrence Winship, editor of the *Boston Globe*, took Monroe Stearns and me to the Union Oyster House for lunch.

Winship said the bidding, which started at twenty-five hundred dollars, kept escalating as both newspapers tried to close a deal. When the *Herald* stopped at twenty-eight thousand dollars, the *Globe* acquired the rights with a bid of thirty-two thousand dollars. Winship told us it was the largest sum ever paid in this country for second serial rights with one big exception. Colonel House's memoirs of Woodrow Wilson commanded fifty thousand dollars at a time when that was a tremendous sum.

Winship asked Stearns how Prentice-Hall got the contract for the autobiography. Stearns told us of his first meeting with Sam Nesson in his apartment on Riverside Drive in New York. Nesson came in around midnight with a suitcase full of miscellaneous Curleyana which, he assured Monroe, could be turned into a best seller. "Nesson was at least six sheets to the wind," Monroe told us. (*I'd Do It Again!* never became a best seller, but it did make the *New York Times* list one week.)

After looking through the material, Monroe accepted the project and hired me to write the book.

The lead review in *Time* magazine included a photograph of a jaunty, top-hatted Curley swinging a cane. Comparing the book with Edwin O'Connor's *The Last Hurrah*, *Time* commented:

> His own story is at once a better and a poorer work than O'Connor's— better because Curley's self-portrait is more revealing, human and tragic: poorer because, whatever else he may be, Curley is not a writer. His suitcase full of anecdotes, memoranda, unchecked recollections and trivia was turned down by two publishers before Prentice-Hall hired Author John Henry Cutler, a Jack-of-all-writing, to bring some order out of the accumulated memories of a lifetime.

Time had good reason for calling me "a Jack-of-all-writing." The New England *Time* correspondent who had interviewed me made this assessment after noting that my literary output had included Sunday newspaper features, two syndicated newspaper columns, several articles for national magazines, including *Esquire, Collier's, Pic,* and *Ford Times*, brief pieces for *Argosy, Shipmate,* and *Leatherneck*, and "fillers" for *Coronet* and *Pageant* magazines; also three adventure books for boys, and book reviews, including a review of Nathaniel Benchley's mystery, *The Visitors* (in which I noted that the only real characters were the ghosts).

By this time I was beginning to think ghostwriters also belonged to some sub-human species. Since it was Curley's story, I had to sound like him, incorporating in the manuscript some of the fustian and flamboyance that are so typical of a politician whose talent was oratorical rather than literary. Curley's wit and humor, clearly identifiable, reflected his gall, irreverence, and ruthlessness. Francis Russell said it succinctly: "[The book] preserves Curley's own style of the informal cliché." The Curley bombast and hippodrome and tailgate oratory which enchanted the populace of Roxbury and South Boston would, of course, prove to any sophisticated book reviewer that "whatever else he may be, Curley is not a writer."

In his upswing days Curley had learned that his followers liked long words. He could call an adversary a "sexagenarian" and make him sound like a pervert. In the Curley lexicon, a police officer was never a cop. He was "a member of the constabulary." A club was a "shillelagh." Curley had spent time in what his uncouth friends might call a "slammer," but Curley would never use that word. He would say, without apologies to Shakespeare, that he had been "in durance vile."

I also knew that in his florid oratory he preferred the longer of two synonyms, the better to accent his Oxfordian delivery. He would say "visitation," not "visit." Since I had heard the man speak so often, I had, through mere osmosis, absorbed some of his locutions and, more especially, his circumlocutions. I went further and coined for him such Curleyesque words as "numbskulduggery."

One night on the way to a bachelor buffet at the home of Lawrence Winship in Sudbury, Massachusetts, I picked up Victor Jones, then managing editor of the *Globe*. En route he asked me whether Curley had objected to my using a tape recorder during our interviews, and he didn't seem to believe me when I said I had never used a tape recorder.

That night Winship had also invited Edwin O'Connor, Monroe Stearns, and Craig Wiley, then trade editor of Houghton Mifflin, one of the two publishers who had rejected the Curley material. Everyone showed up except O'Connor, who, I learned later, considered the Boston Irish political turf his private preserve.

The summer after *The Last Hurrah* was published, Curley sold the house with the shamrock shutters and most of the furniture, Waterford glass, Crown Derby china, and Georgian silver, and moved to a much smaller suburban-colonial house on the other side of Jamaica Pond. Knowing that Curley was once again broke, Governor Foster Furcolo gave him a sinecure job. Curley's health began to fail noticeably, and his mind began to wander. But he responded when Edward R. Murrow ran his *Person-to-Person* television show from the new house. He was also featured on the *Wide, Wide World* television show, for which I wrote part of the script. The "secretary" Nesson had provided to record Curley's ad-libbing was totally inept, as Curley discovered before he ripped a notebook out of her hands and brusquely told her to get out of the room (one of Nesson's offices). I had never seen the "secretary" before or since, but I had a good idea of her calling. One thing I deleted from the final script was another reference to "widening the Mississippi."

When Prentice-Hall sent Nesson a check for sixteen thousand dollars, I assumed the money belonged to Curley, and I asked him about it. He nodded, but didn't say a word. That night Nesson called me in Duxbury and rebuked me for mentioning the money. I didn't know at the time that Nesson owned the copyright, and still don't know whether Curley got all or any part of that sixteen thousand dollars.

There was another puzzling and still unsolved circumstance. Just before Columbia Pictures released its film version of *The Last Hurrah*, Curley, after seeing a preview, sued Columbia for "irreparable damage to a valuable property." He was referring to *I'd Do It Again!* After Columbia settled the suit out of court for twenty-five thousand dollars, it was discovered that the lawyer to whom the check was made out was fictitious. Also, the stamp on the release form was that of a fictitious notary. Curley said his signature had been forged. Nobody has ever learned who got the money, but Curley and others had a good idea. When Curley renewed his threat of a suit, Columbia settled for an additional fifteen thousand dollars. That money went to Curley.

After his death in November 1958, Curley lay on a bier in the Great Hall of the State House for two days as 100,000 people filed past. Loudon Wainwright, a writer for *Life* magazine, paid me a modest fee for identifying some of the dignitaries who were paying their last respects. Mike Ward helped. Around noon, we drove to Mike's house in Brighton. Loudon took notes as Mike talked. Suddenly I could see that Wainwright got exactly what he wanted, and he recorded it in his piece in his magazine:

> The people loved him as the sow's ear, not as the silk purse. But that wasn't enough for him. He wanted to be kind of an intellectual, but he was playing the sunfield there and couldn't always see the ball.

Lawrence Winship, editor in chief of the *Boston Globe*, which had bought second serial rights to the book two weeks before publication, asked me to write a brief story of how I had collaborated with Curley on his book. The story began on the front page of the *Boston Sunday Globe*. Winship said he would pay a hundred dollars for the piece, but he actually paid me twice that amount. A few excerpts from my account:

In writing *I'd Do It Again!*, Curley's main problem was one of selection. His life as a public servant was comparatively well known, but what about the early years when he lived in drudgery on a waterfront slum in Roxbury? What were his parents like? What games did he play, and where was he educated? Curley had to think back almost eighty years to find some of the answers he needed.

One day last August I drove him back to the neighborhood where he was born and reared. He pointed to the drug store on the corner of Massachusetts Avenue and Northampton Street. "Stephen Gale owned it when I earned two dollars and fifty cents a week," he said. "A generous soul, Stephen."

Another pause before the Northampton Street tenement where Curley was born. "Not much to look at now," he said. "And it wasn't much to look at eighty years ago, either."

A turn into an alley and there was the dismal three-decker where the Curleys next lived. "The rent was high for my mother and father," Curley remarks. "Six or seven dollars a month, if memory serves."

Curley was enjoying this rekindling of almost forgotten associations, and at every turn there was a corner or a building that added a page to his book—the intersection of Northampton and Washington streets where he used to peddle the *Boston Globe,* the tenements up whose creaking stairs he lugged a barrel of flour, the grocery store where he politicked with customers while the boss glared. Curley has a faraway look in his eyes when the car stops before the quarters of the first Tammany Club, scene of many a riot. Here Curley pounded his gavel, heard hard-luck stories, and dodged brass spittoons. He indicates another dingy building that housed Tammany later, and just down the street is Hibernian Hall, whose rafters echoed Curley oratory. Also on Hampden Street is the site of the saloon managed by Curley for a few months in 1905. He dispensed beer and bar whiskey in "this poor man's club," but he stuck to ginger ale and orange pop.

And thus did Curley refresh his memory and recreate with the finesse of a masterful raconteur all the little known facts and incidents—all the pathos and humor and tragedy and struggle—of his early life. The neighborhood was a picturesque arena that generated heated political controversy, and here the political maestro learned to "think ahead of the mob," as he puts it. Few old-timers are left who remember the verbal mayhem Jim Curley and Tom Joyce exchanged. There were fights with others, and since Curley has almost total recall, the stormy contention that rocked the County Galway annex comes to life.

"I've never been afraid to make the bold move," Curley says. "I think that is why my life has been so much of an adventure." When he talks about *I'd Do It Again!*, which he thought of calling "Saint and Sinner," you can tell it was an adventure for him to put it together. It was fun to reminisce with old friends, he says. "I like everything that's old," he adds, quoting Oliver Goldsmith: "Old friends, old times, old manners, old books, old wine." There is a pause. "Everything old, in fact, except old Republicans."

In *The Great Interlude*, Francis Russell called the autobiography "a rambling and uneven book, often dulled by the memory of obscure and forgotten ward-heelers, but on the other hand, enlivened by the brazen candor of Curley's admissions."

What put Curley in his confessional mood? The way it came about was ironical. After serving for five months in the Federal Correction Penitentiary at Danbury, Connecticut, for using the mails to defraud, Curley told an old critic, Joseph Dinneen, that the Boston press had always been rough on him. Dinneen himself had pilloried Curley in the *Atlantic Monthly*, in an article titled "Kingfish of Massachusetts." The rumor got around that Curley had tried to buy every copy of the magazine he could lay his hands on, but there were enough readers to be scandalized. I had already discovered that there was nothing new in the disappearance of scurrilous literature that made Curleyism sound like a disease.

After excerpting those several hundred bound volumes in Curley's basement, I spent time at the Boston Public Library reading everything that had been written on the man. One morning in Curley's library I chatted with him and his wife about a difficulty I had encountered.

"A few articles have been neatly cut from the bound volumes. Apparently you or some of your followers thought they were too critical," I said.

Curley nodded in mock sympathy.

"According to the *Periodical Index*," I went on, "one of the articles was written by Joe Dinneen. None of the favorable articles is missing." By this time Curley's look of mock concern was amusing. "Too bad, it was a pity," he said. "All the inconvenience . . ."

"But I read those articles," I said. "I got Photostats from the New York Public Library." Curley turned to his wife, but the smile I expected was missing. "Gertrude," he said, "this young man already knows too much about me." I finally got used to that missing smile.

Dinneen had been brutal but factual in his *Atlantic* piece, depicting Curley's unprecedented arrogance and recklessness during his term as governor. Curley had filled the alcoves and corridors of the State House with sinecures for his cronies, operating at the State level with the same callous indifference he had shown his critics on the municipal level. When members of the Finance Commission pried into the scandals, they were bribed or fired. Curley broke speed records all over the state in his black limousine with its S-1 plates, preceded by State Police motorcycle escorts with sirens wailing. Curley's military aides wore gaudy blue-and-gold braid uniforms, looking as if they had popped out of a Gilbert & Sullivan production. In one accident a State trooper was injured, in another a trooper was killed. In his indifference, Curley was beginning to act like a Latin dictator. He did, in fact, fancy himself as a dictator, and when he told me about his meeting with Mussolini in Rome, he gave the impression that he dominated the conversation. He probably did.

I had a personal glimpse of Governor Curley at the Harvard Tercentenary in 1936, when I received my doctorate. Curley arrived at the Yard escorted by scarlet-coated National Lancers, drums beating and trumpets sounding as the cavalcade passed a grim-faced President Franklin Roosevelt. It was an incredible exhibition of bad taste, perhaps meant to be a deliberate farce—a resentful Irishman's bold show of defiance in a Brahmin setting. Curley was furious that day when he did not receive the customary doctor of laws degree given previous governors. The Harvard Board of Overseers were obviously rebuking him for his outlandish performance as a governor of the Commonwealth.

There was one humorous sidelight that has never been reported. When the valedictorian lauded the *gubernator noster clarissimus* ("our most illustrious governor") I watched Curley, who was sitting on stage with his legs crossed. He was cupping a yawn when the assembly applauded the introductory words of the valedictorian, and there wasn't even a snicker when Curley joined in the applause, not realizing it was meant for him.

After listening to Curley's complaint about the media, Dinneen offered to write a biography, and it was published as *The Purple Shamrock*. Although Curley was not yet in a complete confessional mood, he did make many surprisingly frank revelations, which his wife found anything but amusing. Curley was so pleased he gave City Hall's visitors copies bearing his autograph. (Later the Curley "autograph" was signed by one of his secretaries at City Hall, Larry Costello. Many copies of *I'd Do It Again!* bear Costello's expert imitation of the Curley signature.)

Dinneen did not tell everything, nor did I later. I couldn't at that time. Dinneen said nothing about Curley's Machiavellian practice of raising city assessments just before he left office to turn the wrath of the business community on his successor. Dinneen did say Curley's income skyrocketed

141

while he was in office, but was soon gone when he was between terms, because of his constant handouts. I learned later that when Curley needed money between terms he went to his friend Henry Pierce, president of the Merchants Cooperative Bank of Boston, and mortgaged to the hilt the house with the shamrock shutters. How do I know? Mr. Pierce told me.

In one interview, Francis Curley told a reporter his father made a million dollars three times and lost it four times. In another interview, Francis, whose Celtic imagination often ran away with his intelligence, said his father went broke three times after becoming a millionaire twice. "What he took with his right hand he gave with his left. It was part of the system," Francis said.

During one of our interviews, Curley told me he never worried about money. "There was always some other source." It is no secret, of course, as Dinneen noted, that no contract was ever awarded that did not have a generous cut for Curley. The cumshaw was substantial since Mayor Curley built health spas, parks, playgrounds, three beaches, the El Street Bathhouse, an extension of the rapid transit, and the Sumner Tunnel under Boston Harbor to East Boston.

One afternoon, when I was driving Curley from Jamaica Plain to his summer home in North Scituate, we passed his housing project at Columbia Point. "It's now a vertical slum," he said. Another afternoon he asked me to stop to read an inscription on a bridge in Neponset, stating Curley had built it. Curley was proud of his achievements. And why shouldn't he be?

When *The Last Hurrah* was published in 1956, *Globe* editor Lawrence Winship sent Curley a copy and asked him to review it. Curley returned the book warning of his intention to sue the author, Edwin O'Connor, since it was evident that the leading character, Frank Skeffington, was a thinly disguised Curley. But he changed his mind when he realized the novel endeared him to its readers, maximizing his benevolence while minimizing his ruthlessness. The mercurial Curley for a time signed his name Skeffington, and when I asked him whether he was indeed that character, he solemnly nodded. Instead of taking O'Connor to court, Curley thanked him. "As an aftermath," Russell wrote in *The Great Interlude*, "he decided to write his autobiography as Skeffington by putting into a book what Dinneen had either not known or discreetly omitted."

Curley was at his best when skewering pomposity or ridiculing an opponent, but his humor often took the form of deep-cutting sarcasm, and on occasion he could be childish, as well as ruthless. One night at a political rally at Tremont Temple, he met his future arch rival, John F. Fitzgerald,

"Honey Fitz," on the platform and threatened to "plug him on the jaw." He reserved some of his puerility for barbershops. One afternoon while he was getting shaved at Young's Hotel, Honey Fitz came over to congratulate him for winning a mayoral election. When Curley ignored his outstretched hand, Fitzgerald said, "You've got me wrong, Jim." A few minutes later, when Curley got out of the chair, he glared at Fitzgerald. "No, John, I have you dead right. You are the last man in the world who ought to desert me." Curley then turned on his heel and walked out.

Curley despised former underlings who later turned against him. Maurice Tobin, while serving as Curley's confidential secretary, learned everything he could during one four-year term when Curley was mayor. Then, armed with all the necessary inside information, he ran against Curley, defeating him in 1937 and 1940. Tobin later went on to become governor of Massachusetts and secretary of labor in the Truman administration.

In the 1930s the Statler barbershop was usually crowded on Saturday mornings, when more than a dozen barbers were working. Shortly after the 1937 election, Curley, again a private citizen, walked in, nodded affably to everyone, and sat down in Andy More's chair. Andy was about to wrap the hair cloth around Curley when the ex-mayor saw Maurice Tobin beside him reading a newspaper while getting a haircut. Curley pulled off the apron, got out of the chair, and reached for his hat. He would not, he said, be in the same room with a perfidious hack politician.

He was in another vindictive mood one morning in Sam Nesson's office when I asked him to sign his autobiography for Mike Ward, who had committed the unpardonable sin of trying to upstage His Honor during the preparation of the book. Curley, wearing his snap-brim gray hat, sat down and in his flowing script, penned: "For Mike Ward, one of my understrappers."

In the 1950s Curley's biggest political rival was John Hynes, a former Curley aide who, as city clerk, took over as mayor when Curley went to the penitentiary in Danbury. Hynes later defeated Curley three times in his bid for re-election as mayor. Curley derisively referred to Hynes as "the little clerk," but John, ever loyal, never lost his respect for "the boss." Seriously ill when George Curley died in 1970, Hynes, against the advice of his family and physician, got out of bed to attend the funeral. He died later that day.

Curley was especially cruel to Honey Fitz, whom he displaced as the Irish chieftain. To force Fitzgerald out of the 1913 mayoral race, Curley revived a scandal involving Fitzgerald and a cigarette girl named Toodles Ryan, who had been his mistress for years. Curley circulated a jingle to mortify the former mayor: "Toodles' ass and a whiskey glass made a horse's ass out of me." Curley also hired a university professor to deliver a lecture at Dorchester High School on "Graft in Ancient Times *v.* Graft in Modern Times," a ridiculous analogy lampooning the admittedly corrupt regime of Fitzgerald's.

Curley, of course, professed ignorance when I asked him about Toodles, but he admitted he had hired a Fordham history professor to prepare three lectures on graft. "The last two proved to be unnecessary," he gravely said.

He denied complicity in another campaign caper in 1934 when he beat Gaspar Bacon in the race for governor.

His cronies would drive up in a black limousine to groups of WPA workers and a patrician voice would catch their attention: "You loafers ought to be ashamed of yourselves. Get to work, you lazy bums." When the limousine sped off the cursing laborers could read the sign on the rear bumper: "Gaspar Griswold Bacon for Governor."

Reviews of this book were both good and bad. Willard Edwards in the *Chicago Sunday Tribune* wrote:

> Here's a rollicking autobiography—with unabashed revelations of skulduggery—which reviews fifty years of Boston Irish politics. An impish humor pervades the pages, stirring a chuckle a minute. . . . He spices his story with hundreds of anecdotes, most of them hugely amusing.

Arthur M. Schlesinger, Jr. in the May 25, 1957, issue of the *Saturday Review*, gave a fair assessment:

> One would wish that there were more documentation in the book; also that more care had been exercised to get facts straight and not, for example, make Anthony Drexel Biddle Roosevelt's Attorney General or place the Harvard Tercentenary in 1935 or put the Stevenson Boston rally in December 1956, several weeks after the election. But I suppose these things are not important. For better or worse, Curley has outwitted O'Connor and reclaimed Skeffington for his own.

Chapter Nineteen
SURROGATE WRITING

After completing the Curley book, the second assignment Monroe gave me was to "cut and bridge" a manuscript of more than eleven hundred pages written by the notorious "Red Light Bandit," Caryl Chessman. I reduced this manuscript to 271 pages, and it was published in 1957.

Chessman had already written two best sellers. *Cell 2455 Death Row*, published in 1954, was an international best seller that was translated into fourteen languages and issued in seventeen foreign countries. *Trial By Ordeal*, published in 1955, which continued the story of his life on San Quentin's death row, was also widely translated and widely read. His third book, which was not as successful, was *The Face of Justice*. Like the first two, it was made into a movie.

The Face of Justice had to be written in secret and transcribed in the dead of night in a race against time and the executioner. Each day the manuscript had to be hidden to prevent its discovery when prison officials searched the author and his cell on San Quentin's Death Row. The manuscript was spirited out of the prison by means that Monroe Stearns discovered. One night, when I was watching a rerun of the film based on this book, Chessman's female attorney tried to find out how the book had been "spirited" out. Chessman was noncommittal. It happened this way:

After Chessman wrote his first two books, Harley Teets, the harried warden of San Quentin, denied him permission to write another book. When prison guards saw him working at night in his always-lighted cell they thought he was working on legal briefs. Actually, he was penning *The Face of Justice*, writing first in longhand, then typing the copy, using a separate piece of carbon paper for each page. After he flushed the longhand version and the typescript down the toilet, all that remained were sheets of carbon paper. These were smuggled out of his cell, photostated, and sent to an agent, who engaged Prentice-Hall to publish the book. Then Monroe Stearns hired me to edit the photostats.

Warden Teets had the right to confine Chessman physically, to incarcerate his body, but he didn't own Chessman's soul, and the convict refused to allow him to put his mind in a cell. Nevertheless, Teets was irked, as *Time* magazine indicated. The warden had no idea how the manuscript had been written, despite the surveillance, let alone how it got to a publisher. *Time* also reported Chessman's threat that if the publisher cut his story he might send one of his men around. I pondered this as I cut the fat out of the narrative, along with the adjectives. Chessman often used four adjectives when one or none would have done. I also deleted some of the ranting of this psychopath, who had a genius rating.

The book boiled down to an impassioned plea that capital punishment was an evil scar across the face of justice. Chessman had been under sentence of death for nine years, at that time longer than any other person in this country's history. During all those years he fought fiercely against what he claimed was an unjust trial and conviction. He became a worldwide symbol of a determined struggle for justice against the forces of prejudice and false accusations. In his trilogy he expounded on the causes of crime, the treatment of criminals, and the ineffectuality of capital punishment.

During the Depression of the early 1930s, Chessman first got into trouble by stealing milk and groceries from neighbors' doorsteps to keep his family alive. In his psychopathic hatred of authority he committed a series of petty crimes in the Los Angeles area and wound up in a reformatory, where he learned shorthand and typing and read widely.

After his release from the reformatory, he was arrested, jailed again, escaped, was recaptured, and finally was convicted on sixteen charges, including rape and murder. By this time he was well known as the "Red Light Bandit." He was sentenced to death for violating California's "Little Lindbergh Law." Caryl Chessman, who never benefited from the repeal of the Little Lindbergh Law, died in the gas chamber at San Quentin.

The Face of Justice, like the earlier book, went into foreign editions. The book was especially popular in Scandinavian countries. While in London, I was startled to see the malevolent-looking effigy of Chessman in Madame Tussaud's Wax Museum.

Monroe then asked me to edit *All About Men*, written by Dr. Joseph Peck.

This book, which sold more than eighty thousand copies in hardcover, was syndicated in about a hundred newspapers, and was on the *New York Times* best seller list for thirty-three consecutive weeks.

Born in the last quarter of the nineteenth century, Dr. Peck was one of the first physicians in pioneer Utah, serving settlers in a section of the great American desert the size of Connecticut. He served a tribe of Gosiute Indians, delivered more than two thousand babies, and was for years a member of the Utah State Board of Health. At the age of sixty he retired and began his career as a writer. I take little credit for some of the glowing book reviews, since I merely translated into prose the witty and sage observations of a physician who told me in one letter: "The only things I have written for the past thirty years are prescriptions."

Critics called his book "exceedingly funny, wise and comforting and tartly written" and "a humorous and salty approach to the art of living. It is at once a serious and light look at the emotional problems of man."

Dr. Peck was living in retirement on a farm in the Sierra Nevada foothills when he wrote his 110-page manuscript, which I amplified into 260 pages.

Between my two books on the *Clipper*, Monroe gave me another interesting assignment.

I am especially proud of the rewrite job I did on *Secret Diary of Red China*, which was named on two different lists of the best hundred books of 1961. Again, "smuggling" was involved.

The author was an educator who wandered around China after being ousted by the Communists from his teaching post. This book was a diary between the lines of a classic novel, which was smuggled out of Red China and sent to a Chinese friend in California. This person—anything but a professional writer—translated the diary into ninety pages of typescript, and this was sent to me by Monroe Stearns.

It was a question of putting flesh on the bones. I had to recast every sentence of this fascinating but choppy manuscript. Noting that the wife of the teacher-author was nameless, I called her Yellow Jonquil. After a casual mention at the beginning of the diary that she was pregnant, her husband seemed to forget her condition, so at strategic points in the narrative, I mentioned some of her stirrings. Here and there I added emotional reflections of the characters, including a brief dialogue in the diary, which I expanded to 240 pages.

"If you keep a green bough in your heart and keep hoping, the day will come when a bird will light on it and sing," Yellow Jonquil said. "Yellow Jonquil is right," Prosperity said. "We must keep a green bough in our heart."

I stole most of those words from a column by the sportswriter Bill

Cunningham. I don't know which writer Cunningham stole them from, but they sounded Chinese to me.

During this period of surrogate authorship I learned some of the techniques needed to put a book together. Yes, it was much more complicated than writing adventure books for adolescent boys.

By the time I was doctoring manuscripts, Carl Brandt, my agent, had died, and since I was working directly with Monroe Stearns, I had no pressing need for another agent. Then, out of the blue, a former Hollywood agent for actors got in touch and asked if I was interested in writing the autobiography of a former New York mayor named William O'Dwyer, today largely remembered for marrying a beautiful model named Sloan Simpson and decamping to Mexico as U.S. ambassador after President Harry Truman appointed him in 1950, thereby avoiding a detailed inquiry about his conduct during his two terms as mayor.

Carlton Cole, who had read the Curley autobiography, drew up the collateral contract with the publisher, Julian Meissner, and Bill O'Dwyer's brother, Paul. This arrangement proved to be the kiss of death.

Paul O'Dwyer, although personally congenial, was difficult to deal with. Although he had been in the U.S. since the age of eighteen, he had somehow managed to preserve a brogue that was pure County Mayo.

At the outset everything came up roses. The publisher gave me a five thousand dollar advance and Paul, who had wanted to limit my share of a possible movie to five percent, finally agreed to fifteen percent. Also in the package was a free round trip to Mexico City, where Bill was living in a penthouse suite on the roof of the Prince Hotel.

The night before the flight Paul took me to dinner at Tim Costello's celebrated bar, where I talked to Tim and A. J. Liebling, who was then writing for the *New Yorker*. Tim's place was a favorite watering spot for that magazine's writers. The tape recorder Paul wanted me to take to Mexico didn't work, and it was just as well, as I had never felt the need of one.

After several dinner meetings at the Algonquin Hotel with Paul O'Dwyer and Carlton Cole, I met Mayor William O'Dwyer one afternoon in his hotel room at the St. Moritz. In his informal way he corrected me when I addressed him as "Your Honor." "Bill," he said. When I mentioned *I'd Do It Again!*, he remained impassive. "The auld sod," was all he said. Over the years I learned that the big city mayors I met, unlike governors, didn't stand on their dignity. I was on a first-name basis with Mayors

O'Dwyer, John Hynes, John Collins, and Kevin White. The single exception was Jim—beg your pardon—the Honorable James Michael Curley.

Bill O'Dwyer had a taxi waiting at the airport in Mexico City. I was aware of the ascent into Mexico City, which is about seventy-five hundred feet above sea level. I had never previously been any higher above sea level than Hanover, New Hampshire. I remember feeling dizzy and nauseated that first day in Mexico City. My room was on the floor below Bill's comfortable penthouse suite.

I was in Mexico for an enlightening and at times fascinating eight days. Bill had a Hungarian chef with whom he conversed in Spanish. One day after a crab crepe lunch, Bill was still hungry. "*Nada mas para mi?*" he asked. My Spanish, now fluency-faded, was fair at the time, and I knew what he was saying. "Isn't there any more for me?"

I learned from the first day that it was a good idea to get all possible interviewing in before Bill had his third scotch. Our sessions were occasionally interrupted by celebrity-minded visitors. During the evening cocktail hour Bill would read aloud from a book of poetry, or from a book by an Irish writer. One night we had dinner at the Rivoli on the outskirts of the city, and I had my first close-up of Rita Hayworth, whose red-haired radiance illumined the adjoining table. I waited for Bill to introduce her to me, but he apparently didn't know her well enough.

Bill had often mentioned a *New York Times* reporter named John Siegenthaler, who at this time was editor of the *Chattanooga Times*. At my request, Bill arranged a flight to Tennessee (at his expense) so I could interview Siegenthaler on my way home. The editor took me to dinner and invited me to spend the night with his family in his comfortable mountainside house. He gave me some inside information, and I got the impression that he considered Bill honest.

During those relaxed days in Mexico City, Paul often called to see how things were going, and of course, we never told him that the interviews were not going as fast as the scotch. Nevertheless, I came home with a bundle of readable copy.

Soon thereafter, Bill O'Dwyer moved back to the St. Moritz Hotel, across from Central Park in New York. For about three months I stayed at the Harvard Club of New York, returning to Duxbury every weekend. During the first few weeks I spent part of the day going through the O'Dwyer files at the municipal library, standard operating procedure for any biographer. Thereafter I spent most days and nights in Bill's company. I would walk from the Harvard Club in mid-morning to the St. Moritz to have a cup of coffee with Bill, who wore a blue silk robe over his underwear. No pajamas. Often with him in his suite was a lovely looking nocturnal companion who shall remain nameless. When I wasn't interviewing former associates of O'Dwyer's during his mayoralty, I was constantly in his company. I was surprised one day when we stepped into an elevator at the St. Moritz Hotel to find Walter Winchell standing alone, head bent and hat brim pulled down over his eyes. I wondered why O'Dwyer and Winchell didn't have a single word to say to each other. Was Bill still smarting about something Winchell had said about him in his column? Bill and I went to several social functions, including one bar mitzvah, where he introduced me to Jim Farley. Bill O'Dwyer had one nice habit in common with Gene Tunney. He would never let me pick up a tab.

Several times in taxis I would ask the cabbie what had become of former Mayor William O'Dwyer. Responses varied. "That crook?" one said. "Don't you know he stole a million bucks and lammed to Mexico?" Bill never showed any emotion, whether the driver's comments were flattering or denunciatory. When we got out of the cab, I would hand the cabbie an extra tip. "By the way, this is Mayor William O'Dwyer." Talk about glazed looks and sagging jaws.

In a chapter of the unpublished autobiography, which was to have been titled *The Higher They Climb*, I quoted Bill O'Dwyer:

> I volunteered to attend the hearings of the Senate Crime Investigating Committee in March 1951, because I felt my testimony might help destroy organized crime in the U.S. . . . .
>
> While I was grilled by the committee, President Aleman sent his personal plane to return me to Mexico. . . . I remember sitting alone at the Embassy when Sloan and her mother, who had been in Acapulco, returned. I was not merely a physical wreck. Sloan immediately sensed that I was just as broken in spirit.
>
> "*Pajarito*," she said, "what have they done to you?" All I could recall was sitting in the Foley building perspiring under hot lights and television cameras. I remembered losing my temper and giving a few answers to the outrageous questions. I could remember Senator Charles Tobey, playing the role of a smirking gnome, sarcastically asking why an associate of mine had attended a cocktail party in Frank Costello's apartment. "Why did you go—to carry a bag?" Millions of televiewers must have laughed at that sally.

It was Mayor Jimmy Walker who said, "Nobody can buy a mayor of New York, but almost anyone can sell him." During my work on the

150

O'Dwyer manuscript I learned of gangland infiltration in every pocket of the metropolis. Joe Adonis, a big-time racketeer, contributed twenty-five thousand dollars to Fiorello LaGuardia's campaign in 1933, and there was little that the "Little Flower" could do about it. He let Adonis alone, but in 1937, when Adonis backed his opponent, LaGuardia called him "a gangster and leader of the underworld."

I had a long session with John Murtaugh, who was then chief magistrate of New York. He told me how the Department of Investigation had exposed police corruption in 1944 when its agents raided a grocery store in Harlem. Seized on the premises was a ledger containing the exact bribes paid to police personnel, mentioning plainclothesmen, patrolmen, detectives, and superior officers, including lieutenants and captains. The payoffs ranged from one dollar to thirty dollars. One code notation referred to a "lone wolf." Later a retired detective boasted of having been known as "the lone wolf," and this led to the investigation. It turned out that the Greek proprietor of the grocery store, who had been taking a night course in bookkeeping, was perfecting his technique by keeping a ledger.

Bill was a glib raconteur:

> I recall a rainy night when I was tending bar in the Oak Room of the Plaza. At one table Arnold Daly, the actor, was sitting with Gentleman Jim Corbett and the New York Giants baseball manager, tough John McGraw. Corbett was sipping lemonade while the other two were boozing. Suddenly, Daly started quoting from Shakespeare. McGraw pounded the table. "For Christ's sake, Arnie, shut up." With a fight brewing, Corbett, the heavyweight boxing champ, rose and like a minister admonishing his flock, stretched out his hands. "Gentlemen, gentlemen," he said. "Please, gentlemen."

The shrewd scrappy Bill O'Dwyer was not cut out to be a barkeep. This Irishman from County Mayo, who had just missed taking holy orders, had landed in New York City in 1910 with twenty-five dollars in his pocket. After paying a month's rent in advance at a West Side boarding house, he took a twenty-dollar-a-week job as a laborer, later working as a longshoreman and a plasterer's helper. Meanwhile he studied nights at Fordham University Law School.

In 1916 he married Catherine ("Kitty") Lenihan, a telephone operator and skilled pianist whom he had met while taking evening law courses. By 1917 he was earning a thousand dollars a year as a patrolman on the toughest waterfront beat in Brooklyn. He never completely recovered from the experience of having to shoot a man. He left the force in 1923 after being

151

admitted to the New York Bar and opened an office. Nine years later, he was named a New York City magistrate. As a judge he was known for his common sense. He offered a toper the choice between jail and spending three hours alone with a bottle of whiskey.

I was interested in the experimental methods he used later when he sat in Brooklyn's new adolescent court. Here all youths between sixteen and nineteen were tried. Before passing judgment Judge O'Dwyer consulted with welfare workers, the clergy, and probation officers.

Some of the tall tales Bill heard in the adolescent and magistrate courts would have been grist for O. Henry's mill. One youth said he had stolen a car "under the influence of a full moon." His lawyer told the magistrate that while the lad was normally law abiding, he sometimes acted irrationally under the influence of a full moon. Bill sent him to a reformatory. Only in a city the size of New York would detectives be assigned to handle "full mooners," a term that stems from days of witchcraft, when a new moon was believed to make people act queerly. One boy told O'Dwyer he stole an alarm clock so he could get to work on time to help support his family. "He and another vandal had broken a plateglass window and walked away with four alarm clocks," O'Dwyer told me.

To give me an intimate idea of what happened in court, Bill arranged for me to sit on the bench with a magistrate who was his former associate. I heard one Brooklyn youngster explain why he had slashed a boy with a butcher's knife. "He called me names." The magistrate turned to me. "What do you think I should do with this kid?" I was glad I didn't have to make the decision. The magistrate sent him to a reform school. That morning I saw more than a dozen young offenders stand before the bench. I didn't pass sentence on any of them.

After getting background information from veteran reporters at City Hall, I asked O'Dwyer to invite the "Wolf Pack," as they were called, to his St. Moritz suite. As the evening waxed convivial, two newsmen told me O'Dwyer had promised to let them write his autobiography. Next day O'Dwyer, in his usual impassive way, said: "I hope you got something out of the boys last night. That party cost me $190."

During an interview at the Harvard Club with Sloan Simpson, Bill's ex-wife, whom he had married after the death of Kitty, she told me about the breakdown her husband had had after the grueling Kefauver hearings, which I had seen on TV in Duxbury. She became more reticent when I asked her about what *Life* magazine said of her toreador consort in Madrid.

"The guy was about three inches shorter than I," she said, as if that

152

explained everything. She invited me to a party that Saturday night, adding that Faye Emerson, the glamorous actress, would be there, but when she mentioned some of the things that went on at these celebrity gatherings, I figured a country boy like me would be safer back in Duxbury. A couple of weeks later Bill invited her to a small dinner party at his hotel suite. The fourth person present was His Honor's mistress.

I had sessions with current and former city officials, deputy mayors, judges, detectives, and a few characters who seemed to come out of a Damon Runyon story. Broadway Johnny O'Connor told me about the night he had taken a young William O'Dwyer to former Mayor Jimmy Walker's apartment. Walker, warning O'Dwyer of the hazards of the job, said "cheers have short echoes." But he encouraged O'Dwyer to run. Broadway Johnny was a mysterious person who operated out of a book-lined second-story office not far from Times Square. I got the impression that he was more familiar with the literature of the *Police Gazette* than, say, *War and Peace*. He agreed to join Bill and me for a chat at the St. Moritz, and as we waited for a taxi he nudged my elbow. "See that guy?" The guy was a swarthy six-footer wearing a wide-brimmed hat. "He's the leading bookie in New York." Johnny would tell me no more about him.

During the conversation in the St. Moritz, I got another distinct impression. Broadway Johnny was in no way awed by the former two-term mayor. It was as if he had something on Bill O'Dwyer—a kind of veiled threat. During that session I saw Bill angry for the first time. I forget the context, but Broadway Johnny, in commenting on some honor Bill had received, acidly remarked that any day now one could expect some university to award a "degree in mopery." Bill stood up, his perpendicularity marred only by a slight bulge in the mid-section, and blasted Johnny. Johnny left almost immediately, and that was the last I saw of him. At the time I thought, what undercover stories he could write.

I saw another angry Bill O'Dwyer the night of the Wolf Pack meeting in his suite. A *New York Times* reporter, one of several who thought he was the final choice to be the O'Dwyer biographer, kept asking in a slurred, drunken tone whether the room was bugged. He became so offensive I suggested it might be a good idea if someone dropped him out the window. After another innuendo about Bill's integrity while mayor, Bill threw the book at him. After the party, I left with the reporter, feeling he might be a source of some otherwise unobtainable data. We stopped in a couple of bars, but finally his comments slurred into gibberish, and I left him and walked back to the Harvard Club.

I also spent an afternoon with Grover Whalen, the best-known city greeter of his era, whose autobiography I had read. One night Paul O'Dwyer took me to a political banquet where Whalen was master of ceremonies. Whalen was so drunk he could hardly complete a sentence.

During those months of research in New York I learned that Bill O'Dwyer had enemies in high circles. Also in low circles. Magazine writers like Mike Stern talked about such items as huge reserves of scotch whiskey in the Mexico environs, and of his mysterious ample and continuing income, even though he had said that after two terms as mayor he was down to his last thousand dollars. He ran a law firm in Mexico City that was affiliated with Paul's prosperous law firm on Wall Street in New York, and that, ostensibly, was the source of his current income. One subtle enemy in the low circle was his former press secretary while he was serving his second term as mayor. In a subtle way this mini-bureaucrat—let's call him John—objected to having a hick from Boston do an autobiography of a mayor of New York. On the surface, John obliged when Bill asked him to cooperate with my efforts. But only on the surface.

One late afternoon, John arranged a meeting for me with a burly dese-dem-dose character who, he said, would fill me in on certain mysterious circumstances connected with the district attorney's prosecution of principals in the story of Murder, Incorporated. Left alone with this hulk, I taxied him to the Harvard Club and sat down in a corner table in the semi-twilight of the barroom. I was conscious of his discomfort in such elegant surroundings. He kept his hat on, and although he looked to me like a confirmed barfly, he declined a drink. He seemed at all times to be looking past me or over my head. As friendly as a cobra entrancing a mongoose, he kept asking me if I had this or that mobster in my narrative. The inescapable inference, I gathered, was that this would be a watered-down version of the seamy side of the O'Dwyer memoir.

I was glad when he left. I could breathe more easily.

In 1938 Governor Herbert Lehman had appointed O'Dwyer a County Court Judge in Brooklyn, and he was later elected to that post for a fourteen-year term at a yearly salary of twenty-five thousand dollars. In 1939, when he was elected district attorney for Brooklyn, he accepted a salary cut of five thousand dollars, but it paid off. Less than three months after he took office in 1940, he had solved fifty-six underworld murders, most of them linked. The court trials that followed were sensational, and the mobster ring involved became nationally known as "Murder, Inc."

Until this time it was almost common practice to release gangsters and

154

racketeers for lack of legal evidence. O'Dwyer used what he called "applied psychology" to get a series of convictions. He told me he would tell one mobster that one of his confederates had confessed, in that way inducing the racketeer to admit his complicity.

Bill O'Dwyer was district attorney when the gangsters included Pittsburgh Phil, Louis Lepke, and the fiendish Abe Reles, whose favorite weapons were icepicks and garottes. In Brooklyn, I had a session with the prosecutor who sent Lepke to the chair. He was then a professor of law at Brooklyn College. I had two sessions with one of the detectives who had kept Reles in protective custody at the Half Moon Hotel in Brooklyn. In a sardonic way he told me that Reles either fell or was pushed to his death from an upper window in the hotel. When I asked why the gangster's body was so far from the base of the Half Moon, he shrugged. The inference was clear. Someone had pushed Reles out the window. He was the kind of mobster whom other gangsters despised.

One afternoon session I was with Raymond Jones, a Harlem political boss who was held next in esteem in Harlem to the late Congressman Adam Clayton Powell. I taxied to Harlem to talk to him in his office. I still have a vision of the hostile glances and curt statements as I asked directions on the way to his office. A Harlem cop was so rude that I got the impression that he was telling me the best way to get lost. I finally saw Mr. Jones, and I got the immediate impression that I was listening to the Kingfish in the old *Amos and Andy* TV show. He gave me some documentary anecdotes.

When I got back to the city I was told what a foolish chance I had taken. Someone at the Harvard Club told me I had taken a risk venturing alone in that part of Harlem.

I spent hours with the corpulent Mike Quill, the best known New York union organizer of his era. Mike, the story went, returned to Ireland every year to renew a brogue that was even thicker than Paul O'Dwyer's. Mike, a great admirer of Bill, shut off all his phones and gave me all the time I wanted. He told me of the behind-the-scene chats he had had with O'Dwyer at Gracie Mansion.

Everything was proceeding smoothly until I started prying into the Jim Moran affair. According to the collateral contract, Paul O'Dwyer had to approve everything that went into the book. When it was obvious that he wanted a whitewash of his brother, Bill, I reminded him of a threat a writer named Michael Stern had made to Carlton Cole. Stern had written a devastating attack in *Esquire* on O'Dwyer after Bill moved to Mexico, and he told Cole he would expose any attempt by me to gloss over certain facts. This didn't bother Paul O'Dwyer, but it worried me.

One morning in the St. Moritz suite, Bill sat silently chain-smoking while Paul asked me, in substance, to keep Moran out of the book. Paul was the kind of literary critic who thinks Shakespeare's *Hamlet* would still be a good story if the melancholy Dane were left out. Moran, who had been fire commissioner during O'Dwyer terms, was found guilty of a huge shakedown racket and was sent to Sing-Sing. He was a principal in any O'Dwyer story, but I could never convince Paul of that. Moran died in Sing-Sing.

I had another problem. The publisher wanted more "romance" in the narrative. I had written about how Bill had met, courted, and married a former telephone operator, but when I asked him for more details, he simply clammed up. Kitty, he ungallantly said, was an alcoholic, and during the years before she died, he would often come home to find her passed out. The crowning blow was a weekend I spent with the Paul O'Dwyers at their farm in upper New York State. I had hoped to get a lot of background information, but I came up dry. By this time I was disgusted with the project, which had seemed so promising.

When Paul asked me to sign a release to the effect that I would never write a book on his brother, I refused. But Paul has no cause to worry, especially if he thinks anyone will ever write such a book without mentioning principals like Jim Moran.

Soon, outside of New York, Bill, whom I liked so much, was almost forgotten. He died a few years later. Jimmy Walker was right. Cheers have short echoes.

I saw a lot of Gene Tunney in New York City when I was assigned to write the autobiography of Mayor William O'Dwyer. We occasionally had lunch at the Biltmore and I remember pleasant afternoons at the Lotos Club. I didn't see much of him when I returned to Duxbury after the war. Our most interesting meeting followed a call he made one Sunday night in 1964 from the Ritz-Carlton in Boston. Tunney said, "President Kennedy has kicked me off my Maine island, and I plan to spend a couple of days on Martha's Vineyard. I'll be back at John's Island Tuesday. Why don't you and Bobbie come up for a visit?"

"It was a memorable visit," Bobbie recalled.

We drove from Duxbury one beautiful summer day to the little town of

Bristol, Maine. We were headed for the summer home of Gene and Polly Tunney. From the dock, we could look across and see John's Island, where we were to spend two days. Leaving our car in a garage near the dock, we looked out at the bay and saw Gene rowing, bare from the waist up, his well-publicized muscles bulging with every pull of the oars. Thinking that was to be our means of transportation to the island, we grabbed our bags. But Polly soon followed in a sizeable motor launch and away we went.

We were taken for a whirlwind tour of the waters around the island, then back to the comfortable summer home of the Tunney's where we enjoyed a fascinating evening hearing about President Kennedy's visit.

During the evening, Gene and John went down into the wine cellar to see what the presidential party had imbibed. Well, they drank a lot of scotch and some wine, but otherwise everything was intact.

The next day we boarded the launch and motored across the bay to the mainland to be guests of Polly's sister. We all sat on a deck overlooking the bay and listened to Gene tell of some of the people he had known—George Bernard Shaw, F. Scott Fitzgerald, and Ernest Hemingway, especially.

Gene told of one late afternoon in Paris when he was sitting at a table at the Ritz bar, presided over by the famed Charles, whom Bobbie and I met twice when we were in Paris. Gene was talking to a well-known sports writer, W. O. McGeehan, when F. Scott Fitzgerald joined them. A drink or two later, Fitzgerald got pugnacious, and Gene had to calm him down.

"Scott often gets that way after he has a few drinks," Gene said. "Hemingway did, too, but he never challenged me." Those weren't Gene's exact words, but that is substantially what he said.

Gene's caretaker told us how the Secret Service men had rigged lights so there was not a shadow left on the island, which is about eight miles long. He said JFK had brought his rocking chair with him. Gene placed two books on a table, hoping the President would autograph them. One was *Profiles in Courage*. The other was my book, *Honey Fitz: Three Steps to the White House*. I had sent Gene this book, just as I had sent him every other book I wrote. Kennedy signed *Profiles in Courage*. Alas, he did not sign the book beside it.

Gene Tunney died in 1978 at the age of eighty. He took with him an exciting segment of the Roaring Twenties that was enriched by heroes like Babe Ruth, Jack Dempsey, Red Grange, Bobby Jones, Bill Tilden, and the Four Horsemen of Notre Dame. "But," wrote Joseph Durson in the November 11 edition of the *New York Times*, "the only one who could recite

157

Shakespeare, lecture at Yale, match wits with George Bernard Shaw—and beat Dempsey—was Gene Tunney."

There are times to remember, and there are people you will never forget. The one single person I never shall forget left us too suddenly. The man is Gene Tunney, the private person who did so much for me. But there was one thing he refused to do.

He wouldn't let me write his autobiography. It would have been a good book.

Chapter Twenty
PUT IT ON THE FRONT PAGE, PLEASE!

If writers hang around the Harvard Club of New York's bar long enough someone will ask them to write a book. That's how I met the late Sumner Putnam in 1959, when he was president of Ives Washburn, Inc., New York. Sumner, who was the brother of Eliot Putnam, former headmaster at Noble & Greenough School, told me he would soon be in Nantucket to talk to an author, and he suggested stopping in Duxbury on his way back to New York to discuss a book I might write for him. He mentioned Eleanora Sears, the vibrant horsewoman of the North Shore, who had often broken into print for such feats as walking from Boston to Providence.

Bobbie and I were having lunch at Jimmy's Harborside Restaurant, in Boston, about a week later, when I saw Victor Jones and Daniel O'Brien, two of the top editors of the *Boston Globe*. I sat down for a moment with them and asked what they thought of a possible biography of Eleanora Sears.

"I think the book might sell," Jones said, "to members of the Myopia Hunt Club."

It was a beautiful day in mid-June of 1959 when Sumner dropped by our Cape on Washington Street. Over his single martini, he mentioned that he learned at Westwinds Book Shop that Bobbie and I published a weekly newspaper. "How about doing a book on the *Duxbury Clipper*?" he asked. I was pleasantly shocked by the idea. "And," he continued, "I can see that you are a writer who needs a deadline, so I'll give you until November 1."

Bobbie liked Sumner Putnam so much she went down to the fish market to buy some crabmeat. During Duxbury summers she often serves crabmeat luncheons to favorite guests. Besides, she and the publisher had ancestors in common. They were both related to the Sumners who owned the part of Canton, Massachusetts, that didn't belong to the Draper families.

Writing *Put It On the Front Page, Please!* was so much fun. The prose didn't flow, it gushed as Bobbie and I summed up the delightful experiences we had had in putting a weekly into orbit. The book was a kind of running diary involving the activities of our friends, neighbors, and town officials.

The little book, completed a month ahead of schedule, was the only one I had ever written that didn't get many bad reviews. How do you think

Bobbie and I reacted when the *New York Times*, in its review of *Put It On the Front Page, Please!* called the *Clipper*, "One of the gayest weekly mirrors of New England small town life. . . . If you are planning to start a paper, by all means read Mr. Cutler's book. . . . In any event, you will find here a stimulating view of country life in America."

The *Globe* was kind: "For lively humorous reading there has been nothing recently as delightful as *Put It On the Front Page, Please!* And for a portrait of a town there has been nothing for a long time even to approach it in vividness."

I fished out a review from the *Boston Sunday Post* by the late Olga Owens Huckins, who talked Rachel Carson into writing *Silent Spring* after Olga found seven dead robins on her Duxbury lawn: "The best book ever written on newspapering, and I have read them all."

Alice Dixon Bond in the *Boston Sunday Herald* wrote:

"This book is as jolly and entertaining as its evocative title. . . . It is an entertaining and informative addition to the summer reading lists. The Cutlers are amusing people to visit for an afternoon and their *Clipper* voyage of ten years has all the madcap pace and zany humor of a Moss Hart comedy."

Although the book didn't sell well, it was placed on the shelves of scores of libraries around the country, and it is still used in some college journalism courses.

Bobbie and I were more puzzled than daunted when we received a letter from William Heath, editor of the *American Editor*:

> I thought your book charming, edifying, and even inspiring—not to say humorous—and therefore deserving my attention until I reached paragraphs three and four on page 120. They shook my standards of journalism so heavily I almost decided to send the book back to the publisher. But I read on. My indecision has become serious. Will you please send me a copy of your paper? I'm sure it will help me make up my mind.

I immediately looked up the two paragraphs in *Put It On the Front Page, Please!* I read:

> At another cocktail party, a guest sounded off about the panty-waisted *Clipper*, which refused to print scandalous news. On the way home, he was arrested for driving under the influence and driving so as to endanger. The next time I met him, I couldn't resist teasing him.

160

"That was an interesting item, I know. Please accept my apology for not printing it."

The Associated Press took note of the *Clipper* on March 15, 1965:

John Henry Cutler, who quit as professor of languages at Dartmouth because he wasn't making enough money, decided in 1950 that Duxbury needed a weekly newspaper. The decision was not universally approved.

"Look son," said a long-time Duxbury resident, "do you have rocks in your head? There just plain isn't enough news in Duxbury."

The long-time resident had a point. In 1950, Duxbury was a serene town of three thousand persons on the Massachusetts shore some thirty-five miles from Boston. It had had distinguished history of three hundred and fifty years without benefit of a local newspaper and an apparent willingness to maintain what Cutler calls the "status quorum."

This intentional pun referred to the "oligarchy" in Duxbury.

One amusing incident occurred when Robert Bergenheim wrote a review in the *Christian Science Monitor*. Here is an excerpt from his review:

While Mr. Cutler makes it clear that he did most of the things which should have put him in bankruptcy, he also had a safety line that pulled him through successfully. Not at all easy to come by, he had a writer, editor, circulation manager, advertising manager, production chief, bill collector, and brain truster all wrapped up in one. Of course, it is his wife. She also takes care of him, the house, and their five children. At first one might think Mr. Cutler too modest or chivalrous in giving all the credit to his wife. But as the objective newsman that he is, Mr. Cutler allows her to say a few words of her own in this story of their joint endeavors. This raises only one question—which no doubt occurred to Mr. Cutler. Why didn't he let her write the whole book?

Bergenheim added this cryptic note:

Some readers might be disillusioned to discover that some editors write letters to themselves in order to liven up the letter to the editor column, but it is a successful way to get editorials read.

Several years later Robert Bergenheim moved to Duxbury and Barbara Mullowney, by then a realtor, gave a cocktail party in his honor. She took me over to meet him.

161

"Oh, I know John Cutler," he said. "I reviewed one of his books in the *Monitor*."

"Yes," I said. "I remember that you told your readers that Bobbie should have written the whole book." He smiled.

"Well, the wifely disclaimer Bobbie wrote to the editor after my review proved my point. It was a very well written letter."

Here is the letter Bergenheim refers to:

> The *Clipper*'s success can only in the wildness of your reviewer's imagination be ascribed to my being a writer, editor, circulation manager, advertising manager, production chief, bill collector, and brain truster wrapped in one. Mr. Bergenheim's sometimes accurate review contains the silly comment, "She also takes care of him."
>
> This was of course meant to be charitable and true, and to give your readers the impression that John plays drone to my Queen Bee. John writes notably well and has a concise, sprightly style that is my evergreen envy. In ten years, I have written only two *Clipper* editorials, and as for production chief, what is that? Only when John turned to writing books to augment the kind of family income needed to rear five children (three in prep school at the same time) did I do any writing at all to speak of. . . . Someday I think he should write a book that might tentatively be called *What About Book Reviewers?* A sometimes humorous book of this sort would have a captive audience, what, Mr. Bergenheim? . . .
>
> (Editor's Note: Mr. Bergenheim enjoyed this letter as well as the book.)

Bobbie, who was sitting beside me at the Mullowney party, broke into our conversation.

"I don't want you to spill your drink, Mr. Bergenheim," she said, "but I didn't write that letter, John wrote it."

On publication day Sumner Putnam hosted a luncheon at the Boston Harvard Club. Alison Arnold, society editor of the *Boston Herald*, and later one of the most popular columnists the *Clipper* had ever had, wrote in her column the next day:

> A small luncheon was given at the Harvard Club yesterday to celebrate the publication of *Put It On the Front Page, Please!* Present were the Cutlers, Mr. Sumner Putnam, president of Ives Washburn, Inc., Charles Norton and Phoebe Adams of the *Atlantic Monthly*, Edward Laycock of the *Boston Globe*, Roderick Nordall of the *Christian Science Monitor*, Mrs. Alice Dixon Bond and Edward Devin of the *Herald*, Morton DeWolfe, and Mrs. Oliver Barker, owner of Westwinds Bookstore in Duxbury.

I remember when Charles Norton turned to me: "Listen Cutler, don't be chastened by your own disabilities." Phoebe-Lou Adams, who married the former editor of the *Atlantic Monthly*, Edward Weeks, wrote a brief review of *Front Page* for the *Atlantic*.

Shortly after *Put It On the Front Page, Please!* had been published, Professor Theodore Morrison of Harvard, whom I had first met at the Breadloaf Writers Conference in 1947, dropped in one summer day with his nephew, who was an editorial writer for the *Wall Street Journal*. He was considering leaving the *Journal* and was interested in publishing a weekly newspaper in Vermont or New Hampshire, and he thought of the *Duxbury Clipper* as a model to follow.

The *Duxbury Clipper*, in the early 1950s, was still struggling to get into orbit, and there were times when Bobbie and I regretted rejecting an offer to sell the sheet in 1952 for a thousand dollars. Bobbie and I muddled along, however, with the help of the Sunday features I kept selling to the *Boston Post* and, much more occasionally, to the *Toronto Star Weekly*.

The *Clipper* was beginning to attract attention outside of Duxbury. On September 29, 1960, the *Publisher's Auxiliary* named me "Editor of the Week."

In addition to a book review, the editorial page ran a long feature article on "Mr. and Mrs. Clipper":

> Cutler learned quickly that local news, like local loyalty, makes or breaks a weekly paper. Early in the *Clipper*'s career, he wrote:
>
> As far as a country (we said country, not hick) editor is concerned, it's more important that Ed Noyes and Bill White won the finals in a cribbage tournament than that the United States declared war on Sweden and Switzerland the same day. If Joe Stalin married Lana Turner or if Harry Truman admitted he was ever wrong, there would be no mention of it in the *Clipper*, although some may consider these things the greatest news stories since the Crucifixion. If, however, my friend Tom Lawson says, I'd like to come to your beach party but I have to mow the lawn this afternoon, that's news.

The sequel to *Put It On the Front Page, Please!*, *Cancel My Subscription, Please!*, didn't fare as well, since by the time of its publication, in 1965, the *Clipper* had grown in content, circulation, and perhaps prestige. Part of the appeal of the first book was our goofs and pratfalls, candidly related.

In a column headed "Looks at Authors and Books," Robert Cromie caught the essence of the book:

163

Duxbury is a place where two candidates applied for a job as policeman and one was chosen because the only available uniform fitted him.

In Duxbury, your opponents in the Legion bridge tournament are a barber and a bank president, his partner.

The cuisine at Chez Lucien (formerly the Winsor House) is almost on a par with Maxim's (in Paris) because it is prepared by Lucien Vivas, former chef on the French line *Liberté*.

And in Duxbury one of the most distinguished of Harvard professors may be seen on Saturdays on the main street, dressed in sneakers and blue jeans, bank presidents golf for two-bits a hole, and while there are three Bradford roads, there is only one traffic light.

Like all papers everywhere the *Clipper* prints letters from readers, and some letters seem to have a special flavor. Consider this properly polite request which appeared in the Letters column:

"Will the slobs who dump empty liquor bottles onto the private lot of Bumblebee Lane please refrain from doing so?"

Or this, from a housewife through whose kitchen window an unopened beer can had been thrown:

"Being a newcomer I want to inquire whether this is a local custom I should get used to."

In 1965 the *Clipper* ran a "Why I Like Duxbury" contest. Dixon White took top honors. My Harvard classmate Russell Seaver was runner up. Here is what Dixon White wrote:

Duxbury is many things to me and my family. It is a Colonial home on a quiet street. It is a white sail on blue water. It is a winnowing black duck at sunset. It is a rural mailbox standing sentry duty by a rose covered arbor.

Duxbury is a lonely sweep of beach. It is gnarled pitchpine or a blackjack oak. Duxbury is an autumnal cranberry bog. It is the laughter of children in the distance on a winter day. It is the smell of salt and the sound of surf. It is the feeling of hot sand under bare feet.

Duxbury is a stately white church rising out of green foliage. But Duxbury is more than all this. Duxbury is a vibrant way of life. It is a prime example of Town Meeting government: government by the people, of the people, and definitely with the people's best interests at heart.

Some towns are perfectly nice places in which to live. Our town is more than this. It is vitally alive and has a personal character which has been chiseled out of an adamant Yankee heritage.

As evidence of my sincerity, I submit my mortgage. I love my town.

When the *Duxbury Clipper* switched from a free-distribution to paid-circulation basis in 1963, we expected that some of our involuntary subscribers would sound off in colorful language and refuse to pay a nickel for another copy of the *Clipper*. Bobbie and I didn't want to be embarrassed by asking so many people whom we knew to take out paid subscriptions, so we hired an outsider to make the calls. He was impressed by the response.

The fact that we were then writing a sequel to *Put It On the Front Page, Please!* with the tentative title of *Cancel My Subscription, Please!* might have had something to do with our hope that violent reactions would be recorded.

Well, nobody slammed the *Clipper*. Nobody said it was too left, too right, too backward, or too forward.

Then we received a letter from a former Duxbury resident, Mrs. Howard Douglas of Garden Grove, California.

> Dear *Duxbury Clipper*:
> I HATE the *Clipper* because it makes me homesick as all get-out.
> I HATE the *Clipper* because it is one of the very last rural papers to have the little news items in it which people want to know.
> I HATE the *Clipper* because I lived and grew up in a small town, where vital information such as Mr. and Mrs. X returning from a shopping trip to Boston, or the church picnic, was given priority over the national and international world crises, bickerings, backbitings, and hoopla; your paper gives each person and your own town priority over Khrushchev, Ooomba Boombah, Fidel Castro; which makes me MAD, because our local so-called "family newspaper" has graduated from this type of news.

By the late 1950s, things were looking up. Before the *Clipper* was launched, John Griffin and other Boston editors I had written for would refer to the project as "Cutler's Folly," but the *Clipper* by 1957 was cruising through calmer waters. I was also busy with other activities. I was lecturing at schools and women's clubs, and guest-moderating the WNAC radio program, "Alcoholism is Everybody's Business."

I was on the board of directors of the Boston Committee on Alcoholism and a member of the board of the Massachusetts Council for Public Schools. Working with its chairman, Graham Winslow, was a delightful experience. We traveled around the state visiting overcrowded classrooms and meeting top-echelon personnel in the field of education. One evening I had a long informal talk with Roy Larsen, then a senior editor of *Time* magazine.

After serving on the Massachusetts Council for Public Schools as publicity director, I later had the same assignment with the Statewide Committee for Increased Aid to Public Schools.

In 1955 my agent, Carl Brandt, got a contract from *Ford Times* to produce a special New England edition. At Carl's request, I submitted a list of pieces I could write, and he accepted two at five hundred dollars each, even though both contained fewer than two hundred words. One was on the Pilgrim Fort in Plymouth, the other on the Peabody Museum in Cambridge. I wrote these articles in three or four hours. It was one of the ups that compensated for the more frequent downs.

Bobbie's father, Dr. James Batcheller Sumner, died on August 12, 1955. Here is an excerpt taken from the *Buffalo Courier-Express*:

> Dr. Sumner, whose retirement in July terminated a forty-one year career as a Cornell faculty member, received the Nobel prize in 1946 for isolating an enzyme.
>
> A native of Canton, Massachusetts, he attended Roxbury (Massachusetts) Latin School and received his Bachelor of Arts, Master of Arts, and Doctor of Philosophy degrees from Harvard University. He continued his academic studies at the University of Brussels.
>
> He taught at Mt. Allison College, Sackville, New Brunswick, in 1911 and was research director in 1911 and 1912 at Worcester (Massachusetts) Polytechnic Institute.
>
> Fifteen years after he went to Cornell in 1914 as an assistant professor of biochemistry, he became a full professor.
>
> He was a Guggenheim Fellow in 1937 and was awarded the Scheele Medal the same year in Stockholm.
>
> Dr. Sumner was a member of the American Society of Biologists and Chemists, the American Academy of the Advancement of Science, the Society for Experimental Biology and Medicine, Sigma XI and Phi Kappa Phi. . . .
>
> With Dr. Karl Myrback of Sweden, he co-authored a book titled *The Enzymes.*
>
> Survivors are his wife, Mrs. Mary Morrison Beyer Sumner; three sons, Jacques, Frederick and John; two daughters, Mrs. John Cutler and Mrs. Edward Gamard, and a sister, Miss Amie May Sumner.

At a weekly newspaper convention on Block Island I met a high salaried *Time* magazine writer who had left the magazine to publish a small weekly in New Hampshire. One of the most flattering letters came from the author of a charming book on a weekly newspaper that was published in Pennsylvania. And thereby hangs a tale.

Bobbie's mother, Cid Ricketts Sumner, in the 1960s had been writing her *Tammy* books and some of them were filmed. Debbie Reynolds was the wholesome heroine in one *Tammy* film, and Sandra Dee, who talked, said *Time* magazine, as if she had a mouthful of walnuts, starred in another. One afternoon Cid invited us to the Ritz-Carlton in Boston to meet Sandra and her advance man, who turned out to be my old friend from Breadloaf days, Paul Camey. Sandra was so demure, with her melting look, I couldn't picture her hauling a catfish out of the muddy Mississippi.

"Our studio talked about filming your book *Put It On the Front Page, Please!*," Camey said. "And if we hadn't filmed *It Happens Every Thursday* a few years ago, we would have done it." Paul was referring to the book written in 1951 by Jane Stevenson McIlvaine. It was filmed in 1953, with Loretta Young and John Forsythe playing the leads. After my book *Put It on the Front Page, Please!* was published in 1960, Jane McIlvaine sent me a letter saying how much she and her husband enjoyed the book. Bobbie and I were impressed with the similarity between *Put It on the Front Page, Please!* and *It Happens Every Thursday.*

Paul thought my book was a few cuts above that horrible short story "Thyme and the Tide" which he had read aloud on the porch at the writers' conference. But, alas, no movie. I tried to visualize Hollywood actors who would have played the parts of Police Chief Jimmy O'Neil, Tom Lawson, and Bobbie. Bobbie's role? Well, Greer Garson could have played it, but better still, Bette Davis.

Monroe Stearns and Carlton Cole thought a book on Sherman Billingsley and The Stork Club would sell. One afternoon the three of us sat down and talked over the idea with Billingsley. After an hour or so of conversation, he excused himself and went up to his nearby office, saying he would return shortly. We all agreed that he sounded receptive, but if memory serves, Monroe said Billingsley might hesitate to tell his story because his career as a former bootlegger might embarrass his family. Suddenly I remembered a column I had written on Billingsley in my syndicated feature. The Stork Club host had a special table that was bugged, I had written. It was a fair bet that Billingsley was up in his private office "listening in" at that very moment.

It was another little adventure. Sherman never gave us the green light, but as the months passed, this was of no great concern. I was beginning to write books of my own.

Chapter Twenty-one
THE LAST HURRAH, IN FACT, NOT FICTION

In the 1960s, when an editor at Viking Press offered me advances of five thousand dollars each for writing three biographies, I was rebuffed every time. When I called Vannevar Bush at the Massachusetts Institute of Technology he gruffly told me he could write his own book. When I drove to Harwichport one summer morning to discuss a biography with Attorney Joseph Welch, a star of the Army-McCarthy Hearings, he said, "Well, Cutler, there is no hurry." He died about a year later. Dr. Paul Dudley White never got past the mildly interested stage. Welch and White were then timely subjects, Welch because of the televised hearings, White because he was President Eisenhower's physician.

Monroe Stearns suggested a biography of Herbert Bayard Swope— one I would like to have written—but his widow said no. A physician who had something to do with the estate of Bernard MacFadden asked me to do a biography of the eccentric physical culturist, adding that he had all the basic material, but I couldn't find a publisher.

I turned down one assignment myself. Attorney Ray Baldwin, a former member of a prestigious law firm that handled the famed Lotta Crabtree trial, invited me to write a book on the celebrated case. He had all the documentary material, including correspondence, catalogued in his attic. Sumner Putnam vetoed this idea in favor of a sequel to *Put It On the Front Page, Please!* so in 1965 I wrote *Cancel My Subscription, Please!* Some of the reviewers aptly noted that it didn't have the same appeal as the first book, but it did get some acclaim.

Even though I had a publisher and my agent approved, I rejected the idea of writing a book on alcoholism. At the time I was public relations director for the Boston Committee on Alcoholism, the first committee of its kind (not to be confused with Alcoholics Anonymous) in the U.S. I felt that Elizabeth Whitney, one of the founders, was much better qualified to write such a book. Since then, she has written two books on the subject, *The Lonely Sickness* and *Living With Alcoholism*. Later she edited and wrote two chapters of *World Dialogue on Alcohol and Drug Dependence*, an anthology of fifteen articles by the top contemporary authorities on alcoholism.

In between two books I wrote on the *Clipper*, Sumner Putnam asked me to write a book about women along the lines of *All About Men*. My agent, Paul Reynolds, told me I couldn't treat women the way Dr. Peck had dealt with men. "Women don't like to be spoofed. Make the book serious and factual, recording the changes in the status of women during the past half century."

What About Women?, written in 1960, had some good reviews, but it didn't sell. It was written several years too soon. Elizabeth Hardwick, former wife of the Pulitzer Prize-winning poet Robert Lowell, summed things up in her review in the *Atlantic Monthly*: "Cutler's book is a series of clever and witty essays, but it doesn't necessarily belong on your shelf." (When I met Miss Hardwick and her husband a few years earlier at a cocktail party in Duxbury, where they lived, I recall that when she accepted a third old-fashioned, Robert Lowell gave her a dirty look that suggested he didn't approve of noon cocktails. Sotto voce, she told him where to head in.)

"This," said the *Library Journal*, "is not a collection of generalities; it is highly factual in content, is readable and informative and, because of the author's sense of humor, often truly entertaining as well. Strongly recommended for all (even the smallest libraries)."

I didn't get rich on *What About Women?* but again I had fun. In her long, favorable review in the *New York Herald Tribune*, Eugenia Shepherd said a cop gave her a ticket when she drove down a wrong lane while she was distracted by a comment in my book (about the superiority of women drivers). She added, "John Cutler ought to pay my fine." The WOR interviewer had been less willing to accept my assessment of women drivers, suggesting that I try driving behind a woman sometime on a New York freeway. The most favorable review was written by the women's-page editor of the *New York Times*.

In a single day I was on five shows. The first was a telephone interview on a Connecticut radio show at 9 A.M. At one o'clock, I was one of four on a panel that included two other authors and one physician, on Betty Furness's popular midday TV show. Viewers phoned in questions, not all of them trivial. When a woman asked me how much she should pay babysitters, I thought the question silly enough to deserve a silly answer. "That depends," I said, "on whether you leave caviar or liverwurst in the fridge." A few weeks after the Betty Furness Show I was again a panelist, on Boston's Bob Kennedy talk show. I remember only two of the other panelists—Betty Friedan, author of *The Feminine Mystique*, and Phyllis McGinley.

Before the television appearance, Betty Furness served us coffee and sandwiches. After the show I was with her in the studio limousine when her chauffeur drove me back to the Harvard Club. She was cordial and warm.

Later that afternoon I sat in my room at the Harvard Club and at three-thirty tuned in to a taped radio show. I was startled to hear the interviewer refer to me as "one of the top authorities on women." I wasn't even a top authority on Bobbie.

Late that night during an interview at Leon and Eddie's, a master of ceremonies asked me some more silly questions. He wanted to know whether it was easier for a woman to write a book about men than it was for a man to write one about women. (What man, what woman?) I didn't have the vaguest idea. That brief appearance was around 11 P.M. on my way to a scheduled appearance on the Long John Nebel all-night show.

Nebel, then considered the dean of all-night radio talk show hosts, had early in his career concentrated on interviewing hypnotists, UFO freaks, in the words of *Time* magazine, "sundry other pitchmen of the occult." *Time* noted that Long John (he was six foot-five inches) was an eighth-grade dropout with a "quicksilver tongue" who had been a carnival huckster, mind reader, and auctioneer before joining Manhattan's WOR in 1956.

I was in the torture chamber for almost four hours, but it seemed more like four days. Almost immediately I sensed that the basic idea was to embarrass "experts" by making them seem stupid. The foppish Paris Flammond was armed with all kinds of reference books, including encyclopedias and the *World Almanac*, to refute statements made by victims of his inquisition. At one point I threatened to bolt from the studio, but Long John deftly maneuvered a truce.

In the second half of the "entertainment," all three panelists became friendlier, and Long John even read a few telegrams from listeners encouraging me to "give it to them." This, apparently, was also part of the formula. Listeners included drunk and sober post-midnight diner patrons, truck drivers, and other non-scholars who drool with pleasure when pomposity of any kind is skewered. I should have realized this when Paris Flammond told me one of their recent guests was the famed anthropologist Ashley Montagu, who had just written his book *Natural Superiority of Women*. To Paris, Ashley Montagu was "an unmitigated ass." I have often wondered how Flammond described me to later victims—I mean guests.

After the verbal massacre I had no difficulty, even in my dazed condition, in finding a bar that was open. I needed a tranquilizer. And as I sipped a bourbon and soda I thought of sending Long John a note suggesting a better name for his show: "Target Practice." Or, better still, "Bringing Up Fodder."

In my writing career I have felt at times like Stephen Leacock's horse that went galloping off in all directions. The Curley autobiography changed this. It led eventually into the field of contemporary political biography, and since I had dug deeply into Massachusetts terrain, it brought other regional assignments. Because of my successful collaboration with Curley, Monroe Stearns, by this time trade editor of the Bobbs Merrill Company, Inc., commissioned me to write the biography of John F. Fitzgerald, Curley's old adversary.

Mike Ryan wrote in the *Irish Echo*:

> President John Fitzgerald Kennedy told a reporter: "I think Grampa was worthy of remembrance partly because of his life, which followed a classic American pattern. . . . But I'll always remember him best for his personal qualities . . . for his matchless vitality and spirit which enabled him to move forward steadily through the peaks and valleys of a long, strenuous life."
>
> This is the complete story of that life, the life of a master politician who is credited with founding an American political dynasty comparable to that of the Adamses, the Lodges, and the LaFollettes.
>
> It is the story, again to quote President Kennedy, of "a poor boy of parents who emigrated to this country from Ireland, became twice Mayor of Boston and received many honors and distinctions from his fellow citizens."
>
> Honey Fitz's story necessarily embraces the stories of his charming daughter, Rose, the mother of the President, who has been called "the spark plug that makes the Kennedy political wheel spin so successfully"; of his financial genius son-in-law, Joseph P. Kennedy, former U.S. Ambassador to Great Britain and friend and adviser of presidents; of the President's other grandfather, Pat Kennedy, himself an able politician; and of the early years of the President himself. This fascinating picture of the career of one man and of a brilliant family illumines the entire American political scene of the past eighty years as well as the present.

The day I signed the contract Monroe and I had lunch at the Harvard Club of New York. "Just think," he said, "you have already completed a third of your research." True. There was so much of James Michael in the manuscript, Monroe later asked me to delete some of it. "At times I thought I was reading a biography of Curley."

I was happy to get this assignment, and took it unkindly when a friend asked me if I planned to become "a Boswell of the Gutter." The late Carl Santheson, who ran a fish market in Duxbury, wanted to know why I couldn't find more dignified persons to write about. Think of it! Curley, Chessman—and now John F. Fitzgerald. Santheson reminded me of the aristocratic old lady who wondered about all the veneration given to the painting "Whistler's Mother."

"After all," she said, "she was only a MacNeill of North Carolina."

Despite the head start I had, thanks to the Curley research, there was a lot more digging to do. The real story of Fitzgerald unfolded after scores of interviews. One of my former Dartmouth students was the son of John I. Fitzgerald (no relation to Honey Fitz) who, in his day, was one of the political bosses in a district young Jack Kennedy needed to win during his first contest for Congress, in 1946. That brought Kennedy into contact with John I. Fitzgerald Jr., who told me he often met Kennedy, then a student at Harvard, at a drugstore at the foot of Beacon Hill. "We would have a chocolate soda or a cup of coffee before going on a date."

I got some precious information from an author's query in the *New York Times*, and I persuaded J. J. Smith to put another query in his *Herald Traveler* gossipy column, "Hub-bub." That brought results. I read the few magazine pieces on Fitzgerald, but on this assignment my basic skeletal source of information was the *Boston Post*, then out of print, but at the time of Fitzgerald the leading political paper in New England. (At one time its circulation was larger than that of the *New York Times*.) This forced me to spend months in the periodical room of the Boston Public Library going through almost fifty years of bound copies of the *Boston Post*. Tedious, but rewarding, as I traced the chronological thread of the story. It gave me the framework I needed before the personal interviews with principals in the story.

One morning in the periodical room I met a Harvard Graduate School student who was studying for a Ph.D. in history. When I told him what I was doing, he loaned me a thesis he had written on corruption in Massachusetts. This original document got me off to a good start as I gradually learned that John F. was much more of a rogue than was James Michael.

The first thing Honey Fitz did when he was elected mayor for the first time was to gain personal control of all the city departments except the schools and police. He fired physicians from the board of health and replaced them with saloon keepers. His new superintendent of public buildings was another saloon keeper, and he made a bartender, who had been expelled from the legislature, superintendent of streets. The city found it was paying double for some paving blocks. It had paid for both sides. He added eight deputy sealers to the department of weights and measures and created the job of city dermatologist for a crony, just as future conniver Michael Ward would create the job of inspector of brooms. (The superintendent of public works didn't think an inspector was needed until Mike arranged for his pals to break so many brooms.)

Honey Fitz, who could not do enough for his Dearos, as his followers were called, invented such jobs for them as tea warmers, tree climbers, wipers, rubber-boot repairers, and watchmen to watch other watchmen. Johnny's brother Henry was in charge of most of the graft. The word was, "See Henry."

On April 23, 1987, in the *New York Review of Books*, Francis Russell wrote a review of *The Fitzgeralds and the Kennedys*, by Doris Kearns Goodwin. In it he said:

> In his two terms as mayor he built a city hall annex, schools, a zoo, an aquarium, parks, municipal buildings, a multitude of public lavatories. And from whatever was built, he took his cut. 'Burglars in the House,' John Cutler called his chapter on the mayor's first term in *Honey Fitz*, perhaps the best account of Boston's ward and city politics of that era.

I thoroughly agree with another appraisal of *Honey Fitz* made by Russell in his review:

> That Honey Fitz, if he had not been undercut by the Toodles scandal, had the potential of becoming a national political figure, as Mrs. Goodwin claims, is simply not so. Essentially he was a mountebank, a shrewd, obstreperous local politician. *Sweet Adeline* was not only his theme song but his swan song. (Reprinted with permission from *The New York Review of Books*. Copyright ©1987 Nyrev, Inc.)

My anchor man was the late Frank Buxton. Frank, who was like a father to me, had won the Pulitzer Prize in journalism when he was editor of the old *Boston Herald* during the reign of the Little Napoleon, also known as the dynamic buccaneer, of the Dear Old North End. Frank knew Honey Fitz intimately.

I used to sit for hours with Frank in his apartment in Brookline, and often invited him to lunch at the Harvard Club of Boston. He brought along any friends he thought might help me with the research. At one luncheon he invited Leonard Weildon, Anson Smith, and Alden Hoag, the entire editorial staff of the *Boston Herald*. This was a treat for me, since Alden Hoag was the *Boston Evening Transcript* editor-in-chief who had given me my first newspaper job. Alden was a brilliant editor with a good sense of humor.

One man I wanted to sit down with was Joseph Kane, whose mother was the sister of Joe Kennedy's mother. Kane was a behind-the-scenes strategist, a hard-nosed professional who had helped unseat John F. Fitzgerald in a scandalous Congressional race in 1917.

Joe Kane had an unlisted telephone number at his Brookline apartment, but I tracked him to the Waldorf Restaurant across from Old City Hall. Here, three or four evenings a week, Joe met with old and new political cronies over cups of coffee. For the first two nights I sat near them, listening to their appraisals of Massachusetts politics, while being completely ignored. Except for Kane, the most memorable character was the loud Patrick J. (Patsy) Mulkern, who rocked with laughter one evening while talking about President Kennedy.

"Jack Kennedy, president of the United States of America! Jesus Christ, I remember when I used to get girls for him and Ken O'Donnell, when they lived in the apartment on Bowdoin Street. And him, president of the United States!"

The unofficial political Kennedy headquarters on Bowdoin Street was used by Jack and Bob Kennedy and Kenneth O'Donnell, and later it was the temporary home of Jacqueline's son, John.

Patsy would rant and guffaw until Kane told him to shut up. Then he would walk over to a nearby Liggett's drugstore for his nightly frappe and sandwich. No charge. His girlfriend worked there.

On the third night, Kane asked Attorney Donal Sullivan, a friend of mine, who I was. Finally able to talk to Kane, I invited him to my interviewing headquarters, the Harvard Club. At first the bourbon cocktails before lunch didn't thaw him, but by the third meeting, I saw the beginning of a smile.

"A couple of other Kennedy biographers have talked to me," he said, "but I didn't tell them much. But I like you." To prove it, he gave me a rare sepia print of two men on horseback taken at a hunt club in Asheville, North Carolina, early in the century. Honey Fitz was on one horse, Patrick Kennedy, Joe Kennedy's father, on the other. This photo was taken before Joe Kennedy met Rose, daughter of Honey Fitz. Pat Kennedy, the son of P.

J. Kennedy, who ran a saloon in East Boston, was, like Honey Fitz, a political boss. He ran East Boston while Fitzgerald ran the North End.

The sepia print, which is included in my biography, also appeared in *Life* magazine and *McLean's* of Canada. Bobbie and I had returned from a dinner party around midnight one Saturday when a call came from an editor of *Life* asking permission to use the photograph.

On the same day at the Harvard Club, Joe Kane gave me a corkscrew, which also had an interesting history. I gave it to the Kennedy Library at the request of the curator. It is important because its lettering shows that Patrick Kennedy was not merely a saloon keeper. He was also a liquor importer. (Joe Kennedy made millions from importing liquor immediately after repeal of the Volstead Act.) Earlier Kennedy biographers apparently didn't know Pat was more than the owner of a bar.

Gail Cameron, who had profiled Rose Kennedy for the *Ladies' Home Journal*, was working on a biography of Mrs. Kennedy (published as *Rose*), when she called me from her home in Connecticut for an interview. Bobbie and I invited the Camerons to dinner, and during cocktail hour I showed Gail the corkscrew. She copied the lettering in her notebook. For some reason she went out of her way to tell me I would be wasting my time interviewing Mrs. Vincent (Marie) Green, one of Rose Kennedy's oldest friends and a former classmate at a convent school. I found my interview with Marie Green helpful, however, and even more so a few years later, when I took her to lunch while writing the biography of Cardinal Cushing. (That day, she had just returned from a two-week visit with Rose in Hyannis Port, just three days after the tragedy at Chappaquiddick. Mrs. Green said Mary Jo Kopechne was not mentioned.)

As we rose to go to dinner, I asked Gail Cameron for the corkscrew. Without a redeeming blush, she reached into her pocketbook and pulled it out. I wonder if Joe Kane would have given me the gadget if he had realized its intrinsic value.

Kane, who gave me marvelous background information, spilled enough family secrets to irk Joe Kennedy, who later asked me where I got certain facts. I told him. "Joe Kane thinks he knows everything," Kennedy said.

Kane told me a story I left out of the book against the wishes of Paul Reynolds, my agent. When the Joseph Kennedys lived in Cohasset they were considered parvenus—too nouveau riche for some of the affluent residents, who thought Rose put on airs when her chauffeur, Harry Pattison, drove her around town in her plum-colored Rolls Royce. In any case, when

Joe tried to get into the Cohasset Golf Club, he was turned down. This was especially humiliating, said Harry Pattison, because his man-of-all-errands, Edward Moore (for whom Ted Kennedy is named), was a member of the Cohasset Club. "And Eddie," said Pattison, "lived in the gardener's cottage on the Kennedy grounds." Just to be sure of this sidebar, I checked it with a still-living member of the then admissions committee at Cohasset Golf Club. I gave this information later to Richard Whalen, who was our guest for a week in Duxbury while writing his best seller, *The Founding Father.* He used it in his story.

Harry Pattison, who showed me favorite Kennedy haunts as I drove him around town, took me to the cove where Jack and his brothers and sisters swam. Harry spoke highly of Jack's grandfather, Patrick Kennedy, who used to come down Sundays during the summer, always with an armful of toys for his grandchildren. Pat used to take the Nantasket steamer from Rowe's Wharf, and Harry would meet him at the pier in Hull, where Honey Fitz had a summer home for several years.

By the time I was deep in research, few of Grandpa's contemporaries were living. Among them were Clement Norton and Michael Ward, both former chairmen of the Boston School Committee, at the time a political base for ambitious politicians anxious to learn about corruption from the ground up. Francis Russell was thinking of machine politicians like Clem Norton when he wrote in *The Great Interlude* about the "heavy-jowled, heavy-paunched Neanderthal types. The shoulders of their suits were vast and padded, their ties were handpainted in rainbow tints, and their eyes had that curiously beady look that one finds only in politicians, undertakers, and professional baseball players." If Mike Ward was everyone's idea of a machine politician, Clem Norton was even more so.

Years ago the *Boston Globe* caught the essence of Norton in a lead paragraph: "The stocky, ruddy-faced man stood by the statue of the Goddess of Wisdom on the steps of the Boston Public Library and jabbed a finger toward the other side of Copley Square. 'It was there that I last talked to John Kennedy—are you following me?' said Clem Norton in a controlled whisper. 'I said to him, "Listen, kid . . . ." ' "

I often stood on those same steps with Clem, trying to stand firm as he jabbed his forefinger—not in the direction of Copley Square—but into my chest. Francis Russell claims the record for being Norton-nudged around the rotunda of the older part of the Boston Public Library, but in my time I also have been thrown for a loss of at least a hundred yards.

During my research in the periodical room, there were frequent interruptions as Clem distracted me with conspiratorial whispers. He kept a daily log of George Curley, who was drinking himself to death. "I just left him having his nooners at a bar down the street. Not yet one o'clock and he's half gone," Clem once said.

Clem, who knows more about everything political than I know about anything, kept asking how I was handling this or that. How was I going to treat the Roosevelt-Kennedy falling-out that followed the Ambassador's embarrassing conduct at the Court of St. James? While addressing a large Jewish audience in Boston, Senator Jacob Javits, of New York, emphasized that Jack Kennedy was "the son of his father." The audience knew what he was referring to: Joseph Kennedy was considered an anti-Semite who, as U.S. Ambassador to England, had voiced support for Hitler before the war.

Others have suspected why Ambassador Joe refused to wear knee pants and stockings, following the tradition of the U.S. Ambassadors to the Court of St. James, but Clem Norton knew for a fact. "Joe has fat legs—piano legs, do you follow me?" He wore long pants. Clem, at one point, had Francis Russell, author of *Tragedy in Dedham*, convinced that Sacco and Vanzetti were fall guys for the Morelli gang in Providence, but you could never tell people like Governor Alvah Fuller or President Abbot Lawrence Lowell of Harvard that, Clem told me—do you follow? I didn't follow Clem. I retreated around the Boston Public Library.

As I kept trying to pry information from Clem, it dawned on me that I gave more than I received. One day in 1961, Joe Kennedy called me from Hyannis Port, saying he kept getting anonymous postcards from "someone who doesn't like you. And this person has read your manuscript." I insisted that nobody had read my manuscript except Bobbie, but Joe didn't believe me. He didn't believe me until I suggested that those postcards might be from Clem Norton, who had once been his informal chauffeur in New York City. I told Kennedy how Norton kept asking me questions at the library.

"You know," he said, "it could be Clem Norton. It sounds like him."

I deliberately repeated this conversation one morning in the periodical room during one of Clem's interruptive visits. Clem and I were eyeball to eyeball, and I didn't miss the look of guilt in those beady eyes. "Moreover," I said, "Joe Kennedy knows who is sending those anonymous postcards."

"He does?"

"He does. And so do I." Clem left for one of his imaginary appointments.

Clem Norton, the last of the authentic Hibernian politicians, was mercurial, likable, bizarre, and boring, and he brought new meaning to the

177

word eccentric. Whenever I invited him to have a cup of coffee at a restaurant near the Boston Public Library, I was never sure he would make it all the way. Twice while walking along with me, he suddenly, without a word of explanation, turned, jogged a few steps, and hurried back to the library. Did he think I expected him to pick up the tab? I didn't dare ask him.

Clem had been going to the library for over half a century. For years, recognized as the local political guru by the late Francis X. Moloney, the assistant librarian and a good friend of mine, Clem used a cubbyhole in a private part of the library, where he spent hours riffling through biographies and scores of magazines and newspapers, picking up tidbits which he jotted down on wads of paper. He then collated the facts and sold features to a newspaper.

I had first met Norton at the library while researching the Curley story. Curley didn't act like other Roxbury kids, Clem would say. He didn't play baseball or football or compete in sports. Norton didn't seem to know that Curley used to skate at Hawes Pond in Brookline. One morning when I drove Curley to his doctor's office on Beacon Street, across from the pond, I said I used to go skating as a youngster at Hawes Pond. Curley nodded, "So did I. The quicksand . . ." I was startled. Mention of quicksand was a nostalgic touch for kids who skated there. We remembered the legend of a horse and ice wagon sinking through the quicksand into the bottom which, we were solemnly told, had no bottom.

During our conversation at the library—monologues would be a better word, since Clem seldom interrupted himself except to ask if you were following him—I often suspected that Clem knew a lot more about Curley, Honey Fitz, and the Kennedys than he let on. I became even more convinced of this when I learned he was working on an autobiography. But once in a while, in a particularly expansive mood, he would drop sidelights.

One morning he mentioned a birthday party held a generation ago at the Parker House for Mayor John Fitzgerald. Noticing a little boy waiting in the corridor, Clem asked who he was. Jack Kennedy said he was waiting for his Grandpa, Honey Fitz, whereupon Clem led him into the hall, lifted him onto a table, introduced him, and prompted him to point to the honored guest and say, "This is the best grandpa a child ever had." You got the impression from that historic moment that their relationship was warm and intimate and that it continued after Jack Kennedy went to the White House. Clem said:

I told him that when other people were around, it would be Mr. President this—Mr. President that, but when we're alone I'll still call you 'kid,' the same as when I first met you.

Clem was a friend of Edwin O'Connor, and he is proud of the fact that the novelist used him as a model for Charlie Hennessey in *The Last Hurrah*. Hennessey was the pudgy, garrulous, derby-hatted politician who, in the movie version of the novel, was shown stuffing free cigars into his pockets at an Irish wake. Charlie was a slap-you-on-the-back city councilor, a gadfly who later had a current counterpart in Albert ("Dapper") O'Neil on the Boston City Council.

If Clem Norton ever wrote a book, it might be more of a fictional autobiography, for as both Francis Russell and I learned through the years of library association with him, his Gaelic imagination persistently clouded the truth. It was one thing for a novelist like O'Connor to model a character after Clem Norton, another thing for a nonfiction writer attempting to re-create the Irish-Yankee confrontation during the early decades of the twentieth century.

For example, during the Curley research, I was sitting with Sam Nesson one morning in the Curley library. Nesson motioned toward a library shelf. "See those Shakespeare books? Curley knows every line in every book." Clem Norton had a different version. Although he exaggerated when he told a reporter that Curley had the finest Shakespearean library in Boston, he came much nearer the truth when he added, "and you know, not one of those books has ever been opened." The truth was that Curley, in his mayoral days, had a mysterious bachelor secretary named Standish Wilcox who provided him with all the quotes he needed from Shakespeare and the Bible. Norton was the one who told me that Curley used to speak of "John Shakespeare" until Clem advised him to change the John to William.

Nevertheless, Edwin O'Connor came to like his Charlie Hennessey. Occasionally, even after the publication of *The Last Hurrah*, the novelist would invite Clem to a bachelor dinner to soak up more of his mannerisms. One night Clem commented on O'Connor's delicate souffles. "That was a good puddin', Ed." When this bit of gourmet criticism was picked up by a Boston newspaper, I teased Clem about it. It was the only time I ever saw the man embarrassed. "It really *was* pudding," he said.

One night, after a session at the Boston Public Library, I took Clem to the nearby Red Coach Grill for dinner. After his two Manhattans (he seldom drank) Clem told me the "no, no, no" story, which Edwin O'Connor used so effectively against me. Young Johnny Fitz, who found himself an orphan

179

while in his first year at Harvard Medical School, later tearfully told political rallies how he had to fend for his family. "I had to take care of all six of my brothers." He didn't mention that two of his brothers were several years older than he. "I washed the dishes, scrubbed floors, sifted ashes, and brought scuttles of coal up three flights of creaky stairs. I even washed the faces of the younger boys every day and often dressed them." Clem Norton added to that piteous story. "When relatives offered to help, Johnny would say, 'no, no, no. It is my trust to take care of the family.' "

"Yet no one could say that Johnny Fitz was Alger all the way," Francis Russell wrote. More of that when we come to O'Connor's lead review of *Honey Fitz* in the *New York Times*.

If another reviewer was correct when he called *Honey Fitz* "the best book ever written on municipal politics in action," much of the credit should go to Mike Ward, not Clem Norton. Just after I submitted the Curley manuscript to Prentice-Hall, I received a call from Ward, the Hibernian Machiavelli of the Curley era. "You and I should get together and write a book called *What Curley Forgot*," he said. It was no wild overstatement. Clem, for once, was right when he told me, "You could write two books about Curley, and both of them would be interesting."

I remembered Mike Ward's casual comment in 1960 when Bobbs Merrill commissioned me to write *Honey Fitz*. After this book was published, Mike took me to a fundraiser at the Statler. Among the speakers were elder statesman James Michael Curley and Senator John F. Kennedy, who spoke briefly, as becomes a rising statesman. "Tonight let's hear from the old pro, Governor Curley," he said. After the banquet Kennedy and Ward found themselves in an elevator on the way up to a private gathering.

"How did I do in the Cutler book?" Kennedy asked.

"Not so good," Mike said. "But I did okay."

I had good reason to be grateful to Mike for all the priceless background information he gave me. Mike, in his retirement, owned a modest duplex that became a kind of political mecca in an obscure neighborhood in Brighton, and many a conspiracy was hatched in his kitchen and humble living room, which was just off and within audible distance of the bathroom. I spent hundreds of hours listening to his incredible tales of roguery. It was a weird experience. For one thing, every time Mike left the room, his wife, a former chorus girl, would slip into her faded dance costume and go into a high-kicking act. She would disappear when Mike returned, and never once did he allude to her bizarre behavior. During those educational mornings there was a steady stream of droppers-in, who came upstairs without bothering to ring the front door bell. Henry Cabot Lodge and Leverett Saltonstall used to sit around the kitchen table or in the living room with Mike, and Jim Farley usually consulted him when he came to Boston.

I met the deputy superintendent of Boston schools, an old-time humorist named Benny Drohan, and dozens of politicians and bureaucrats. One morning Mike proudly introduced me to two ex-convicts. One, who boasted of having had only one "stop" (i.e., jail term), gleefully recounted how he had used tear gas to hold up the Harvard Coop in Cambridge. Trying to match his felonious friend, the other convict, a burly former hijacker, boasted that while in Federal Correctional Institute of Danbury, he had occupied a cell earlier occupied by Mayor Curley. He considered that a great honor.

Before Mike moved from Roxbury to his duplex, his predecessor in the State Senate was the Republican Martin Hayes, who had a big following in Brighton and environs. Mike reversed that quickly, with the help of thousands of mattress voters. He told me without embarrassment about cemetery names that he added to his list, and when Lt. Governor Leverett Saltonstall launched an investigation, Mike had a crony steal Saltonstall's stationery, then used it to give instructions to the investigators. "The investigated were telling the investigators what to do," Mike said.

One morning Mike invited Mamie O'Toole to his flat to meet me. "Mamie, tell John how we used to invalidate the ballots."

"I was a teller, and I used to put lead from a pencil under my fingernail," Mamie said, with her pretty Irish smile. "I added a cross for Mike when someone voted for his opponent. This meant the ballot didn't count."

"There are few shrewder politicians in Boston—or anywhere else— than Michael J. Ward," the *Boston Post* had noted. I can add that there are few bolder politicians. Mike once took me into the chambers of a judge in the Roxbury District Court. "You know, Harold," he said to the judge, "you remind me of a San Francisco pimp." Another time he introduced me to the foreman of a Boston school-department supply room. "You have a son, don't you, John, who plays baseball?" He turned to his friend. "Give him a catcher's mitt." What could I do? Say I couldn't take it because I wasn't a thief?

Mike also told me how he had stolen City Hall furniture for his political organization, the Jefferson Club. One Saturday, when City Hall was closed, Mike sent cronies wearing overalls to carry out office furniture, explaining to the custodian that new furniture was to be moved in Monday. "The poor sap wound up helping my boys put the stuff into the freight elevator." Mike also had a story about a character named John ("Wimpy") Hare.

> Wimpy was running against my candidate, but he didn't know it. When he came to me for advice, I told him his weak spot was Ward Four. I advised him to station himself on election day at the Ira Allen School and to pass out cards. "Be sure to smile at everyone." Later Wimpy discovered that the Ira Allen School was not in his district.

Another Ward trick was to send baskets of fruit from S. S. Pierce & Company to poor people and ask that the bill be sent to him, giving the name of some wealthy Republican opponent who, if he refused to honor the bill, lost a vote.

Mike was at his best when impersonating Curley. While serving as secretary to Mayor Curley, he would use his well-modulated Curley accent to get jobs for his friends. "I'd call the superintendent of the Street Department and tell him that I, the Mayor, wanted to put some men to work, then I'd send over my buddies for the jobs." Later, while Curley was governor, Mike would pick up the telephone, call a top official and say, "This is the governor, I am sending a gentleman over for some employment. I'm sure you'll find a good position for him." Once he phoned a department head and asked every consideration for his "first cousin." Mike didn't know his "first cousin" was black.

Mike, who said he operated on the theory that whoever controls the streets of Cairo controls Egypt, told me his greatest pleasure, from his earliest days in politics, was to tease Proper Bostonians. While chairman of the Boston School Committee, he told the press his committee was considering bringing Eamon DeValera to Boston as superintendent of schools. "American citizenship is not necessary, and I can't for the life of me think of a better man for the job." Mike also said Harvard should have made Jim Farley its president after Abbot Lawrence Lowell resigned.

Yes, it was Mike who made my book an authentic mirror of municipal—and often crooked—politics in action.

One question I wanted answered was why Joe Kennedy, with all his millions, never donated a cent to his alma mater, Harvard. Attorney Oscar Hausserman, who, like Robert Benchley, had been in the A. D. Club with Kennedy at Harvard, where they were classmates, gave me the answer.

Joe was miffed because he was never made an overseer, nor did he ever receive an honorary degree from Harvard. The third reason was trivial, said Hausserman: "I was sitting beside Joe at the Harvard–Yale game when his son Joe was a senior. When young Joe didn't get into the game, his father ran over to the bench after the game and blasted Coach Dick Harlow." After being appointed by President Franklin Delano Roosevelt as the first secretary of the Securities and Exchange Commission and later made Ambassador to the Court of St. James, Kennedy felt he deserved an honorary degree from Harvard.

Hausserman showed me the program of a play performed at the twenty-fifth reunion of his class. In one skit, Joe Kennedy, wearing a top hat and spats, comes into an office, hangs up his coat, and phones FDR in Washington. "Okay, Frank," he says, "I'm here. You can start the country."

After I completed a semifinal draft of the book I sent the manuscript to Joe Kennedy. A few weeks later the telephone rang. "Is John Cutler there? This is Joe Kennedy." I was about to say, "Really? This is Nelson Rockefeller." But it was indeed the former ambassador. We had a long talk, and I wish I had taped it.

"Rose liked the first half of your manuscript," he said, "and I liked the second." He went on to say that none of the biographers "got my father right, but you came closer than any of them." Then, when I asked him why he didn't write his own memoirs, he said, "That's what Jack is always telling me." Jack was president of the United States at the time.

"But you made a few mistakes," he went on. "For instance, that business about my calling up President Roosevelt and wearing spats and so on. That never happened."

"Oscar Hausserman showed the program of the play performed at your twenty-fifth reunion," I said. "I read all that myself."

Suddenly Joe remembered. But he had a few other questions. "Where do you writers get the idea that I make so much money?"

"I got the impression when I read Richard Whelan's article in *Fortune* magazine," I said. "Whelan said you were worth from four hundred to six hundred million dollars." I couldn't see him, but I suspected he was smiling.

"I am leaving for New York tomorrow," he said. "I'd be glad to talk to you as long as you like. You can call my secretary, Diane Winters, here in Hyannis Port to make arrangements. She'll give you my private phone number and address."

I was elated. Now I could check out some of the stories I had heard.

One story had Tom Mix and his horse clop-clopping into Joe's bank when he was president—the youngest bank president in the United States. He also invited Gertrude Ederle to the bank for publicity purposes just after she had swum the English Channel. I wondered if I dared ask him about his affair with Gloria Swanson, but I never was able to sit down with Joe Kennedy. Before I could get to New York, he had his stroke.

That was the first of a few major disappointments. Daniel Green, the publicity director of Bobbs Merrill, had arranged a television interview for me with Robert Kennedy, then Attorney General of the United States, at the National Booksellers Convention in a hotel in Washington, D.C. I was to hand Bob Kennedy a copy of his grandfather's biography. I was heading for the front door of my house on Washington Street when the telephone rang. It was Dan Green, public relations director for Bobbs Merrill.

"The whole thing has been called off," he said. "Someone gave Bob Kennedy a copy of Ed O'Connor's review in the *New York Times*."

I was crushed. A devastating review, which Dan Green called "a dreadful pan," and now this. A book that might have been a best seller was off to a bad start. I wasn't consoled a couple of months later when I read in a Boston newspaper that Rose Kennedy was seen deplaning in Hyannis Port with a copy of my book under her arm.

In the *Chicago Tribune*, Fanny Butcher compared the book with an exciting novel.

Here are excerpts from her review:

> Anyone who read Edwin O'Connor's *The Last Hurrah*, anyone who is interested in politics, anyone who doesn't know a thing about how elections are won and lost but is fascinated by the way humans tick, will find *Honey Fitz* completely absorbing. . . .
>
> John Cutler, a newspaper man, has written not only a biography of a man but a history of a period in American politics which was as bizarre as the most imaginative writer of fiction could dream up.

The week before in her *Chicago Tribune* column, "The Literary Spotlight," Fanny Butcher had written:

> The Pulitzer Prize for fiction went this year to Edwin O'Connor, author of *The Edge of Sadness*. Many thought that the prize was given not only for that book but in memory of O'Connor's previous novel, *The Last Hurrah*, which just missed getting the prize. It survived that defeat to become a national best seller. . . . There has just been published . . . a biography of Honey Fitz, another mayor of Boston, John F. Fitzgerald, President Kennedy's grandfather and namesake.
>
> It was written by John Henry Cutler, who turns a literary X-ray machine

184

on Curley which reveals much that *The Last Hurrah* did not, as well as on the hero, Honey Fitz. Curley looked on Fitzgerald (his senior by eleven years) as his mentor and his ideal until there arose between them an epic political feud, a vocal donnybrook with no holds barred. . . . Cutler's book is a history of Boston politics during the days when Fitzgerald and Curley were drum majors of as brassy a political band as any city could boast. . . . It is as factual as a weather report, but as irresistibly funny—and sad—as Emmett Kelly, the master clown.

O'Connor's review proved to be the kiss of death. It kept my book off a lot of bookstore shelves.

O'Connor's first paragraph quoted those Horatio Algeresque words of young Johnny Fitz, who, after the death of his parents, had rejected the notion of having relatives take care of his brothers.

"No, no, no," he said. "I will take care of them."

Then Mr. O'Connor quoted a similar passage from a book by Horatio Alger. Why the editors let him get away with it I have no idea, but O'Connor ascribed the exact words of Fitzgerald to me. O'Connor's cup probably didn't run over when he read the review in the *Saturday Review* written by Ben Bradley, when he was Washington bureau chief of *Newsweek* magazine: "Here is *The Last Hurrah* in fact, not fiction." (Bradley is the retired editor of the *Washington Post*.) I didn't believe Clem Norton when he told me O'Connor regretted his pan of *Honey Fitz* so much he cried, but I think he should have cried, since it was more of a vicious attack than an objective review.

George Frazier told me Ed O'Connor had mentioned that I was "too soft" on Fitzgerald, and that Ted Kennedy had said I was "too hard." Ted's office called me twice asking for a copy of *Honey Fitz,* and the publisher also asked if I could find a copy for him. I told a Kennedy staffer that I would send Ted a book if he gave me a usable anecdote for a biography I was writing on Senator Edward Brooke. He didn't and I didn't.

But, at the request of Doris Kearns Goodwin, who had interviewed me a few times for her wonderful book, *The Fitzgeralds and The Kennedys*, I sent a copy of *Honey Fitz* to Eunice Kennedy Shriver, who was staying with her mother at their Palm Beach home. Mrs. Shriver sent me a gracious thank you note:

Dear Mr. Cutler:
Thank you so much for the copy of your book, *Honey Fitz.*

My mother is staying with me this week, and she doesn't read because of her eyes. I have read her several chapters, and she will comment, "Oh, I remember that!" She was so devoted to her father, and speaks of him all the time.

Thank you very much for the special efforts you took to get this book to me. I shall cherish it, and I hope to meet you soon.

In August 1972, when I was invited to speak at the Star Island Writers Conference, in New Hampshire, I was astounded to note that the program listed me as "a winner of the O. Henry Short Story Prize." I had never come close to writing a saleable short story. During the two-day conference, I was asked why I didn't write a biography of Edwin O'Connor: "I can't see him as a subject," I said. "I would much prefer to review his autobiography."

George Frazier wrote in his *Boston Globe* column: "Ed O'Connor to the O'Contrary, John Cutler's book is absolutely absorbing."

In a letter to George Frazier dated November 8, 1962, Joe McCarthy, a Hearst syndicated writer, wrote:

> P.S. I forgot to mention the other day that I think John Cutler's *Honey Fitz* is indeed a high class and valuable job of interesting research and I can't understand whatever possessed Ed O'Connor to write such a vehement attack on it in the *Times Book Review*.

There was a sequel to the O'Connor review. One afternoon I had a telephone call from a Dr. Henry FitzGerald, who lived in nearby Quincy. He asked if he could bring his weekend guest, who was the night managing editor of the *New York Times*, down that evening. He also wanted me to autograph two copies of *Honey Fitz*. He said his guest was so displeased with O'Connor's review of my book that he had arranged for Charles Poore to do a second review. And that is precisely what happened.

A few excerpts from Poore's review:

> They tell in the folklore of Boston about the day Honey Fitz—former Mayor John F. Fitzgerald—was standing in the Custom House Tower when a guide arrived with Hollanders desiring a panoramic view of the Dublin of America.
>
> Honey Fitz for once in his public career did not immediately start singing "Sweet Adeline." However, he greeted them cordially.
>
> "Ladies and gentlemen," he said, "many years ago, when I was Burgomeister of Boston, the German people were among our best citizens."

At which point the guide whispered to Honey Fitz urgently: "Sir, they are Dutch."

"But, the Dutch," he continued suavely, "were my favorites." (Copyright ©1962 by The New York Times Company. Reprinted by permission.)

The Charles Poore review also mentioned that John Fitzgerald Kennedy "entered the White House and continued his naval career sporadically on a small yacht that goes with the office. He called it the *Honey Fitz*."

One edition of the *New York Times* had a three-column panel showing President Kennedy sitting on his famous rocking chair on the stern deck of a vessel that looked more like a tub than a Presidential yacht. Painted on the stern were the words "Honey Fitz."

The symbolism was obvious. (He was reading *Honey Fitz* in the panel.)

About a year after the publication of the book, Richard Whalen called me from New York to say The New American Library had commissioned him to write the biography of Joe Kennedy. (I should have thought of this first.) He asked me to have lunch with him in Boston. He had read *Honey Fitz*, he said, and thought I could help him. I invited him to spend the night with us in Duxbury, and we liked him so much we asked him to stay for the next six days. I advised him to concentrate on the latter part of Joe Kennedy's life, since I had completed most of the excavating of terrain in his early life. He did precisely that, crediting my book more than fifty times in his early chapters.

I introduced him to Frank Buxton and others who gave him useful information. Dick, who had written for both *Time* and *Fortune*, was a highly skilled writer, and I was surprised that he hadn't written more books since his definitive biography, a best seller that made the Book of the Month Club when it was published in 1964. Since then his only book has been *Catch the Falling Flag*. Whalen was one of President Nixon's speech writers until he became disillusioned and quit.

Bobbie answered the telephone one stormy night when Dick called from the Statler in Boston. He said he and his wife, Joan, had rented a car and would like to drive to Duxbury to see us. Bobbie said we would be delighted to have them, but she warned of the hazards of driving in a blizzard. But they came, with a bottle of pink champagne, and we spent a wonderful evening with them. Dick gave us a copy of his book, inscribed: "January 23, 1965. On this night the author returned to the scene of the crime, to rejoice with John and Bobbie, who offer warm hospitality to wayward writers. Affectionately, Richard J. Whalen."

It was a final pleasant touch to a pleasant assignment.

Another pleasant touch were Rose Kennedy's words in her book *Times to Remember* when she called me a leading historian of the Boston political scene. She recounted an anecdote in almost the same words that appeared in my biography of her father. Here is the original story as I wrote it in *Honey Fitz*:

> On primary day he and Jack went to the polls with his Fitzgerald grandparents, then went to see a movie, *A Night in Casablanca*. When the votes were counted, Honey Fitz hopped onto a table and danced a jig as he led the singing of "Sweet Adeline." . . . After the victory celebration, Billy Sullivan, a former assistant attorney general, patted Honey Fitz on the back.
>
> "Congratulations, John F," he said. "Some day . . . who knows? . . . Young Jack here may be governor of the Commonwealth."
>
> "Governor?" Honey Fitz smiled. "Some day that young man will be president of the United States."

Attorney Richard Cotter, a Duxbury friend, gave me that story. He witnessed the scene.

Years before I wrote *Honey Fitz*, Mary Clemens, a reporter for the *Boston Globe*, had asked me to collaborate with her on a biography of Rose Kennedy. Mary had interviewed Rose several times, while I was never able to have a single session with her. Something interfered with that project, and perhaps it was just as well. Gail Cameron took care of it.

Joe Kennedy had told me that his wife liked the first part of my manuscript. I never learned whether she also liked the second part.

The martini luncheon is part of the ritual for signing a contract for a book or mulling over ideas for a new book. I was always excited when Paul Reynolds, while he was my agent, took me to lunch to talk things over at the Century Club, just a block down from the Harvard Club of New York.

One pleasant recollection of Reynolds and the Century Club goes back to 1963, when I hoped to work with Rocky Marciano on his life story—an autobiography or biography, which Reynolds and I figured was bound to be turned into a film and a good, if not best seller. A few months after the publication of *Cardinal Cushing of Boston*, the late George Swartz, well known in Massachusetts as president of the "Hundred Club," asked if I was interested in such a book. Swartz was Rocky Marciano's business manager. As an old boxing fan, I was, of course, delighted, and a few days later we talked things over at the Harvard Club of Boston. After lunch, I sat in George's insurance office on Newbury Street while he called Marciano at the Carlyle Hotel in New York. Swartz outlined the plan but was unable to go into details, because Marciano told him he was about to leave for the airport for a flight to Beverly Hills, California. I could hear Rocky say, "Who is John Henry Cushing?"

Meanwhile, I asked Gene Tunney to help with the project. Tunney sent me a letter saying he had called his friend Rocky at Jack Dempsey's Restaurant where, said Gene, Rocky often dropped in. Gene enclosed a copy of another letter he had sent to Rocky advising him to tell his story, "while you are still affectionately remembered."

The project was on hold the day Paul Reynolds took me to lunch. (Paul sometimes said, "I will feed you a lunch.") I asked Reynolds what kind of advance we could expect on the Marciano story, adding that I was willing to give Marciano any share he wanted. That's because I knew how generous Rocky was! And I was sure that if the book were filmed, Rocky would give me a cut.

"At least ten thousand dollars, maybe fifteen," Reynolds said. He paused. "It could even be twenty." But, as matters turned out, even this inducement—perhaps a trifle to a celebrity like Marciano—was not immediately sufficiently persuasive to the former heavyweight champion, and about two months later he died in the Midwest in a small plane crash.

Chapter Twenty-two
IT COULD HAPPEN ONLY THERE

On September 28, 1962, at the University of Mississippi in Oxford, Governor Ross Barnett of Mississippi marshaled the police might of his state against one man, James Meredith. Bobbie and I happened to be in the vicinity while on a two-week tour of the Deep South.

It was a lovely warm day as we left Memphis early in the afternoon, headed for Jackson, Mississippi. As residents of New England we felt the strangeness of driving along a state highway on an autumnal day of soft greens and golds. No crispness in the air, and instead of the russets, crimsons, and yellows touching up the fading green foliage, we drove along a narrow ribbon of highway flanked by unfamiliar trees draped with Spanish moss and long stretches of kudzu vines that hid trees from our view. Every hour on the hour the radio was on, as it had been during the drive across Pennsylvania and down the Ohio Valley into Kentucky and Tennessee. Now, as we sped along an almost deserted highway we heard the one o'clock news. The gently tree-shaded, spreading campus of the University of Mississippi was becoming a battleground. Still fresh in our minds was the morning tour of the once embattled fields of Vicksburg, as a radio commentator mentioned that the Mississippi crisis was the gravest since the Civil War. At this very moment, it appeared, a university campus was awaiting an ugly test of raw force between national and state authority over the attempt of Negro James Meredith to register at Ole Miss.

We stopped for gas and a tight-lipped attendant glanced at our Massachusetts plates. He was overtly polite but tense, and not until he was wiping the windshield did he speak.

"They kill that nigger yet?" he said.

"What do you think is going to happen today in Oxford?" I asked. I knew it only as the home of Ole Miss and a tiny town to which the late William Faulkner had for the most part brought honor.

"There's going to be bloodshed," the attendant said. "Nobody's going to force Mississippi to take that nigger. This man Ross Barnett is tough. He used to be a criminal lawyer, and he'll fight it all the way. He'll go to jail or die before he lets that nigger in Ole Miss."

190

He told us it was about fifty miles to Oxford. A few miles down the road we took a left turn and drove through William Faulkner's lovely little community. As we approached the university campus, the streets were lined with cars. We passed a sound truck wondering whether its equipment was for radio, television, or both. With our Massachusetts plates, we felt conspicuous as we drove past the main gateway to the campus, and some of the hard looks noted did nothing to make us savor the traditional warm hospitality of Mississippi. We parked in front of the administration building, not far from the alumni building that housed the truculent Governor Ross Barnett, who was still huffing and puffing and about to blow himself in. A dozen regular policeman lounged around the front steps of the administration building.

There were no federal marshals on the campus of Ole Miss. The day before, Ross Barnett, flanked by sturdy Mississippi troopers, had turned back two federal men who had accompanied Meredith to the campus, and from that point on, the governor was, in the words of the southern editor Ralph McGill, "making pious statements about law and order when the inevitable harvest of preachments of defiance and nonexistent state sovereignty was (soon to be) so fearsomely reached."

The students of Ole Miss—many of whom earlier had been in the mob cheering the governor's defiance of federal power—were relaxed and smiling. We saw them sauntering from class to student union, chatting and skylarking. Some of the coeds gave a hint as to why two consecutive Miss Americas came from the campus of Ole Miss.

"Welcome to Ole Miss—everybody speaks" said a sign meant for freshman at one of the doors of the building James Meredith hoped to penetrate with the support of federal officers if he was to register.

On the greensward of the rolling campus was the ugly brown mark of a cross fashioned of fiber and laid on the grass at night and burned.

On a dormitory windowsill—draped and not flaunted—was a Confederate flag. Not far from this campus the clay mound over the grave of William Faulkner, who did not always praise the South, was, a reporter said, "still raw and red but already eroding. There is no marker on it yet, but there are flowers." He added that it was on a hillside, as Faulkner had wished, and under an oak, also as he had wished. And a tree had sprinkled green acorns among the flowers.

And now we come to the grimmer side of our story. From the main gates to the steps of the administration building we saw some three hundred officers. Some were police chiefs from nearby towns. Some of the men

191

didn't look like police officers. They wore black trousers and black shoes, and all had armbands fashioned from shredded white sheets. It was just suggestive enough of the Ku Klux Klan to add a macabre touch to the proceedings. We asked one elderly gentlemen with a wisp of a white mustache who he and his associates were.

"I am a sheriff," he said. "So are all the others. Every county in Mississippi is represented here today." None of the sheriffs was armed, and most of them looked as if political pull, rather than brawn, accounted for their status.

But not so the hundreds of state and county police marshaled by Governor Barnett at Oxford, as well as at the state capital in Jackson. The helmeted state troopers had clubs and side arms, and nobody doubted that they would use the clubs, at least. Later, Barnett would speak about the "oppressive might" of the United States forces. What of the oppressive might marshaled by him against a quiet, intelligent man of twenty-nine who had spent nine years in the U.S. Air Force?

The afternoon wore on, and the hard glint of the sun was on the live oaks, cherry laurels, pecan trees, and magnolias. The cameraman was right. Despite radio reports, Meredith would probably not put in an appearance on this Friday afternoon.

The next morning in Jackson we read an inflammatory editorial in the *Clarion-Ledger*. To the editorialists of this sheet, KKK stood for "Know Knothing Kennedys."

Meredith enrolled on September 30. Some students were seen leaving the campus with packed suitcases. At one point more than half the students in the dormitories had checked out. That terrible yet glorious first day when Meredith was a student at Ole Miss, he was the only member of his Spanish class.

Then came Barnett's capitulation. At the capital in Jackson, this demagogue, who had once vowed to go to jail rather than see Ole Miss integrated, blamed the disorder on the marshals. He said they were "inexperienced, nervous, and trigger happy." And this demagogue, who would sit in the U.S. Senate as the nefarious Theodore Bilbo had sat before him in the same tradition, had incited to insurrection the fanatic adults and teenage hoodlums who set such a bad example for General Walker. Many well-meaning Mississippians were swayed by the most extreme White Citizen Council groups, who were Ku Klux Klanners at heart.

It was in 1848 that President Edward Everett of Harvard made a classic remark that every student at Ole Miss should remember. It was in answer to certain students who objected to the college's admitting a Negro.

"If this boy passes the examination," said Everett, "he will be admitted; and if the white students choose to withdraw, all the income of the college will be devoted to his education."

Shortly after our experience in Mississippi we received a letter from a highly esteemed friend, Frank Buxton, former editor in chief of the *Boston Herald*. He said in part:

"The outrageous conduct of the governor of Mississippi and General Walker and local courts in the South reflects on them, not on the nation as a whole. I feel ashamed of some of my fellow countrymen, but not of my country."

Chapter Twenty-three
CLIPPER CORRESPONDENTS

The *Clipper* is mailed to one or more subscribers in forty-nine states—all except the culturally deprived state of Wyoming—and it also goes to many parts of the world, including Indonesia and Africa. One former Duxbury resident pays $200 a year to have his *Clipper* airmailed to him in Hong Kong.

Duxbury residents keep three local travel agencies busy booking trips to faraway places. The *Clipper* needs no paid "foreign correspondents" when Duxbury residents provide first-hand accounts of world events. Over the years many of these intimate glimpses have found their way to the pages of the *Clipper*, giving exciting details which are not always found in magazines like *Time* and *Newsweek*.

One letter of particular interest was written two days after the disastrous earthquake in Alaska on March 27, 1964. Here are graphic excerpts from a long letter which came from a *Clipper* subscriber in Anchorage, Alaska:

> The earth under our feet seemed to be rolling in both directions at once. The walls rippled and swayed, as did the picture windows. It seemed as if the whole earth had gone into convulsions. By this time everything in the whole house was flying in all directions. Books flew off the shelves and everything fell from the mantel over the fireplace. Lamps toppled over and all the plants were a jumbled mess on the rug. Then Jack yelled to clear out.
>
> I started down the street toward the corner, six houses away. There are two blocks of homes on Inlet Bluff. I looked down toward the bluff, and even when I saw water and no houses, didn't realize that all the homes below us had dropped into the Inlet. Two entire blocks of homes below us had been completely wiped out—more than a hundred beautiful homes stretching about a mile along the bluff. We also learned that the whole downtown of Anchorage was demolished. . . .
>
> The quake moved some glaciers as much as half a mile. It dropped rivers and lakes into the ground. Our whole area out here in Turnagain has been

moved eight feet closer to the Inlet. Kodiak Island dropped eight feet, and Valdez was raised fourteen feet.

Over the years one of the most popular features of the *Clipper* has been "Sounding Off," a letters-to-the-editor column that allows any resident to write his own editorial of praise or blame.

"Sounding Off reminds me of a nudist colony," one reader wrote, "in that it is a place to air your differences."

One letter led to an interesting bit of research.

"Since Ashdod is a part of Duxbury, I would like to know more about this part of town as it was years ago, for I am descended from people who lived there."

In an ensuing issue I wrote, "While there are many stories to tell of Ashdod, the most absorbing concerns the Triune Immersionists who expected the world to end in Ashdod in 1909."

END OF THE WORLD WAS POSTPONED was bannered on the front page of the September 24, 1909, edition of the *Boston Post*. The lead story told of the Triune Immersionists then in the Duxbury community awaiting the prophesied end of creation. The believers, many of whom had given away their worldly possessions to skeptics, according to former Police Chief James O'Neil, who was at one time Duxbury's entire police force, "are still maintaining their frenzied exaltation," reported the *Post*, "protesting that the end is near, but that it has been postponed for only a few days."

By this time, many members of the sect, having given up hope for an immediate end of the world, had gone home, "but Ashdod, where their little temple is, is still crowded with hysterical radicals who are expecting every moment to be their last, and seeing the preliminary signs of the breakup of creation in every incident at all out of the normal."

Exhausted after an all-night meeting, the Triune Immersionists were led to believe that the moment of truth would come at three o'clock on the following afternoon. Here is the *Boston Post* version:

> Five minutes before the hour neared, they dropped on their knees and remained until one minute before three, when they arose in a body and raised their arms awaiting the coming. They retained this attitude, all apparently ready to depart without a murmur, until one, two, three minutes past the hour had ticked off and some gazed at each other with expressions of surprise that they still remained on earth, and were unable to realize that they were again mistaken in their expectations. Undaunted, however, by this, they immedi-

ately began further preparation, many exclaiming that God was giving them more time, as some of the band were not as yet ready to depart.

After we published this story in 1961 there were a few amusing sequels.

One Duxbury old timer, who wished to remain unidentified, remembers turn-of-the-century prophecies in Duxbury of the end of the world.

In 1900 or 1901, three Jehovah's Witnesses were excused from Duxbury schools to await the world's end. At this time, as Miss Adele Burgess recalls, a resident named Stanley Evans ran a cobbler's shop in what is now Bos'n's Locker. Stan was affectionately known as "Skinny Miserly," because he was a clutchpenny. On the day the world was supposed to end, he stood outside his shop and handed out coins to kids who passed by. When the world didn't end, he demanded his money back.

There is another story about a ministerial member of a religious sect who had a small pond behind his house. He instructed his faithful followers to renounce all worldly goods by throwing their valuables, including watches, jewelry, and coins, into his pond. Concealed beneath the surface, the story goes, he had a net into which the worldly possessions were collected and salvaged.

A saltwater town is inevitably a source of tragic stories we wish we didn't have to publish. Duxbury Bay can be a gracious host, but even a sun-splashed afternoon can suddenly be marred by squalls capable of capsizing boats. The bay, because of the high short chop caused by a strong tidal current rushing down the channel, has claimed victims. In April 1961, a young Duxbury honeymoon couple who lived near the waterfront left their supper simmering on the stove while they went out for a sail. The twenty-three-year-old bridegroom was later pulled out of the Cape Cod Canal, and his bride was never found. Their twelve-foot sailboat washed ashore at Scusset Beach, Sagamore.

In late August of that same year, David and Meg, our sixteen-year-old twins, were involved in a near tragedy. They were among ten teenagers who almost drowned in Duxbury Bay when an overloaded motorboat sank shortly after midnight.

After having a picnic on Saquish Beach across the bay, the group headed for the Duxbury Yacht Club just after the turn of the tide. Two of the boys held up the outboard motor to keep it from scraping bottom as water gushed over the stern and finally swamped the boat, which sank around 12:30 A.M. The group decided to swim for shore after discarding their sneakers and most of their clothes. The tide was still low enough for them to walk part of the way just after the boat sank.

After sloshing along the mud flats for about two hundred yards, the water got deep enough to force them to swim. They split into three groups with only seven life preservers among them. After swimming for half an hour, and trying to stay together, they saw a light from a boat that was heading for the Duxbury Yacht Club. In unison they shouted for help, but nobody heard them.

Some shore-dwellers, unaware of a possible impending tragedy, complained of their shouting. The boys and girls were still yelling, and singing to keep up their spirits, when finally they spotted a light from a boat stranded on the flats.

After swimming another hundred yards, they found they could touch bottom. They pushed forward and climbed aboard the stranded boat on the flats. A few minutes later the rest of the exhausted group joined them, and the skipper provided the group with warm gear.

Offshore, three cars were blinking their headlights. The skipper flashed back an improvised "A-Okay" signal, and, after waiting for twenty minutes of incoming tide, they cruised to the Yacht Club. The police, who had tagged their cars, had no idea of the danger they had been in and were shocked when they found out.

It was almost 3 A.M. that Sunday morning when Meg and David came home soaking wet from that Saquish picnic. Although Meg looked completely miserable, with a bad case of poison sumac—a plant they had used for their picnic fire—she didn't have one word of complaint. She merely apologized for getting home so late. Bobbie and I didn't learn until the next morning what had happened.

"It was almost a miracle that none of them was injured or drowned," said Harbormaster Vic Nickerson. "They were lucky to have made it, lucky it was a calm night, with little wind; lucky the water was warm, and lucky that visibility was good."

Meg, by the way, is the most creative of our children. She has a deep love of literature and is a promising poet. As a young woman she was more interested in art and, after graduating from the Winsor School, in Boston, she attended Briarcliff College in New York and The Boston Museum School. Several years later she received a degree in American Literature from George Washington University. She has also done graduate work at the University of Maryland and, for several years, taught English as a second language.

Meg and her husband, Jim Chandler, live in Silver Spring, Maryland, just outside Washington, D.C. Jim, a graduate of Duke University, has a master's degree in International Relations from the University of Kentucky and a law degree from George Washington University. While in law school, he clerked for Clark Clifford. After a brief stint at the U.S. Environmental Protection Agency, he has spent his entire career as legal adviser to the International Joint Commission, an agency of the State Department which oversees border issues between the U.S. and Canada.

In the fall of 1959, two Duxbury boys found the body of Cameron Ives, an investment counselor, washed ashore on Duxbury Beach after he had been reported missing for ten days. He had been shot through the head; his boat was found drifting on a nearby beach.

Ives had disappeared on September 7, exactly a year to the day after Richard Tingey of Quincy, a nuclear power expert at the Fore River Shipyard, had disappeared from his sloop while sailing off Scituate. The battered hulk of his boat was found near the spot where the two boys found the Ives body.

One of Duxbury's most dramatic marine incidents occurred on August 10, 1965, to Billy Sawyer. In the next day's issue of the *Boston Globe*, Harold Kaese wrote in part:

> Billy is skipper and harpooner of the *Cachalot*, the fishing boat given him by his father, Bill Sawyer of Duxbury, Boston and Watertown banker and sportsman.
>
> With the help of a plane spotter, two swordfish had already been ironed. This was the third fish—at 3:30 in the afternoon of a sunny day.
>
> The *Cachalot* sneaked up until its eighteen-foot pulpit was nearly over the fish, then wham—the strong right arm of the harpooner had sent the spear into its target.
>
> Instead of erupting in a takeoff for the bottom, the swordfish lay stunned, wondering what had hit him.
>
> Young Billy hurried back off the pulpit to throw overboard the keg—to which the harpoon is attached by a four hundred-foot line.
>
> As he stepped on deck, his foot landed in a coil of the six-foot auxiliary line which connects an inflated inner tube to the main line.
>
> At that instant, the fish bolted. Over the side shot Sawyer, his left leg snared in a half hitch in the auxiliary line.

When Sawyer hit the water, the fish paused briefly, giving him a chance to reach for his new clasp knife. He couldn't find it. The occasion, he admitted, called for a sheath knife.

Then, before the three boys left on the *Cachalot* could move, the fish blasted off as though the next stop was China.

Young Sawyer went down so fast his red shirt faded from view like the red light on a supersonic jet.

"I remember three thoughts: What'll it be like being dead? Mom and Dad have lost their boy. And, God help me. Then I was loose. The inner tube was beside me. I grabbed it and shot to the surface."

There is another unforgettable story to tell about the *Cachalot*. The senior William Sawyer of Duxbury used his own airplane to spot the swordfish he harpooned. In the summer of 1961, he took his forty-foot sports-fisherman out along the northern edge of the Gulf Stream, just south of Martha's Vineyard. One guest aboard was Amos Smalley, an eighty-three-year old harpooner out of Gay Head, Martha's Vineyard, who hadn't put to sea since 1910. Like the legendary Ishmael of *Moby-Dick* fame, Smalley is the only man in history known to have struck an all-white cachalot.

In 1902, Smalley was harpooner on the bow of a whaling boat containing a crew of eight. Around five o'clock one afternoon, in a quiet sea, the spout of a sperm whale was sighted a mile off the weather bow. Amos Smalley's assignment was to harpoon the whale.

In his book, *Thar She Blows*, Chester S. Howland noted that during the time from the sighting to the lowering of the boats, the whale sounded and was about a mile away, where his enormous shining white body could be seen "far down in the sea."

Smalley and his crew followed the rising whale until it broke the waves a hundred feet away. The whale swam away from the boats, his body submerged, but part of his head lifted above the waves with every spouting. Smalley threw his harpoon with an explosive bomb attached and after it struck, the whale went down.

"Presently," wrote Howland, "the great white whale was seen coming up through a deep column of water and sixty feet of his body was thrown out of the sea; but the anticipation of a wild chase was turned to disappointment, for the terrific explosion of the bomb, so well darted, had ruptured the beast's great heart and lungs and the spotless white skin was made gory by a thick stream of clotted blood which poured out of the nostrils. After another bomb was shot into the dying whale, it rolled fin out, a dead whale lying in a crimson ocean."

199

Soon thereafter, Amos Smalley retired with a unique record. He had harpooned an all-white sperm whale. It has been said that this very monster may have been the murderous beast that destroyed the *Pequod* and her crew with the single exception of the bow oarsman—Ishmael.

Chapter Twenty-four
THE WORST DAY

In 1957 Cid Ricketts Sumner wrote *Traveler in the Wilderness*. I asked her how she got involved in such an unusual venture. She told me she had read this ad in the personals column of the *Saturday Review*. The ad read as follows:

> Explore with top boatmen and renowned wilderness photographer down Green and Colorado Rivers. Expedition leaves Green River, Wyoming June 10 on 60-day journey to Lake Mead through fabulous canyons including Grand Canyon. Re-live voyage Major Powell made in 1869. Requirement: ruggedness! Inquire Charles Eggert, Barrytown, New York.

When Charles Eggert, the leader of the expedition, asked Cid why she wanted to go on this dangerous adventure, she wrote him:

> My life is of little real importance. I would try not to be a nuisance. I have been a medical student. I am old enough not to be disturbed in the company of men (no matter what may be their physiological necessities). My children are of age and independent. No one is in actual need of my presence. I am at that place in life when I can feel altogether reckless, adventurous, ripe for whatever fun can be wrung from existence. Do not imagine that I am trying to commit suicide via your expedition. I love life and people and shall to my last gasp. When I go abroad I carry a note saying, 'Just bury me where I fall and no to-do about it. Notify John Cutler, Duxbury, Mass.' This would apply to your expedition. I would like to write up the voyage from the point of view of one woman to fourteen men. If at the last moment you need my fare and are willing to take a chance on me, let me know, will you? I'll fly out to Green River.

Eggert at this point gave in, so Cid went on the expedition, the only woman in the crew. The movie made of the canyon trip was shown all over the country, including a showing at The First Parish Church in Duxbury.

In 1964, with the publication of *Saddle Your Dreams*, Cid Ricketts

Sumner celebrated the appearance of her twelfth book. She had previously made a pony-trek in Scotland and was a member of horseback over the trackless Hardangervidda in northern Europe, pony-trekked through the Cairngorms, Invernesshire, Scotland. In *Saddle Your Dreams*, she recounts how she followed Robert Louis Stevenson's trip through the Cévennes, in France. The title of her book comes from Mary Webb's *Precious Bane*, chapter six: "Saddle your dreams before you ride 'em."

This was the Cid Ricketts Sumner for whom her family gathered in West Virginia in October 1990, for her centennial. None of us will ever forget the tragedy that involved Cid and her grandson, our son John.

The pain is still there and it will always be there. To lose a child is the worst thing that can happen to a parent.

To tell what happened, I must go back about twenty years. John Ricketts Cutler, our youngest child, was born in 1954. He was a bright, normal boy with many friends. He did well in school, and he excelled in baseball, football, and in athletics in general. His eighth-grade Duxbury football coach said he was disappointed when Ricky went away to Noble & Greenough on a five-day boarding basis. Lee Sargent, a nephew of former Massachusetts Governor Francis Sargent, was his freshman football coach at Nobles. One afternoon after football practice, Lee Sargent, noticing Bobbie and me hiding behind a tree so Ricky couldn't see us, asked, "Are you Ricky's parents?" We said we were, fearing we were about to hear something bad about Ricky. "I just want you to know," said Sargent, "that I am building the football team around Ricky."

Ricky was an honor student whose report cards included parenthetical remarks. One comment: "He is the shoulders of his class."

Ricky had not wanted to go away to school. He would have been happier to stay in Duxbury with his friends. At the very least, Bobbie and I felt later, we should have given him the opportunity to choose a school rather than push him into a prep school we had chosen. But off he went and he did well for two years. In his third year, he developed inexplicable fears—nameless dreads. We consulted a leading pediatric psychiatrist, Dr. George Gardner, a close friend of our family. He told us not to worry. "It's just adolescent turmoil. I've had dozens of cases like this. Ricky will outgrow it."

Nevertheless, on Dr. Gardner's advice we took Ricky to a psychiatrist at Children's Hospital, who advised one session a week for a few months. Rick went from school by cab every Friday. Some of the other students began to tease him: "We know where you're going." Ricky, an unusually sensitive child, was hurt and embarrassed.

One evening a master caught him smoking marijuana. Eliot Putnam, the headmaster, called us and asked us to meet him the next day at the school. We drove so fast a state trooper pulled us over. Noticing how frantic we were the trooper let us go with a warning to "take it easy."

Eliot Putnam said he would have to suspend Ricky for three days, adding that he had also suspended two other students. It was over the Columbus Day weekend, and Putnam said Ricky would return the following Tuesday.

Ricky was terribly upset by the suspension, but he said nothing.

On Thursday evenings, Bobbie's mother, Cid, who lived next door, often came in for a drink. On this Thursday in October 1970 she brought some corn pudding, not realizing Ricky was home, but knowing how Ricky loved corn pudding. No one mentioned why Ricky was home.

That night we had two guests for dinner. They left around ten o'clock, and we went to bed. I got up early and happened to glance out the window. Our Buick convertible was gone. Stolen? I went down to Ricky's bedroom. He also was gone. I woke Bobbie and called Rick's brother David, who lived about a mile away, and asked him to go out to look for Ricky. Then I called the Duxbury Police. About two hours later, the police called back: "Your son is just coming into the parking area," the desk officer said. We were relieved, but still apprehensive. We never suspected the horrible news that was about to unfold.

I immediately drove our station wagon to the police station to get Ricky. Captain Thomas Johnson took me into a side room where Ricky was sitting. I listened numbly while Johnson told me that Ricky had confessed that he had killed his grandmother. He had bludgeoned her to death with a steel hammer.

"Why, Ricky, why? Why did you do such an awful thing to your grandmother who loved you so much? I know you loved her, too. And how did you do it?"

"It doesn't matter now," Ricky said. He acted as if he were in a trance.

After driving around town looking for Ricky, David had driven to our house. As he passed Cid's house, he saw a police cruiser and a hearse.

"Oh, God," he said. "Grandmother is dead." He rushed into the house and told Bobbie. "And Ricky killed her," Bobbie said. She had been looking out the window. Meanwhile, Police Chief Henry McNeil insisted on driving me home, noticing how shaken I was. Both of us were crying. I had never seen the chief so disturbed.

Ricky obviously did not fully understand what he had done. He had never shown the slightest tendency toward violence. I suddenly remembered what he had once said: "I'm just like Robert." He apparently had convinced himself that he had inherited mental instability, and wrongly blamed his grandmother. During all the long years of family therapy with social workers at McLean Hospital, no one had ever brought up this subject.

We learned later that he had had several drinks after Bobbie and I had gone to bed, and probably had smoked pot. I remember how stupid I felt about having left the vodka and a bottle of cherry brandy on the counter. Ricky, having drunk too much alcohol, wound up not knowing what he was doing. In any case, what followed was a chilling nightmare. After Bobbie and I had gone to bed, Ricky left his basement room, drank the liquor, and picked up a hammer which I had noticed earlier in the evening lying in the yard. He went over to Cid's house and knocked on the door, hiding the hammer behind his back.

"My mother wants to borrow a frying pan, Grandmother," he said. Then it happened.

Bobbie and I didn't see Ricky again until we went to court two days later. We had to sit in the courtroom while Captain Johnson recounted the tragedy down to the last grim, gory details. Bobbie could not listen. She put her hands over her ears to shut out all sound and leaned against me. Finally the judge spoke.

"This boy is not a criminal," he said. "He is sick." Ricky, sixteen at the time, was fortunate not to have been tried as an adult.

Chief McNeil took Rick to a youth detention center in Roslindale. During the few weeks he stayed there we visited him every day, always mindful of what a psychiatrist had told us: "Don't mention what happened."

Bobbie and I would meet Ricky and a social worker in the chapel and talk. One social worker, a former priest, said our son was always polite, unlike most of the other troubled inmates, "who were a rough bunch." Some of them delighted in teaching Ricky how to hot-wire a car before stealing it.

One day when I drove to the detention center alone, Rick begged me to get him out of there. "They're trying to kill me."

At that time I had been writing a magazine piece on Dr. Jonathan Miller, director of the Department of Youth Services, which was headquartered in Boston. Miller told me he would make immediate arrangements to transfer Ricky to a Westfield detention center. "I'll drive him there myself if I can't get someone to do it tonight," he said.

At Westfield Ricky was treated well, given responsibility, and was taught rappelling. He was taken to Boston University for an evaluation by psychologists, and it was decided that he should be placed in a psychiatric hospital. But where? We called several hospitals. One official especially depressed us. "If the others know what your son has done, they will have nothing to do with him. We cannot take him."

Finally, McLean Hospital in Belmont admitted our son, and he stayed there for five years, diagnosed as paranoid-psychotic. When he came home on weekends he was accompanied by a social worker and often brought as many as fifteen boys and girls with him for cookouts around our swimming pool. Ricky had many friends, including a series of girlfriends, and more and more he showed signs of improving. He finished Arlington High School on the McLean grounds.

During the next few years we took him on several trips—one to Bermuda, another to Florida, a third to Sicily. A year later we went to the Greek Islands and Ricky enjoyed the trip.

Some weeks he seemed more depressed than others. There was always a question of how he would feel from one day to the next. During his last year at Wild Acres halfway house, where he had been transferred, he had a steady girlfriend—a lovely girl who was devoted to him. She often came with him to Duxbury on weekends.

We had bought Ricky a small car two years earlier, and during his last year at Wild Acres we bought him a new Pontiac. He loved it. He usually came home on weekends only with his girlfriend, Laura. He no longer wanted crowded cookouts.

On Mother's Day it had been our custom for a few years to go to the Harvard Club for dinner, taking the whole family. In 1987, Ricky didn't want to go, so Bobbie arranged to have dinner at home. The champagne flowed, dinner was festive, and we were all happy to be together. This was our last happy occasion with Ricky.

We did not see Ricky often during the next few weeks, although we often talked with him on the phone. He came down for some of the activities of Duxbury's 350th celebration. Then, one evening Ricky, Laura, and I were sitting beside our swimming pool, while Bobbie was painting in her tower studio.

"I heard some harsh words," Bobbie said later, "and the next thing I knew a car was starting up. I looked out the window to see Laura and Ricky pulling away."

We had just bought some new pool furniture, when Ricky, who was angry because the pool looked too dirty to swim in, picked up a chair and slammed it into the concrete facing of the pool. I rebuked him, forgetting how sensitive he was. He wanted to pay for the broken chair, but I wouldn't let him.

After Laura and Ricky drove off, I deeply regretted hurting his feelings. The next morning I called him at Wild Acres and apologized, adding that we hoped he would bring Laura down the next weekend. On Thursday, Ricky called to say he could not come down because he had an important meeting and on Saturday had to play in a softball game. He said he would be down on July Fourth, when we usually had a family cookout.

Later we found out that Rick had told Laura not to call him at home that fatal weekend. He gave no reason, but obviously he had made other plans. On the following Monday, Paul O'Neill, director of Wild Acres, called to say Ricky had not returned from the weekend. He wondered if we knew where he was. Thinking he might have been visiting David, Bobbie and I didn't worry at first, but when we found that he had not been at David's, we were terrified. We asked the Belmont police to put out a general broadcast for a missing-person announcement. One day passed, and no news of Ricky. When there was no news the following day, we panicked.

The following morning David called us: "They found him. He is dead." On Wednesday the search party had found him lying in a tall, grassy field on the grounds of McLean Hospital. He had been missing for three days.

The Belmont police had called the Duxbury police, who in turn had called David, not wanting to give Bobbie and me the terrible news. That was the end of everything for Bobbie and me. For a week we stayed away from the Clipper office, most of the time sitting numbly in our living room, scarcely talking. A funeral service was held at the Episcopal church, and later another service was held in the McLean chapel. Bobbie did not attend either. She had been rushed to the hospital where she stayed for ten days, emotionally exhausted.

Summer went on, life went on, but nothing was or ever will be the same. Often, even after three years of grieving, I find Bobbie sitting by herself weeping.

"Whenever there is a fine June day, with an east breeze and white clouds scudding across blue skies, I cry," Bobbie says. "It was the kind of day Ricky loved. Whenever I hear certain songs, I cry. I still go to private places to cry, and I always will."

I did not visit Ricky's grave in Mayflower Cemetery until August 21, 1990. I simply couldn't bear to. In the cemetery I read his marker: "John Ricketts Cutler, 1954–1987." Near Ricky's marker is another grave marker: "Cid Ricketts Sumner, 1890–1970."

For months before he took his own life, Bobbie and I, at his request, had called him John. He never again wanted to be called Ricky.

In 1989 Bobbie and I established the John Ricketts Cutler Memorial Scholarship. The five thousand dollar scholarship goes annually "To a senior who will attend a four-year college and who is an outstanding scholar-athlete as was John Ricketts Cutler."

Chapter Twenty-five
SUCCESS STORIES

Our son David is fond of saying he learned the newspaper business through osmosis.

"The *Duxbury Clipper* was launched when I was six years old," he recalls, "and my parents ran it from the dining room table for nearly ten years. How could I not soak up something about newspapers? I grew up with them."

David, his twin sister, Meg, and Robert used to fold the *Clipper* every Wednesday night, and David, as he grew older, delivered *Clippers*, collected ads, and occasionally wrote stories for the *Clipper*.

Still, his mother and I were moderately surprised when he said he intended to be a newspaperman. He graduated from Colby College in the spring of 1965 and two days later became a general assignment reporter for the *Patriot Ledger*, an afternoon daily in suburban Quincy, Massachusetts. At Colby, David had captained the varsity football team, but he showed relatively little interest in the school newspaper.

David spent five years at the *Patriot Ledger*, sandwiched around a three-year tour in the U.S. Marine Corps. He was commissioned a second lieutenant in January 1967 and by the following September was traipsing around the DMZ in Vietnam as a rifle platoon commander. His mother and I used to publish excerpts of his letters in the *Clipper*.

I was home one early morning in May 1968 when David called from a ship-to-shore radio and said he had been wounded in a firefight near Khe Sahn. He was calling from his hospital bed aboard the USS *Repose,* which was stationed off the Vietnamese coast. He had been shot in both legs and had spent nearly ten hours in a bomb crater before being taken to the ship in a marine helicopter. Later he told us he was hit while trying to rescue his platoon sergeant, Bill Price, who had been shot in the stomach. David had given him the only stretcher and the only available morphine, while he was taken to the hospital ship on a stretcher consisting of two rifles. Sergeant Price, a wise-cracking "lifer" from West Virginia, recovered and later was wheeled to David's room on the hospital ship to thank him.

I remember that ship-to-shore call well. "Don't worry, Dad," said David. "They say I'm in critical condition, but I'll be all right."

After the call I drove to the *Clipper* office to tell Bobbie what happened. A few hours later, two Marines arrived to inform us that David had been shot and was in critical condition.

"Oh, we already know that," said Bobbie. "He says he'll be fine."

The Marines were visibly upset to learn that David's call had pre-empted their official announcement.

After recovering at home for a couple of months and completing a fifteen-month tour at Camp Lejeune, North Carolina, David returned to the *Patriot Ledger*; shortly thereafter, he was named the paper's State House bureau chief.

In the fall of 1971, while working on the Brooke book, I was at the State House to interview Governor Francis Sargent and John Powers of South Boston, former president of the Massachusetts Senate. After the interview, David and I had lunch at the Golden Dome Pub, a local hangout for politicians, lobbyists, and reporters, and David issued a long, low sigh.

"Boy, I wish I could start a weekly newspaper. I don't think I'd like anything better."

"Well, why don't you?" I asked. "Marshfield could sure use one. You know what to do."

Six months later, in April 1972, David and Mike Stearns, the son of my former editor, Monroe, published the first issue of the *Marshfield Mariner*, a sixteen-page tab that, as David has said many times since, "borrowed liberally from the *Duxbury Clipper*." His credo on weekly newspapers—"keep it local"—comes directly from the *Clipper* tradition.

The Mariner was well received and proved to be a modest financial success. Two years later, the boys started another *Mariner*, this one in Norwell, and David began to get the idea that *Mariners* could be published almost everywhere. Four years later, in the fall of 1978, the *Scituate* and *Cohasset Mariners* were born. Along the way, David persuaded Bobbie and me that we needed a printing press, and a printing company was formed.

Actually Bobbie was dead set against going into hock for a $150,000 press, but David and I agreed the investment was worth it. We decided to call the new company Clipper Enterprises, and an enterprise it was. I was sixty-seven when our press arrived at our new *Clipper* headquarters, and later David would say he was amazed that anyone "already past the age of retirement" would go so far out on a financial limb.

David bought out his partner in 1979 and continued to start new

Mariners. By 1980, there were five, and by 1983 there were seven. Occasionally, to help himself out of a financial pinch, David borrowed money from the old man. He said I was easier to deal with than a bank.

In 1988, David owned seventeen newspapers, employed 120 persons, and had annual sales of more than five million dollars. His net, he would admit in hushed tones, was not quite as good as the *Clipper*'s. He had built a new, 18,000-square-foot building in Marshfield and, after buying our share of the printing business, moved the press to the new facility. Along the way, he had accumulated about $3.3 million in debt.

In 1989, David sold the Mariner Newspapers, now among the largest weekly groups in New England, to Capital Cities/ABC Inc., for $7.4 million. He had started seventeen years earlier with one thousand dollars.

He was not immensely impressed with the idea of being a millionaire, and after the sale he continued to serve as publisher, never forgetting, I think, what he learned about weeklies at our dining room table. His son Joshua entered Skidmore College in Saratoga, New York, in the fall of 1990 and joined the staff of the school's newspaper. Our other grandchildren, both David's children, are Benjamin, a freshman at Phillips Academy, Andover, and four year-old Carolyn, a blond bombshell who is a star at nursery school.

George Frazier, whom I had known since Boston Latin days, died in 1974. Here are a few excerpts from a piece I wrote about him for *Harvard* magazine: (The magazine, which accepted my piece, neither paid for it, returned it, nor published it.)

> I can still see George, his straw hat cockily aslant, plunked on a chair at our 25th Harvard reunion in June 1957. George had caught the *Time* review of *I'd Do It Again!*, the autobiography I had just written for Curley, and he wanted to talk about it. We were 1932 classmates, both born on June 10, although I was a year older. "Since we are Gemini," he once told me, "we can't trust each other."
>
> There were college days and nights to remember. The bull sessions in George's dorm. The night George and I went to Moseley's-on-the-Charles to hear a name band. As a jazz illiterate, I listened to George expound on the beat, little dreaming that a few years later he would launch one of the first jazz columns in the nation, called "Sweet and Low-Down," in the *Boston Herald*. This led to his assignment as entertainment editor for *Life* in 1942, continuing through the 1940s. During that period Frazier came to know intimately the great and the near great in the entertainment world.

In his years with *Life* he did pieces on Bogart, Sinatra, Hildegarde, and Tallulah Bankhead.

He consorted with the powerful New York gossip columnists Walter Winchell, Louis Lyons, Earl Wilson, and Louis Sobol, as he made the nightclub circuit, including the Stork Club and "21."

He used to tell me of his convivial bouts with John O'Hara, Ernest Hemingway, and Humphrey Bogart. He mentioned the three thousand dollars he wanted to borrow from Jackie Gleason.

Jackie pulled out his checkbook. "Don't be a piker, George." Gleason wrote out a check for seven thousand dollars.

"And you repaid it," I said.

"Don't be silly. Gleason would have been annoyed."

In the 1950s George spent a week with us in our Washington Street Cape, refusing to explain the Indiana plates on his convertible. It was summer, and my son David and I remember bobbing around Duxbury Harbor with George in our little whaler. Unforgettable were those evening conversational interludes. Then, after putting us to bed, George would retire to his bedroom with a six-pack of beer and spend most of the night reading, arising next day when the sun was on a setting slant.

"Good heavens, that man is still in bed!" our daughter Gail said one afternoon when she came home around three-thirty from the fifth grade.

In June 1962, when our Harvard class had its thirtieth reunion at the Mayflower Hotel in Manomet, Massachusetts, George called from the *Herald* and asked me to pick him up. At the *Herald* he introduced me to David Farrell, noting that I was the author of the newly published book *Honey Fitz*. Farrell gave his version of a sniff. He had read the biography of John F. Kennedy's grandfather, and apparently he didn't like it.

My best memory of the thirtieth reunion was the way our classmates' wives lionized George. Next morning in the *Herald* George wrote a memorable essay on the greasy fried chicken at the class banquet.

"I know it was chicken," he wrote. "I got an affidavit from the Mayflower chef saying so."

On the drive from Boston to Plymouth, George told me he was getting only $350 a week from the *Herald*. He wanted more money. He knew I had written for *Esquire* a profile of one of his predecessors ("Bill Cunningham's Eight-Day Week") and he asked about Cunningham's salary. The answer was $500 a week, plus revenue from his United Features Syndicate column. George said he intended to ask George Minot for a raise.

Instead of giving him a raise, managing editor George Minot fired him.

211

Although Robert Choate (who died in 1963) and the brass at the *Herald* thought George was a great writer, he was a burr under their saddle because of threatened lawsuits. Sometimes, when the editors pruned his copy of possible libelous remarks, George would sneak down to the composing room and persuade a compositor to slug in his copy.

Dave Farrell, who succeeded Minot as managing editor after Hal Clancy became a power on the *Herald* following Choate's death, fired George for his defamatory remarks about Francis Bellotti, who was running for lieutenant governor.

It was during this interlude that George asked me to run a few of his columns in the *Duxbury Clipper*. George and a friend would drive down to our house around 2 or 3 A.M. and pick up a hundred copies of the *Clipper*. Some of them were sold at a drugstore on Charles Street that stayed open most of the night and at the well-known kiosk in Harvard Square. George wanted to prove that any paper that carried his column would sell—even a country weekly like the *Duxbury Clipper*.

I remember later spending a Saturday afternoon at The Players in New York City, playing Guggenheim with George and Monroe Stearns, who was then my editor. We wound up the evening in the wee hours of the morning at the Plaza.

"Come to think of it, George," Monroe said, "you used to live here at the Plaza. I take it you last left the hotel by way of the laundry chute."

Another night George took me into the bar of The Algonquin, where he mentioned he used to sit with John O'Hara when the short-story writer and novelist was "on the sauce." George was nostalgic to the end. He liked old times and old friends, even if they didn't have duende.

He had a well disciplined and, when he chose, a gifted pen, but he often dipped it in acid. Although he never wrote a book, he contemplated writing one he would title *It's About Time*, and he aimed some telling barbs at that magazine. Jim Britt (who used to broadcast the Boston Braves baseball games) was a mutual friend of ours. "A *Time* staffer told me," Britt said, "that Henry Luce told him that Frazier's name was never again to be mentioned in the magazine except in an obituary notice, and on that occasion, Frazier's name was to be misspelled." (In a column George mentioned that Harold Ross in his book *The New Yorker* mentioned him only once, and he spelled his name "Frasier.")

Actually, *Time* often mentioned Frazier, lauding his columns as "a continuing tirade against lapses in taste, morals and common sense," and describing him as "one of the few genuine eccentrics left in daily journalism." *Time* cited him as the oldest contributor ever solicited by Rolling Stone, the rock newspaper. Over the years he also wrote for *Esquire*, *True*, *Collier's*, *Coronet*, and *Note and Go*.

There was the afternoon when I was asked to be a guest on the Haywood Vincent talk show. Haywood was away. The interviewer was George Frazier. I have the tape of that interview, and I treasure it.

Here is part of a *Boston Herald* column George Frazier wrote on November 8, 1962. The boldface type is George's, not mine.

Benisons Among Books

What seems so odd is that the two benisons among the books of 1962 should both be collections of letters and, not only that, but letters written by successful authors. And what may be even odder still is that *The Letters of Oscar Wilde* may, when I get around to reading them, make the blessings three. Until then, however, *Raymond Chandler Speaking* and P. G. Wodehouse's *Author! Author!* will do quite nicely, for they are simply superb. And yet I might have allowed them both to go unnoticed. As it happened, I came upon them quite by chance, without any resounding recommendation, without the purple of press agentry.

But that, of course, is when a book is at its best—when you come upon it by accident, as ol' Holden Caulfield came upon Isak Dinesen's *Out of Africa* **and, for that matter, I came also upon John Cutler's** *Honey Fitz* **and Joe McCarthy's** *In One Ear*, **both of which authors, incidentally, I can call on the telephone any time I please, for they have been close friends of mine for quite a long time.**

But that is why I might never have read *Honey Fitz* and *In One Ear*. After all, there is a certain reluctance to have to pass upon the productions, be they babies or books, of one's friends, and, consequently, you might never have had a word from me about either Mr. Cutler's or Mr. McCarthy's book. But then one night I opened *Honey Fitz*, which had lain unread on my desk for weeks, in the hope that it might provide some old-style political invective that I could quote in a column I had in mind. Having opened it, however, I discovered that I could not, as the saying goes, put it down, for though it has its faults, it is irresistibly readable—and for me not to say so just because I happen to be a friend of the author's would be as dishonest as if I were to praise it if it were a bore. (Reprinted with permission of the Boston Herald.)

It was a Duxbury author, Charles Fountain, who in 1984, wrote a widely acclaimed biography of George Frazier, *Another Man's Poison*. As noted on the dust jacket:

213

Charles Fountain reveals in this vivid portrait, Frazier scanned the contemporary scene for more than four decades in search of this kind of style, the unmistakable magic he called *duende* that sets an original—someone or something—apart from the merely imitative or the downright phoney.

In hundreds of magazine articles and newspaper columns Frazier took the measure of all sorts of people and objects in his inimitable style—an amalgam of playful wit and astringent observation. . . .

As mischievous as Mencken, as cantankerous as Pegler, as elegant as Swope, as individual as columnists come, during his forty-year career George Frazier expressed his stylish views of the world in the pages of *Life*, *Esquire*, *Mademoiselle*, *Down Beat*, the *Boston Herald*, and the *Boston Globe*. For the first time Frazier's life and writing are examined together in this fine biography, which offers generous examples of his work.

In 1975, I received a letter from Dr. Howard B. Gotlieb, chief of Special Collections, Mugar Memorial Library, Boston University.

> Your fine writing is highly admired here, and it is our feeling that future scholars will be studying your life and work. It is important that your manuscripts, papers and correspondence be carefully preserved under optimum archival conditions. Our new library, just completed, will be devoted to the study of contemporary literature. We very much wish the John Henry Cutler Collection to be a part of such a center.

I was pleasantly surprised, but not overwhelmed, to get this letter. I knew that Dr. Gotlieb, originally an archivist and curator of historical manuscripts at Yale University, had moved to Boston University in the early 1960s and had begun to collect the personal papers not only of distinguished twentieth-century authors but also of journalists, mystery writers, cartoonists, movie actors, and less than famous figures.

Over the years Gotlieb has "saved the lives" of more than fifteen hundred persons by assembling an amazing collection of their personal papers, diaries, letters, and memorabilia. Few other university librarians in the early 1960s agreed with Gotlieb that first drafts of potboilers and the private correspondence and news commentators deserved shelf space among the papers of well-known celebrities.

The collection at the Mugar Memorial Library, housed in special vaults, is valued at almost $50 million. Every year more than five thousand researchers, students, journalists, and authors use these collections, which are the largest of their kind in the country. The collection includes the papers of such celebrities as Robert Frost, Bette Davis, Robert Redford, Alistair

Cooke, Joan Fontaine, and George Bernard Shaw, along with U. S. presidents from George Washington to Richard Nixon. The Mugar collection also includes the papers of minor celebrities like John Cutler.

I could not possibly have penned these memoirs without the help of the information housed in the Mugar Memorial Library.

Chapter Twenty-six
CARDINAL CUSHING

My biography of Richard Cardinal Cushing completed a full century of deep excavation in the social, economic, political, and religious terrain in Massachusetts, beginning with the birth of John F. Fitzgerald, in 1863.

I was in my study one summer afternoon when Monroe Stearns called from New York to ask whether I'd like to do a biography of Cardinal Cushing for Hawthorne Books, Inc.

"No thanks," I said. I liked to re-create the careers of colorful characters, but a churchman? A prelate? "I don't know enough about theology," I said.

Monroe said the book would be as much political as religious. With that assurance, and a modest advance, I signed another contract.

It was jolting to find that there had been three previous biographies of the prelate. There was one brief book by John H. Fenton, a *New York Times* correspondent based in Boston. Fenton, in his review of my *Cardinal Cushing of Boston*, called it the best of the lot, and he told my daughter Gail, whose office at the *Boston Herald* was near his, that it was more of a "documentary" than a biography. One biography, written by nuns, was the longest press release I have ever read. The third book, which was sloppily written, had a few asides that apparently irked the prelate—especially its references to his drinking. In a fascinating letter Cushing wrote me he said two of the biographies (it wasn't difficult to guess which) "were not worth the paper they were written on." He asked me to please not write another book, and to show he meant it, he enclosed a prayer. I was puzzled, since he had told his archdiocesan attorney, Henry Leen, that "anyone who wrote *Honey Fitz*, can write a book about me." I was never able to interview this great personality, but his right-hand man, now Bishop Joseph Maguire, told me he liked my Cushing book.

Having been born and raised in Boston, I was ashamed to find out from the outset of my research what a great—and colorful—personality Cushing was. I should have known this. The churchman of the century, he was a warm, compassionate person who was a liaison between the shanty and

216

cutglass Irish of the world of the Fitzgeralds and the Curleys and the Venetian blind and suntan Irish of the Kennedy era.

Cardinal Cushing, although liked and respected by the Brahmins, did not, like his predecessor, Cardinal O'Connell, cater to them. Cushing, despite his great works, remained to the end of his days a simple, unaffected, and unpretentious personality. Once, while showing a group around the cardinal's residence in Brighton, he motioned toward the elegant surroundings. "What do I need with a joint like this?" he asked. "In South Boston we had an outhouse."

Although millions of words have been written about Cushing in newspapers, magazines, and books, I discovered that much of the untold story of his life existed in the recollections of friends, colleagues, clergymen of almost every faith, politicians, and statesmen. Most anecdotes which illumine his personality came from them.

The best files on Cushing were in the library of the *Boston Record American*, where long obituary notices had already been prepared. The librarian had a glazed look when I told him I wanted to go through all the Cushing material. Later I understood when I overheard his assistant say, "Hey, Joe, this guy thinks he's going through all the Cushing clips." There were thousands more clips on Cushing than I had found in the municipal library in New York on Bill O'Dwyer. Reading and excerpting them was a long and terribly tedious job, but it was rewarding.

During almost two years of research, Bobbie and I took our twenty-year-old daughter, Gail, who was then an assistant to Alison Arnold at the *Boston Herald*, to Ireland, in the spring of 1968.

After landing in Shannon we spent the first night in Ireland in the airport motel. Next morning we rented a Fiat and drove through the mist and alternating bright sunshine and drizzle to a beautiful hotel overlooking Lake Killarney, and here we spent the night after a delicious seafood dinner, which included fresh salmon caught in one of the rippling streams that cut through the Emerald Isle.

On the drive from Killarney to Cork City we stopped at a gas station, after an earlier stop to let some slow-moving cows cross the country road. The attendant was a lovely colleen, and a smile lit up her face when we asked directions to Glanworth, the ancestral Cushing (also spelled Cushion) home. "I haven't a clue," she said.

Sean McCarthy, a former lord mayor of Cork, and his wife entertained us on a Sunday afternoon, and in his home we learned the ritual of "the tenth." Mr. McCarthy poured each of us a slug (apparently a tenth of a pint) of whiskey, which we were expected to drink without ice or water. Gail almost gagged, but she was not one to let Americans down. Next morning Sean McCarthy took Bobbie and me to his successor's office at Cork City Hall, and around ten o'clock Lord Mayor Pearse Wyse opened a desk drawer, pulled out a bottle of rye, and handed us our tenth.

In Cork City, I visited area churches, interviewing clergymen who had met Archbishop Cushing when he was in the city. The Reverend Matthew Sheehan, of St. Colman's Seminary, had some amusing stories to tell about Cushing. One had the prelate refusing to enter St. Peter's pearly gates until a photographer arrived.

On our way to Glanworth, not far from Cork City, we had lunch in another pub, where I asked the usual questions of the bartender and waitresses. Suddenly an American woman who lived in Massachusetts came from an adjoining room to our table.

"I overheard you saying you were writing a biography of Cardinal Cushing," she said. "You must get in touch with my sister, Sister Angela Marie, who is now in Columbus, Ohio. On one of the cardinal's trips to Rome, she used to wash and iron his altar linens. He was so fond of her he gave her his cardinal's ring and always called her 'Sister American Express.' " I jotted down the nun's address and promised to write to her when I returned from my trip.

One of the best parts of the trip was the full day we spent in Glanworth, after passing through an early morning marketplace full of farmers whose donkey carts were loaded with produce. We drove across a quaint wooden bridge into the charming village of Glanworth nestled in verdant, rolling hills.

We shared a bottle of sauterne with the Very Reverend Michael Canon Hurley, who told us he had entertained Archbishop Cushing at the dining room table where we were sitting. Canon Hurley pointed out the site of the Cushing homestead and took us into the church that had been refurbished by Cushing in memory of his father. James Fouhy, one of the oldest farmers in the village, remembered the morning Patrick Cushing, on his way to Boston, was driven in an ox cart to the railroad station at Ballyhooly. Canon Hurley had proof that Cushing's grandfather was an Anglican convert.

This friendly village priest gave us directions that led down dusty roads to the tiny thatched cottage of Mrs. John ("Kitty") Tobin, the last of the Dahill descendants in Ireland who had been related to Cushing's mother.

In Waterford, on the way to Dublin, we were entertained by Lord Mayor Colum Kilcullen, who invited us to a reception honoring the victorious soccer team, which had just won the championship of southern Ireland. Earlier we had seen members of the team feted in a glorious parade, banners waving, drums beating, bugles blaring as the spectators cheered. Kilcullen had led the parade and despite his ceremonial duties, invited all three of us to be his guests at an overflowing reception.

The next stop was Dublin.

On the way from Waterford, where we visited the famed Waterford Crystal Factory, to Dublin, we drove through lush, green, rolling hills, some of them rimming crystal-clear lakes and rivers. We stopped at Blarney Castle, where Gail kissed the Blarney Stone, and later we caught a glimpse of the breathtaking Cliffs of Moher. The next stop in our rented Fiat was the Hotel Shelburne in Dublin. We parted with the Fiat before checking into our room, which overlooked St. Stephen's Park. As I looked out our hotel window I had the feeling that I was glancing down at the Public Garden from an upper floor of the Ritz in Boston. Dublin, indeed, reminded us of Boston.

The next morning I spent a few hours in the morgue of the leading newspaper, the *Irish Free Press*, going through the Cushing files. On the following day I was surprised to see my photo in the lead front-page story in the *Irish Press*. I realized for the first time that Cardinal Cushing was held in as high esteem in Dublin as he was in Boston when I read the three-column headline: "Cushing Biographer Visiting Dublin."

That front-page story was the first link in a chain of exciting incidents. During the third day of the week we spent in Dublin, I got a phone call from Peter Kilroy, who, with Walter Mahon-Smith, co-edited the *Catholic Standard*, the leading Irish weekly newspaper. "I knew a Cushing biographer would look for material at the *Irish Free Press*," he said. "One of the editors told me you were staying at the Shelburne."

Peter went on to say that his files were full of Cushing material, partly because his wife, who had been born in Glanworth, was a favorite of the Cardinal. Peter, with surprising candor, said Cushing, when he was an archbishop, had donated five thousand dollars to his weekly for its promotion of the faith. I wondered whether this would have bothered the parishioners of the archdiocese back home who dropped money in Sunday church collection boxes.

When Gail saw the front-page spread she asked how it came about.

"How would you like to have your picture in the *Irish Free Press?*" I asked.

That Saturday afternoon Bobbie and I walked with Gail to the newspaper. We went inside and chatted with one of the editors I had talked to earlier. Bobbie and I told him that Gail had just won the mixed-doubles badminton championship in her age division. That was excuse enough for him to summon a reporter and a photographer. Sunday morning we bought the thick edition of the newspaper, found the picture of our little blonde, and went up to our room, where Gail was having breakfast in bed.

"Sorry, you didn't get into this edition," I said. "Maybe you'll make it tomorrow."

Gail, out of curiosity, started riffling through the paper to see if it came up to the standard of the *Duxbury Clipper*. She was delighted when she saw her picture at the top of an inside column.

Monday morning Peter Kilroy called to ask whether we would like to meet President Eamon deValera. We were thrilled!

I knew a bit about the tall, gaunt Irish leader who had been the last battalion leader to surrender in the famous Easter Rebellion of 1916. After being sentenced to jail for life, he was pardoned a year later, but in the 1918 insurrection he was again jailed. He escaped after finding a key in a cake, and as a stowaway he sneaked into Liverpool disguised as a fireman.

President deValera was far from the man I had once called "a fugitive from a wax museum" in a "Who Is It?" column written in 1940. He couldn't have greeted us more cordially in his gracious and almost shy way, immediately putting the three of us at ease.

He told us about his father, Vivian deValera, a Spanish immigrant who had married an Irish girl. The president's name had been changed from Edward to Eamon. He talked about his battles with the Black and Tans, and when I asked about his trip to New York, he said he had crossed the Atlantic disguised as a stoker. I knew he had been one of the first persons to master the Einstein theory, but when I asked him about it, he switched to the story of how he had fallen in love with a teacher who had flunked him in Gaelic. Later he married her.

President deValera, who was almost blind, fumbled for the telephone when it rang. Gail, with perfect aplomb, picked up the ivory-colored receiver and handed it to him. Feeling that we were overstaying our cordial visit, I edged off my chair when deValera picked up a silver pen set.

"President John Kennedy gave me this when he came to Ireland," he said. He seemed in no hurry to let us go.

One of his aides called a taxi for us, and we drove out of Phoenix Park feeling that we had been in the presence of a great man, a courageous revolutionary who had become a ruler after years of underground activities.

I was saddened to learn later that, at the age of ninety-one, he had entered a Dublin nursing home. An aide said deValera would return to his official residence in Phoenix Park to work every day until President-elect Erskine Childers was inaugurated. DeValera died soon thereafter.

One day we went to Stradbally, northwest of Dublin, to visit the Cosby home. (Bobbie's great-grandmother was a Cosby, who had come with her family from Scotland to Parsippany, New Jersey. At the age of eighteen, she went by stagecoach to rural Mississippi, to teach school, and later married Bobbie's great-grandfather, Edwin Burnley.)

We set out by train, and in an hour and a half, after one change, we arrived at the small town. A taxi took us right there, for everyone seemed to know the Cosbys. We almost were not admitted, for at the gatehouse there was a snarling dog of uncertain origin, and we had to explain to the gatekeeper—a loud, disagreeable woman—just who we were. The taxi driver took us right up to the main entrance of the large stone mansion surrounded by woods, a wide stream, stables, fenced-in corrals, and flower and vegetable gardens. We were greeted by Rear-Admiral and Mrs. Cosby, and after we explained who Bobbie was, they were most cordial. They said they raised ponies and were just off to buy some more. After showing us about fifty ponies, they left us in the capable hands of Admiral Cosby's brother, Major Cosby, who told us he had spent most of his life abroad with the British Army.

He invited us in and after a long search, found a decanter of sherry, which he served with biscuits. We walked around the large rooms. Shabby genteel at its best! Glorious oriental rugs, gleaming Georgian silver, walls jammed with impressive oils—at least sixteen of them by Sir Joshua Reynolds. (Later, at the townhouse, a clerk told us that whenever the Cosbys were broke they would take a Reynolds to London and sell it for enough to live on for many months.) But the upholstered furniture was threadbare, as were the damask draperies. Wallpaper was hanging in ribbons, and on the large polished mahogany dining table was a worn-out toaster, an open box of Kellogg's Corn Flakes, and a jelly glass of milk. We spoke some about family history and bid the major adieu.

While waiting in the railroad station for the train that would return us to Dublin, we chatted with a young Irish woman. After some conversation, she said, "Are all Americans as homely as you two?" Of course she was not referring to our looks, but to our friendliness.

Bobbie said she wasn't too sure.

Since there wasn't enough time during that crowded week to go through the material in the files of the *Catholic Standard*, I gave Peter Kilroy a check for two hundred dollars in return for his promise to send me Xeroxed copies of his material. None of the three earlier Cushing biographies had included most of these stories.

I flew home from Dublin while Bobbie and Gail flew to Rome for another week's vacation.

My anchorman on the Cushing book was John Hynes, who was perhaps the most honest and modest mayor Boston ever had. This time one of our interviewing headquarters was Anthony's Pier Four, Hynes's favorite restaurant. He had carte blanche to invite anyone he wished who, he thought, could contribute something to the biography. At one of our first luncheons, he brought Richard J. Condon, president of the St. Vincent de Paul Society. Anthony Athanas, owner of Pier Four, walked over to our table.

"May I sit down for a moment, Your Honor?"

When a waiter came to take our orders, Anthony ordered a cup of black coffee. He turned to the waiter. "No check," he said.

"Thanks, Anthony," Hynes said, "but today we are guests of John Cutler."

"Thanks, John," I said to Hynes later. "That lunch cost me sixty dollars."

Our guests at another luncheon were Judge Francis X. Morrissey and his brother, a young attorney. My first question to the judge referred to an incident I had read in William Manchester's splendid book *Death of a President*. In a meeting in the Washington, D.C., home of Archbishop O'Boyle, Theodore Sorenson and Sargent Shriver, representing the Kennedy family, had attended to make funeral arrangements for Jack Kennedy with O'Boyle and Cushing. A surprise visitor was Judge Francis Morrissey, who later denied "crashing" the meeting. He bristled when I asked him about this.

Turning to John Hynes, he cocked his thumb in my direction.

"Listen to him, John," he said. "Did you hear what he asked me?" He went on to say that Shriver had invited him to the meeting. During that luncheon he kept stressing the close ties he had had with the late president.

"I had his power of attorney," Francis said.

"That won't do you any good now," his brother said.

I didn't dare ask him how he felt when the Massachusetts Bar Association, with help from the *Boston Globe*, had blocked his appointment to a vacant federal judgeship in the Boston area. Morrissey was a Boston municipal judge when Joe Kennedy had tried to persuade President Kennedy to name him to the post. I knew that Joe Kennedy, on a cruise out of Hyannis Port in his *Marlin*, had told Cushing to ask Morrissey to accept a trust fund for his children as balm for his disappointment. During the drive back to Boston, Cushing discussed the matter with Morrissey, who refused the offer.

One morning I got a phone call from Sister Angela Marie, who said she was temporarily staying at the Stigmatine Fathers' residence in Waltham. She was available for an interview.

When I entered the lobby of the monastery I saw an attractive young woman wearing a miniskirt. I was about to ask her where I could find Sister Angela Marie when she introduced herself. It was Sister American Express.

On the way to Duxbury, we stopped for lunch at the Country Fare in Hingham. When I asked whether she would like a cocktail, she ordered a sidecar, a cocktail I hadn't heard of since college days. I had a martini. I didn't have the courage to order one more unless—

"Would you like a dividend, Marie?" (She had asked me to use the name after making it clear that she wasn't overly fond of the Sister American Express business.)

She nodded. "But you may have to take care of me," she smiled.

This pert and intelligent nun was full of Cushing lore. In our Duxbury living room that afternoon she charmed Bobbie and me with her background stories.

Among leaders of the Italian-American community I interviewed were Joseph DeMambro and Ralph Tedeschi. DeMambro loaned me several scrapbooks, which were full of photos and correspondence he had had with Cushing. I spent an entire morning in Ralph Tedeschi's mansion (that's the word for a huge hilltop house with a marble foyer), and he pulled from the wall any photographs I requested. Some of them appear in the book. Ralph had sold his Tedeschi supermarkets to Stop & Shop, whose president was Sidney Rabb. The day after I interviewed Ralph, I spent an afternoon with Rabb, another Cushing admirer. It was not until I spent another afternoon with Francis Kelly, former lieutenant governor of Massachusetts, that I realized how sick Cardinal Cushing was. From the intimate correspondence (they were close friends), I came away with the idea that Cushing was close to dying.

One of the most pleasant interviews was at the Hotel Statler, where a "boxing ring" was set up in the middle of a crowded auditorium. In each of the four corners was a college president—Nathan Pusey of Harvard, James Perkins of Cornell, Howard Johnson of the Massachusetts Institute of

Technology, and Ray Heffner of Brown. As guests of Charles Werly of Duxbury, who was then a trustee of Cornell University and chairman of the board of the Putnam Fund, Bobbie and I were invited to a private cocktail party in an inner sanctum, where we met the college presidents. When Pusey heard I was doing a biography of Cushing, he said, "This is something you probably won't use, but I had an interesting meeting with the cardinal at his residence."

Pusey then told me about a proposal to allow medical institutions to obtain stray animals from pounds for research. "A few days before a hearing at the State House, Dean George Berry and I went to see Archbishop Cushing. He listened attentively until Dean Berry finished talking."

"How many votes do you have?" Cushing asked.

Pusey smiled. "That's why we came to see you, Your Eminence."

I asked Pusey about a statement Theodore H. White had made in his book *The Making of a President*, in reference to the Nixon-Humphrey campaign: "It was impossible, Nixon's private polls said, for him to carry Massachusetts unless, inconceivably, Cardinal Cushing, President Pusey of Harvard, and the Boston City Council all publicly endorsed him; and even then it would be chancy." Pusey nodded and smiled again.

We discussed another story that had Pusey showing Cushing around Widener Library. When Cushing asked for a standard textbook on canon law, Pusey was embarrassed when a librarian couldn't find a single volume. A closer look revealed the books on canon law were listed under ballistics.

"That story is apocryphal, I'm afraid," Pusey said. Later I found that the same story had been told about William Cardinal O'Connell and Harvard President Abbot Lawrence Lowell.

Charles Werly introduced Bobbie to President Perkins as the daughter of Dr. James B. Sumner, formerly head of the biochemistry department at Cornell and the first Cornell professor ever to win the Nobel Prize. (After he received the Nobel for being the first scientist to isolate an enzyme, Cornell created the department of enzyme chemistry for him.)

During the lunch that preceded what turned out to be debate on student riots, Bobbie and I sat with Charles Werly and one of his Putnam Fund associates, George Putnam. The latter also had a few Cushing stories to tell. Cushing, like Curley, left a long and winding anecdotal trail behind him.

Within a two-year period, all four of those college presidents had resigned.

I had a rewarding exchange of correspondence with Attorney Daniel Kelly of Rye, New York, who for almost half a century had handled the legal affairs of the "Cushion" branch of the family. I was stymied, however, when I tried to interview Cushing's sister, then a saleswoman at Best & Co. in Boston. Cushing had sealed her lips.

Years earlier Frank Buxton had told me of an incident involving Cardinal O'Connell and Mayor Curley at the time when Buxton and O'Connell were trustees of the Boston Public Library. Discussed at one of their meetings was a proposal to display a bust of Curley in the library. O'Connell said something to the effect that there must be some place in the basement where we could put "this monstrosity." Sidney Rabb, who later served as a trustee of the Boston Public Library with Cushing, confirmed this illuminating anecdote.

I came to love Cardinal Cushing not merely because he was the "Churchman of the Century," but also because he was so refreshingly informal. One Sunday, after celebrating a High Mass, he went outside the church and waved to a Knights of Columbus honor guard, who saluted him with sabers. "Why don't you fellows go home?" he said. "The roast beef is getting cold."

No Prince of the Church had the knack of putting children more at ease. At a reception Cushing was moving casually among several hundred adults and children when a four-year-old nuzzled up, gazing at him wide-eyed.

"Hello, little girl. What's your name?"

"Mary."

"My, what a nice name."

As he patted her head, she broke the silence with her high-piping voice. "What's your name?"

"Richard." He exchanged a wave with her as he moved on.

My favorite story about his informality? Cushing himself used to tell about a little boy who lived near the Cardinal's residence. Occasionally, when he went for a stroll, he met the youngster, who always solemnly said, "Hi, Dick." Then he would slip his hand into the prelate's and walk along beside him.

The Cushing biography, which was reviewed in the Boston area only in the *Pilot*, didn't command any substantial second serial rights, especially in comparison with *I'd Do It Again!*, which cost the *Boston Globe* thirty-two thousand dollars. When the *Boston Record-American* ran *Honey Fitz*, its circulation increased by half a million in three weeks. (Only the autobiography of Mae West did better, circulation director Lester Zwick told me.) The *Boston Globe*, after acquiring second serial rights to *Cardinal Cushing of Boston* for twenty-five hundred dollars, sold it to the *Record-American*

225

for five hundred. But Zwick told me his newspaper spent sixty-five thousand dollars in publicity, including radio, television, and ads.

I consider this biography my most important work.

The Cushing biography was condensed in the *Catholic Digest* for which I received one thousand dollars. It was also a Catholic Book Club selection. I was told Rose Kennedy liked it, primarily because she liked Cushing.

Victor Newton, in a November 1970 issue of *Sign,* wrote in part of his favorable review:

> Cutler's biography follows in the wake of such worthy efforts as John Fenton's *Salt of the Earth* and Joseph Dever's *Cushing of Boston*, as well as many others. Certainly no ecclesiastical figure in America has ever been honored in America with as many books, and few lay figures have. The present biography, however, need bow to none of its predecessors. If anything this is the definitive biography of the cardinal to be issued to date. It is in greater depth, evidences more painstaking research and offers more detail than any of the others.

After the cardinal read my biography, he was pleased, according to Bishop Joseph Maguire, who was right-hand man in the Cushing's residence in Brighton.

In the June 30, 1984, issue of *Boston Irish Echo*, Mike Ryan wrote:

> Cutler, seventy-four, admitted that he likes to write about colorful characters whose lives are "illumined" by anecdotes. People have asked him to write books about John Hynes or John McCormack. "Good politicians," Cutler said, "but they had little of the roguish charm and color of a Curley or a Honey Fitz."

John McCormack? How could anyone write a riveting biography of an honest politician who for fifty solid years had dinner every night with his wife?

Except for a few members of the clergy who reviewed the Cushing biography, most of the reviews were favorable. Victor Newton in his review gave an appraisal that was about average:

> The writing here is lucid and engaging. A lengthy book, it holds your interest fast from page one to the final chapter and is further enhanced by a selection of pictures which is sheer nostalgia for those who have followed

Cushing's career to date. When you put down the book, for all its carefree jauntiness, you sense the pathos which marks the life of every man.

Pivoting between the Irish transitional periods, Cushing would officiate at the funerals of both Curley, who'd begun one era, and John Kennedy, the first Irish Brahmin. At both, he prayed in the grating, honest South Boston voice that was his inheritance, and which he was too proud to change.

Cushing himself died just as the biography came out.

Chapter Twenty-seven
SENATOR EDWARD BROOKE

Later in 1970, Reynolds "fed" me another lunch. Mentioning widespread interest in the problems of blacks, he asked whether I knew Senator Edward Brooke. I didn't, having had nothing more than a brief chat with him one afternoon when he addressed a group of weekly newspaper editors at The Parker House. "But I think I can get to him," I said.

The Century Club is a popular haunt for writers and editors. Earlier I had sat "back to back" with Geoffrey Hellman, the facile author whose profiles I had read in the *New Yorker*. On this particular day Reynolds brought over one of the Doubleday editors, Sandy Richardson, and asked whether he was interested in a biography of Brooke. Richardson seemed enthusiastic. In fact, after luncheon, as Reynolds and I were walking downstairs, Richardson called after us to repeat his interest in the project.

Sandy Richardson must have had a third martini that day, because two weeks later Paul Reynolds sent me a copy of a note Richardson had sent him saying the Doubleday editors had decided the book was too "marginal." My discouragement ended a month or so later when Reynolds called me—it was just before Christmas—to say, "You can raise a glass. Bobbs Merrill has accepted the book with an advance of five thousand dollars."

Getting to Brooke was no cinch. I learned later that the Senator had consistently refused publishers' pleas, so it took a great deal of persuasion. I kept prodding Roger Woodworth, Brooke's press secretary, and asking him to make an appointment for me with Brooke in Washington.

I could have written the book without Brooke's consent, but I knew it would be better if I could get firsthand information from him, his sister and mother, his wife and two daughters, and his close friends and colleagues.

Brooke put it this way, after the book was published:

> At first, I didn't want a book because I thought I was too young, hadn't accomplished anything, and thought it premature. John didn't get in touch with me until after he'd talked to a lot of people. Then when I heard about this man . . . who he was . . . what he was . . . and his scholarship, I was really quite flattered, frankly, that he would write about me.

228

I was the one who was flattered. Ed Brooke is one of the most brilliant men I have ever known personally. And, of course, I felt honored to be writing about the first elected black senator in the United States.

After flying to Washington, D.C., for the first interview, I waited all day in the senator's office while his personal secretary came out of the inner office every hour or so to say the senator was sorry to keep me waiting. But the time wasn't wasted. Between the incessant telephone rings, I gleaned some background color from Sally Saltonstall, a niece of Senator Leverett Saltonstall. Sally, whom I twice took to lunch, was one of the two receptionists in the outer office.

In Washington, Brooke lived in the Watergate complex, where his mother and sister had separate apartments. A member of Brooke's senatorial staff arranged my appointment with Senator Brooke's mother. After taking a taxi to Watergate, I was stymied. Nobody could enter unless the unseen person who was monitoring the Watergate complex had been notified beforehand. Apparently someone goofed, because Mr. Anonymous refused to let me in. I waited until a woman carrying a bag of groceries entered and quickly slid through. When I called Mrs. Brooke, she asked me to wait ten minutes. It was so sweltering in her apartment I asked her permission to take off my jacket and loosen my tie.

It was a delightful and profitable visit. Mrs. Brooke showed me dozens of releases from magazines and newspapers and loaned me those I hadn't previously seen, including some notices in the *London Times*. Then, when she showed me a beautiful photograph of her son, I said it simply had to be reproduced on the front cover of the dust jacket. Mrs. Brooke, a gracious person, smiled and told me she would have to think about that. Later Senator Brooke brought me the photo.

Next day I took Salvatore Micchiche to lunch. As the *Boston Globe's* Washington correspondent, Sal gave me some good leads. During that week in Washington, I got a lot of behind-the-scenes data from Brooke's staff— especially from Betsy Warren, the senator's personal secretary. Washington telephone operators who could not reach Brooke at his office, apartment, or home in Newton, Massachusetts, usually called Betsy to locate him.

Betsy Warren told me about the night her home phone rang at eight-thirty. "This is the White House. The president is anxious to speak to Senator Brooke. Do you know where he can be reached?" When Betsy asked if she could take a message, President Nixon came to the phone. "Hello, Miss Warren, this is the president."

"I was about to tell the caller to cut the comedy when it occurred to me that it *did* sound like the president. We chatted for six or seven minutes. And he, not knowing I had a special line, asked why I was working so late."

One afternoon Nancy Dickerson, of NBC, phoned and asked to speak to Betsy. Roger Woodworth, Brooke's campaign manager, thinking he was talking to a friend of Betsy's, said, "Yes, Betsy is here. But I'm afraid she is terribly inebriated right now. You see, she just returned from a martini lunch." Another time, Roger, who spent the night with Bobbie and me in Duxbury to make interviewing easier, told a startled caller that one of the girls on the staff was no longer with the senator, explaining that drugs had been found on her person. Then, realizing it was a serious call, he handed the receiver to the "addict." Roger told me he would sometimes say to a caller, "Call back in a few minutes. She is in the ladies' room."

During a Christmas party, Ann Cunningham, another staffer, had a part in a pageant when the phone rang and someone asked to speak to her. "Sorry, but she can't come to the phone," Roger said. "Ann is dressed in swaddling clothes and is lying in the manger."

A big help in tracing the Brooke family background was Dr. Adelaide Hill, the senator's cousin, who was a professor of sociology and director of Afro-American Studies at Boston University. Dr. Hill, who grew up with Brooke and went to school with him through the early grades, high school, and college, read and corrected early chapters of the manuscript after giving me family background information. Since I am a biographer of the "What porridge ate John Keats?" school, I found Dr. Hill a big help.

John Bottomly was one of the early Brooke supporters who suggested that the best way to get into political orbit in Boston was to get on the Boston Finance Committee. He was right. Bottomly was a principal later in Brooke's most sensational case while he served as district attorney of the Commonwealth—the case of "the Boston strangler." "It was inconceivable," a biographer wrote, "that anything could ever match for sheer horror the series of grossly grotesque stranglings by a sexual psychopath who made fiendish assaults on his victims—all women—and then left them in obscene positions, shockingly exposed as though to debase and degrade them."

Brooke created a special Strangler Investigation Bureau and named Bottomly coordinator of all police efforts to track down the maniac. The strangulations got so much publicity that Earle Stanley Gardner, the master of whodunits, came to Boston to discuss the case with Bottomly. In their exasperation Brooke and Bottomly sought help from Peter Hurkos, a Dutch medium.

A few weeks after his arrest for a series of rapes, Albert DeSalvo told Bottomly he was the strangler, and Bottomly believed him. In my opinion, the real strangler was still in Bridgewater State Hospital in Massachusetts.

Hurkos gave an incredibly accurate description of a man and his cluttered room on the third floor of a shabby rooming house near Boston College. Hurkos even said this man (known as Thomas O'Brien, not his real name) slept on a spring that had no mattress, and took showers downstairs with his shoes on. Hurkos led Bottomly's detectives to the apartment. The man inside, who slammed the door in their face, fitted Peter's description exactly, even to the beaked nose, scar on the left arm, and deformed thumb on his right hand. Bottomly and his men saw all these things when they returned with a search warrant. The man escaped trial by voluntarily committing himself to a mental hospital.

In 1968, Brooke rejected a lucrative offer to play himself in a film based on Gerold Frank's book, *The Strangler*, primarily because the script pointed to DeSalvo as the murderer. In the film Henry Fonda starred as Bottomly, and Tony Curtis played DeSalvo.

Six months after DeSalvo's long confessions ended, Bottomly resigned as assistant attorney general "over matters unrelated to the stranglings." Actually, Brooke, annoyed with him for the way he handled the case of the strangler, gave him his walking papers. They became friends again later.

One day I invited the senator's wife and her daughters, Remi and Edwina, to lunch at the Harvard Club, but when I rang the bell at the Brookes's Newton apartment, Mrs. Brooke invited me in. "It will be easier here," she said. "I want to show you the albums, and we can have lunch." There was no lunch. Around four o'clock Edwina brought us tea and cookies, but I didn't mind, since those four hours were more profitably spent going through scrapbooks and albums.

From outward appearances the Brooke couple were happy, but I suspected their marriage was in jeopardy. As I sat in the living room that day interviewing Remigia, her two daughters, and Remi's second husband, there was an underlying sadness as Remigia, sitting on a hassock near me, commented on the photos of the Brooke family in happier days. There was something wistful about it all. I found Remigia Brooke charming, but her reputed vibrancy seemed muted. I sensed there were family matters which none of us could talk about.

Over the months I interviewed Brooke's college friends, his early business and law partner, those who first got him to run, some of his political enemies, and every member of his staffs in both Boston and Washington offices. Since it was an authorized biography, there were some fascinating stories I couldn't tell. Otto Snowden, head of Freedom House in Roxbury, Boston's Harlem, was a classmate of the senator at Howard University. Some of the tales Otto told me of his handsome friend's ways with the ladies never got into print. I was disappointed when I interviewed one of Brooke's earliest supporters—Alfred Brothers.

When Brooke graduated from Boston University Law School, he shared a two-room suite in a Roxbury building with Brothers, who was a realtor. I had heard the rumor that the sign on the front door of the suite read, "Brooke Brothers." When Alfred said it didn't, I suggested that perhaps it should have.

Early in the summer of 1971 the senator invited Bobbie and me to his annual barbecue at his place in Oak Bluffs, Martha's Vineyard. We took the steamer from Woods Hole to Edgartown and spent the night at the Daggett House, on the main street in Edgartown. That night we had dinner at the Shiretown Inn, across the street from the Daggett House. Here we read the sign on the wall: "No mention of Senator Edward Kennedy, please." It was the motel where Kennedy spent the night after the tragedy at Chappaquiddick. After dinner Bobbie and I took the ferry across the narrow channel to Chappaquiddick.

Next day we spent the afternoon with the Brookes and about 150 of their friends, political associates, office staffs, neighbors, and Republican state officials.

The Brooke compound includes a typical Victorian house, a tennis court, and a building that was once a barn. The barn had one huge room decorated with a dozen vases of wild flowers. All afternoon people played tennis or lolled around sunning themselves in bathing suits, while a few persons were sipping beer at a bar inside the main house.

An elaborate barbecue had been prepared at noon, with long tables of littlenecks, which the senator was opening as fast as he could. There was the tempting aroma of spare ribs sizzling next to heaping dishes of potato salad and watermelon. The guests helped themselves and sat comfortably around the spacious lawn.

Bobbie was especially interested in getting to know Brooke, partly because he was the first black senator ever to be elected in the United States. An ancestor of hers in the middle of the last century was Senator Charles Sumner of Massachusetts, known as "the Great Abolitionist." Bobbie's paternal grandfather was named for him, as was her baby brother, who died in the 1918 influenza epidemic. When Bobbie mentioned the abolitionist, who was once cane-whipped on the Senate floor for his views, Brooke smiled: "As you may surmise, I am a great admirer of Senator Charles Sumner."

That evening we returned to the Daggett House. Before dinner we had cocktails with Roger and Judy Babb. Roger was a state representative. We sat a few yards from the ferry to Chappaquiddick and, as the sun was setting, watched the Chappaquiddick ferry go back and forth.

Edward Brooke's defeat by Paul Tsongas in the 1970 senatorial race shocked blacks the world over, including black populations in the emerging nations of the Third World. (My biography of Brooke, for example, was translated into French by an international publishing house that distributes books in both France and Africa.)

Brooke was a black who twice declined appointments (by Presidents Lyndon Johnson and Richard Nixon) to the United States Supreme Court. He was a symbol of hope to a downtrodden race, even though Senator Brooke looked upon himself as an American, Republican, and black in that order. Until his own family did him in, he had kept a remarkable profile in a state that logically might seem inimical to his interests, for he was a Republican in a state that was overwhelmingly Democratic, a black in a state that was ninety-eight percent white. In his review of my book, W. W. MacDonald, a professor of history at Lamar University in Beaumont, Texas, caught the flavor both of the book and its subject:

> This literate, beautifully written biography is a tribute and testament to the only black U.S. Senator. It is in the traditional biography genre, describing Brooke's early lean years, his educational background, his early defeats for political office, his emergence as a leader of the GOP in Massachusetts, his election as Senator, his arrival as a national political figure, and his political future, particularly his changes to attain national office. Cutler interprets Brooke's amazing success as a combination of talent and his ability to transcend his "blackness" and to appear as a representative of all Americans. Highly recommended for larger collections.

One of the joys of writing contemporary biography is getting an inside look at events which, even if not distorted by the media, are misinterpreted by the public. For example, that stormy Republican primary convention in Worcester in 1962 scarcely showed Elliot Richardson in his usual role of the shining white knight—as the impeccable Brahmin who was above reproach.

When, at this convention, a delegate called Brooke "the white knight in the contest," Richardson said, "The man must be colorblind." Behind the scenes, Richardson, through his partisans, brought color into focus in the primary race for attorney general of Massachusetts, despite the fact that he had previously told a *Boston Globe* reporter that any qualified candidate had a right to run "regardless of creed or color."

On the sweltering day in Worcester in 1960, the contest proved to be the most dramatic seat squirmer in Massachusetts political history. It was also one of the dirtiest conventions. Richardson aides, not content with accusing Brooke of improprieties in his private life, spread the rumor that he beat his wife. Delegates were told that his Communist activities had kept him out of a federal post. There was no question about the fact that Richardson had guns for hire. "Richardson didn't merely want to defeat Brooke," Roger Woodworth told me. "He wanted to *destroy* the boss." There was another rumor that Robert Kennedy, recognizing Brooke as a threat to the Kennedy dynasty in Massachusetts, had the same ambition.

Roger Woodworth showed me a copy of a note passed around at the Worcester convention:

> If you elect a black attorney general, how would you like to have a black governor later?

Richardson partisans went out of their way to drag racism into the campaign.

Brooke's partisans, who couldn't be blamed for trying to counter the smears, circulated reports about Richardson's drunken-driving record in his youth. It was a dirty convention.

Then a dramatic thing happened. After the first ballot it appeared that Richardson had barely won. His jubilant followers danced in the aisles and cheered, and many of them left for their cocktail parties. At this point Francis Alden Wood stepped into the picture. He had attended the convention as a member of the Middlesex delegation for Richardson, but he had been so impressed by Brooke that he changed his mind, and his vote was not recorded on the first ballot. When he challenged the vote, Chairman Leverett Saltonstall ordered a poll of the Middlesex delegation and the resulting figures showed Richardson one vote shy of a simple majority. On the second ballot Wood voted for Brooke, enabling him to squeak by. Francis Alden Wood sent me the newsclip from the *Lowell Sun* telling the complete story.

During the research I went through the files of all the Boston newspapers, every magazine that listed Brooke in the *Periodical Index*, the *New York Times,* and the *Washington Post.* After perusing five years of Maxine Cheshire's gossip column I was surprised to find that Brooke was not mentioned once. He was not a party goer.

In the Brooke venture I developed a deep admiration and respect for a warm, brilliant person who fell into a trap of his own making. Yet he was no worse than the average politician and clearly superior to most politicians. The Gaelic proverb applies to most of them: "If all politicians' sins were written on their forehead, they would all pull their hat down over their eyes."

A month after his defeat by the able Paul Tsongas, Brooke wrote Bobbie and me a letter:

> After the initial period of letdown and bafflement, I have moved into a much more desirable frame of mind: counting my blessings. They are many.
>
> And chief among them are the old cherished friends, who stood with me on the battlement all during this long, traumatic year. I don't think I ever really understood those words in the national anthem—"bombs bursting in air"—until I experienced the phenomenon myself.
>
> You were there, Bobbie and John. And so was the *Clipper.* I have no words adequately enough to thank you both for your loyalty, faith, and friendship.

Chapter Twenty-eight
CELEBRITIES PAST & PRESENT

In October 1990, when Bobbie and I attended the centennial family reunion given in honor of Cid Ricketts Sumner, we were guests of Berry Morgan on her two-hundred acre farm at Summit Point, West Virginia. Berry Morgan, a relative of Cid's, often visited her in Duxbury, and Bobbie and I got to know her well. She wrote several fictional pieces for the *New Yorker* in a quaint Mississippi dialect that was fascinating.

Among other authors who were Duxbury guests of Cid Sumner over the years were Jessamyn West and Evelyn Eaton. One night I asked Miss Eaton if she would read a manuscript I was working on. "I'd be glad to—in hardcover," she said.

My old friend Margaret Coit, who won a Pulitzer for her biography of John Calhoun and later wrote a biography of Bernard Baruch, was an occasional visitor, as was Rachel MacKenzie, who contributed to the *New Yorker*. My favorite author was Margaret Widdemer, a poet and Pulitzer Prize-winning novelist. Bobbie and I met her often when she visited Cid. One night I asked her why it was getting so hard to sell novels.

"Less fiction is published today because life is more exciting—with all the space exploration and technological advances—than any fiction writer could dream up."

Margaret was warm and friendly and a great conversationalist. Bobbie and I met her and Cid later in London and took them to lunch. After Simpson's famed roast beef and Yorkshire pudding, served from a samovar, we were amused when both ladies stuffed rolls and other non-delicacies into their handbags. Their explanation was that after such a sumptuous luncheon, that would be all they needed for supper. We had cocktails with them that evening at their bed-and-breakfast inn.

One puckish guest of Cid's was Maeve Brennan, the Irish-born author of several books, who for several years wrote "The Long-Winded Lady" for the *New Yorker*. Maeve liked Duxbury so much she spent an entire summer in a waterfront apartment with her thirty-nine cats, who roamed around the boatyard roofs to everyone's dismay. Her large dog of questionable ancestry was also a nuisance. Once, on the sundeck of her apartment, he lifted his leg and the resulting stream seeped through the planking onto the head of a man who was about to buy a large boat. The man took off in a hurry—and not in a boat.

Maeve liked to shock people. One night after I took her to dinner at the Winsor House, a friend said to her, "Weren't you afraid John might seduce you?"

"I was afraid he wouldn't," she said.

Early in my writing career I met a lot of other stimulating people. I spent one weekend in New York as a guest of Maurice Ewing, who was a leading oceanographer of his day. He was living on the former Thomas Lamont estate, which is owned by Columbia University. In addition to its scientific laboratories, there were several small garages which housed marine specimens, including ocean bottom core samples which Dr. Ewing had dredged on his oceanographic expeditions. One inch of a core sample might contain the geological history of hundreds of thousands of years of marine life, and some of Ewing's cores were almost twenty feet long. Ewing was the subject of a *Reader's Digest* article in the 1950s.

I spent a few enjoyable afternoons with Harvard Professor Ernest Hooton, a leading anthropologist. I remember one afternoon when we discussed the four stages of alcoholism: jocose, bellicose, lachrymose, and comatose. I insisted that alcohol intensified feelings. If something good happened, a person felt euphoric. If he was angry, he became bellicose, if depressed, lachrymose. Hooton thought the effects of alcohol could not be predicted, and he may have been right.

I interviewed Professor Pitirim Sorokin several times. He had been secretary for Aleksandr Kerenski, a Russian revolutionary leader who was overthrown as prime minister by the Bolshevik Revolution, in November 1917, because of his moderate policies and indecision. Kerenski fled from Petrograd to Paris while Sorokin escaped to the United States. When I interviewed Sorokin, he was chairman of the Department of Sociology at Harvard University. During one interview when I mentioned Vico, the Italian philosopher, Sorokin turned around and confronted me. "You are not a reporter," he said. "How do you know about Vico?" I confessed to him that I had been a Harvard graduate student. The *Boston Sunday Post* ran my feature on Sorokin.

I remember one morning in the early 1950s when Bobbie and I were chatting with her father during one of his winter visits. (He sometimes rented a Duxbury house in the summer.) He asked how I went about writing newspaper features. Instead of answering his question, I queried him about

237

his work. Soon he was giving us a fascinating view of the future of biotechnology. He mentioned synthetic food. Today some of the things he talked about are commonplace. About a week later I sent him an article under one of my pseudonyms, James Sadler, which summarized his informal talk.

"That's how I do it," I said.

Dr. Richard Field, former chairman of the Department of Geophysics at Princeton University, was a close friend and neighbor who occasionally took me to scientific seminars. I wrote a feature on him.

I listed some other Duxbury celebrities in *Put It On the Front Page, Please!*, written in 1960. Here are a few excerpts:

Although it has been some time since the late Burton Holmes (author of *The Burton Holmes Travelogues*) lived in Duxbury, the town has in Cecil Atwater a world traveler whose travelogues have won wide acclaim. Atwater, who has lectured all over the United States, is a fellow of the Royal Photographic Society of Great Britain.

Bishop John Wesley Lord is a summer resident, as was the late William Cardinal O'Connell (whose home, Miramar, is now a seminary); Dr. Richard Cattell, who performed a gall bladder operation on Sir Anthony Eden; Dr. Robert Fleming, founder of the first alcoholism clinic in the United States (he represented the country in an international conference on alcoholism in Geneva, Switzerland). Cattell and Fleming are two of many distinguished physicians who spend their summers in Duxbury. Another was the late Dr. Emma Erving, a friend of Gertrude Stein's, who was physician for Teddy Roosevelt's children and those of other presidents.

Other interesting personalities who have lived in Duxbury are Justice Felix Frankfurter, of the United States Supreme Court (who was denied summer membership in the Duxbury Yacht Club); actress Fanny Davenport and her brother William Seymour, a celebrated actor; Thomas Lawson, author of an autobiography titled *Frenzied Finance*, who summered at the Myles Standish Hotel and gave considerable thought to building his "Dreamwold" here in Duxbury before deciding on a manorial site in nearby Scituate (his grandson Thomas Lawson II, is a resident of Duxbury); Dr. Nathaniel Noyes, well-known in medical circles in the horse and buggy era, who listed among his patients Fanny Davenport and Adelaide Phillips, another great actress; and Judge William Thayer, who presided at the Sacco-Vanzetti trial. The murder for which Sacco and Vanzetti were convicted, incidentally, took place directly in front of the *Observer-Press* in South Braintree, years before the *Duxbury Clipper* was printed there.

Over the years there has been frequent mention in the *Clipper* of Bobbie's mother. *Clipper* readers were especially interested in her novel, *The*

Hornbeam Tree, which opens: "There is a village south of Boston not far enough down to be called the Cape, near enough for rather inconvenient commuting, a typical New England village with green-shuttered white houses, and now and then a gray shingled or a barn-red one with tall elms, lilac hedges and the sea."

If there was any doubt that this typical New England town was dear old Duxbury, Olga Owens Huckins of Powder Point, writing in the *Boston Sunday Post*, dispelled it:

> No Duxburyite can go to LaFleur's or Josselyn's General Store [she noted in a book review] without hearing somebody ask, "What page of *The Hornbeam Tree* are you on?" or "After Peggy finishes reading it, can I have it next?" Letters of praise or protest are published in the *Duxbury Clipper*. Mrs. Sumner's travels, her books, her eleven grandchildren, their parents, and all the relatives that come, part and parcel, to visit her by the sea, keep the social and literary columns of the village paper pretty well stuffed all the time.

When it comes to lovers of wildlife, nobody in Duxbury can touch Mr. and Mrs. Stuart Huckins. They fed wasps with an eye-dropper. A red-shouldered hawk, injured on Clark's Island, patiently let Mr. Huckins approach it and treat it before flying off. The *Clipper* reprinted this item from the Audubon Society's Newsletter:

> Mr. and Mrs. Stuart Huckins of Powder Point feed wild skunks in their living room. Says Mr. Huckins, "They're perfectly friendly, and come regularly for their meals, as many as three at a time. . . . Buffy (our cat) has adopted a live-and-let-live attitude toward the skunks, who reciprocate in about the same manner." Mr. Huckins, a friend of the late Rachel Carson, was credited by the author with suggesting the idea that led to Silent Spring. Mrs. Huckins, often finding dead birds on her property after an aerial spray of DDT, wrote Rachel Carson about it.

The late Alison Arnold, long-time society editor of the old *Boston Herald* and later the *Boston Globe*, wrote countless poems and pieces for the *Clipper* and upon retiring became a weekly columnist. Cleveland Amory spent a month researching her files before he wrote *The Proper Bostonians*. When she became a *Clipper* columnist, Stephen Gifford, who had a long Duxbury background, asked me one night at the Winsor House why I let

Alison Arnold write for the *Clipper*: "Why, she's lived here for only fifty years," he said. "What does she know about Duxbury?"

The late Blair McClosky, who had spent fifty years as a concert and opera singer, was one of our good friends. He authored *Your Voice at Its Best* and *Voice in Song and Speech*. Both books have been translated into Japanese. He was once the director of The Plymouth Rock Center of Music and Drama in Duxbury, and he taught the late President Kennedy how to use his voice without straining it.

During the 1960 campaign, when John F. Kennedy was concerned about the daily grind of speaking from dawn to dusk on his whirlwind tours, he enlisted Blair as a voice therapist, inviting him to travel with him and record his talks and criticize his inflection and delivery. The press had no idea of the vocal exercises Blair McClosky prescribed for Kennedy. For example, Kennedy did most of his "barking" when he took one of his hot baths to ease the pain in his back. In my telephone conversation with Dave Power, he told me that the staff wondered about the strange animal sounds coming from the bathroom. "One night I opened the bathroom door to see what was going on, and the boss looked up from the tub, obviously embarrassed. I heard a funny noise and I expected to find a seal in the bathtub!"

"I had an absolute love for that man," McClosky said.

"Sometimes," according to Harold Banks of the Boston *Record-American*, "the Kennedy days were so crowded that the only contact [McClosky] had with him was one of the hand-signs agreed on between them to guide him in the use of his voice. Sometimes McClosky had to give his instructions while Kennedy was simultaneously poring over a speech, talking to one person and listening to another—and taking it all in without missing anything. And sometimes, McClosky had Kennedy to himself for a few minutes."

McClosky picked up one speech left on a lectern in St. Louis on which Kennedy had made notations on some pages. One was "I saw Blair." McClosky had made sure that Kennedy saw him in the audience so the candidate could glance at him for instructions, and McClosky could respond with a hand-sign.

In the 1962 gubernatorial contest in Massachusetts, Candidate Endicott Peabody also went to Blair for help. One old-line Duxbury Yankee thought this was all right, even though he was a Republican and Peabody was a Democrat.

"But why the devil did McClosky help that other fellow?" he asked.

McClosky, an audience of one, was the first to hear Peabody's inaugural address. While Peabody talked, his tutor suggested changes in tone, inflection, cadence, and emphasis.

McClosky, who gave a series of lectures in German in Vienna, Austria, and Professor Holcombe are not the only Duxbury residents who had close ties with the late president.

The only year Jack Kennedy went out for sailing at Harvard, he won the championship. He and his brother Joe, later killed in World War II, were members of the Harvard intercollegiate championship McMillan Club team. One of his five teammates was Edward Hutton of Duxbury, one of our friends and neighbors and a salt who has won many Duxbury sailing championships.

"Harvard used three skippers," Hutton wrote in the 1939 *Harvard Class Album*. "Loring Reid, '40, started the series, then turned the helm over to Joseph P. Kennedy Jr., '38, after scoring two firsts in five races. Kennedy was an able substitute and kept his craft in the money positions for the remainder of the series. The sail trimmers on this boat were N. Horton Batchelder, '39, and Richard Burnett, '40. The other Crimson boat was skippered by John F. Kennedy, '40, whose three second places in the last three races were an important factor in turning back the vain stern chase of Dartmouth and Williams." Handling sails for Captain Kennedy on this boat were James A. Rousmaniere, '40, and Hutton.

The Kennedy brothers, who supplied the boats, were the winning skippers in the regatta held at the Wianno (Massachusetts) Yacht Club. Hutton was shown with the Kennedy brothers and three other teammates in a photograph published in *Yachting* magazine in August 1938.

When I saw the photo I asked Hutton whether he had ever visited the Kennedy compound at Hyannis Port, and he recalled the day he was sitting with Jack and Joe Kennedy Jr., in the living room of their father's house. Ambassador Kennedy had just returned from London. He shook hands with Hutton and left when a friend told him the White House was on the telephone.

Jack Kennedy had other Duxbury ties. One of the medical specialists who attended Patrick Bouvier Kennedy at Children's Hospital in Boston not long before the infant's father was assassinated was Dr. Stewart B. Clifford, a Duxbury resident who was senior pediatrician at the Boston Lying-In Hospital.

John F. Kennedy was no stranger to Duxbury. The president often expressed his admiration for Dr. Arthur Holcombe. The author of one essay in *College in a Yard*, published in 1957, was John F. Kennedy, who referred to Professor Holcombe as "Sower of the Seed."

> I have known many great teachers at Harvard, many who excelled in showing the enchantment of thought to young men who, in this springtime of youth, were more enchanted with life itself. But the one teacher known to generations of Harvard students who stands out in my memory and personal affection is Arthur Holcombe. Under his direction in a course in American Government, I discovered for the first time the distractions of the Congressional Record, as I studied for one term the rise and eventual political extinguishment of an obscure Republican Congressman from upstate New York.
>
> But Professor Holcombe's greatest impact was not in his erudition but in his personality and character. Dispassionate, reserved, self-restrained, without illusions yet persistently idealistic, he was extraordinarily well equipped with qualities and principles to meet his responsibilities as a teacher and as a citizen. He taught and inspired my father. Forty years later he taught and inspired, with equal brilliance, my younger brother. To them, to me, to all his students, he set a standard to which in later life we could repair.

We were familiar with the next incident mentioned, for we had heard Professor Holcombe tell it:

> Shortly after the 1946 election he remarked to me with unconcealed pride: 'I had the pleasure on election day of voting for three of my former students—one for senator, one for governor and one for congressman—and they were all elected!' It did not matter to him that the party labels were different; they had been his students, they were graduates of Harvard, he respected their capabilities and motives—and that was enough.

The senator elected was Leverett Saltonstall; the governor Robert Bradford of Massachusetts. The congressman was Jack Kennedy.

Professor Holcombe, having already taught Joseph P. Kennedy and Joseph Jr., was interested when Jack Kennedy turned up in his classes.

> Like most undergraduates with a prominent background and ample means, he expected more from college than a mere opportunity to get a bachelor's degree. I knew it would be up to me to persuade him to do his best work in my subjects. His record showed he had superior natural intelligence, and, since he did not have to take any courses unless he thought he would be

242

interested in them, I was bound to regard myself as a failure if he did not pass them with distinction.

Although Jack Kennedy graduated cum laude, Professor Holcombe said he could have won higher honors "if he had directed his impressive energy to that end. But he was a young man of exceptional curiosity and resolute independence, both in thought and action, and set his own goals. He got a great deal out of college and thoroughly enjoyed it."

Dr. Arthur Holcombe, former head of the government department at Harvard, was in Switzerland in the summer of 1959 on a UN mission. "I stayed only a week," he told us. "I missed Duxbury too much to remain any longer."

One afternoon while we were watching his grandson Peter Holcombe play tennis against my son Robert, he talked about Jack Kennedy. "Although I gave him a C, I could see that he was an astute student of government," he said.

Another Duxbury resident is James Southwood, who wrote *Torn Lace Curtain*, a book about the Kennedy family in Hyannis Port from the chauffeur's point of view.

Duxbury has long attracted celebrities and still does. Years ago, James Garfield, grandson of President James B. Garfield, also lived in Duxbury. Here is an excerpt from a letter he wrote the *Clipper* in the early 1950s:

> Dr. Marvin Baty sent me a copy of your *Clipper* in which you ask about the houses that my father and I formerly owned in Duxbury. My father, Harry A. Garfield, was president of Williams College. He first lived in the little cottage on King Caesar Road, which is the second house beyond the Old Sailors' Home. Later he sold that house and lived in the house subsequently sold to Dr. Marvin Baty.
>
> My own house, in which we spent ten summers, was recently purchased by Hamilton Edwards of Powder Point Avenue. . . . We loved Duxbury and were sorry when we had to leave it.

Duxbury is no stranger to celebrities such as the late David Patten, who during World War II was a naval technical advisor and operations officer for General Douglas MacArthur, who awarded him the Legion of Merit in Manila. After the war, Patten, one of the nineteen original chiefs of mission appointed by President Truman to administer the Marshall Plan, went to Portugal with the rank of Minister Plenipotentiary. Also, Eugene McAuliffe, former ambassador to Hungary; the late Llewelyn Thompson, ambassador to Russia, who spent a summer on Clark's Island off Duxbury, a favorite spot of Thoreau and Louisa May Alcott.

Charles Coburn, the actor, wore no monocle when he came to Duxbury, which is informal. I have never seen anyone in town wearing a full dress suit.

Jack Sanford, the San Francisco Giants pitcher of World Series fame, told the *Clipper* he bought a home in Duxbury because he liked "breathing space."

A typical feature in the "around town" section of the *Clipper* would often include tidbits such as:

> Sunday cocktail guests of Larue Brown of Duxbury and Beacon Street, Boston, were Eleanor Roosevelt of New York City, and Mr. and Mrs. Hector Holmes of Duxbury.

Another Duxbury resident is John Malcolm Brinnin, a poet, biographer, and social historian who has taught at several universities. His best-known work is *Dylan Thomas in America*, a biography of the Welsh poet. He has also written a biography of Gertrude Stein, whom he knew in Paris. Gertrude Stein used to come to Duxbury as a friend of Dr. Emma Erving. They met at Smith College and went on to Johns Hopkins University together, where they were medical students. Erving finished and went on to practice in Washington, D.C., for twenty-five years. Stein balked at taking a course in obstetrics, as she felt that subject was not for women. She left in her junior year for literary fields. She was a frequent visitor at Erving's house during the summers of the 1920s.

Truman Capote, like Llewelyn Thompson, spent a summer on Clark's Island, which is a short outboard-motor ride from Duxbury. Both Thompson and Capote occasionally came ashore to shop in Duxbury.

One morning, Bobbie met Capote in Josselyn's Variety Store. Unlike others who gawked at Capote in awe, Bobbie identified herself and said, "I wish you would drop in this afternoon for tea." Capote, in a diffident way, declined. When Bobbie told me about the incident, I said, "You should have invited him over for a double martini. I'm sure he would have accepted."

In John Malcolm Brinnin's biography *Truman Capote: Dear Heart, Old Buddy*, Capote is quoted making a disparaging remark about Duxbury. Brinnin recounts a conversation with Capote in 1958 in which Capote discusses his plans to spend the summer on an island off Massachusetts to finish writing his latest book.

When Brinnin inquires whether the island is Nantucket or the Vineyard, Capote responds, "I wouldn't be caught dead on either one of them. It has to be a place where I can be alone, not a literary ant farm." Brinnin told Capote there weren't any other islands off Massachusetts "unless you mean that string of little ones the Forbes family keeps to itself."

Capote disagreed. "But there is. The only people there are some rich Philadelphia hillbillies who come for the summer and guard it like moon-shiners—except for this one house I'm getting through a friend." Capote was referring to Clark's Island, which is a part of Plymouth.

When Brinnin asks what part of Massachusetts it is near, Capote says, "A little absolute noplace called Duxbury. That's where I'll have to go in an outboard . . . for even so much as a paper clip or a can of soup."

Brinnin sums up his impressions of Clark's Island and Duxbury:

> Unconvinced, I thought no more about this 'little absolute noplace' until I bought a house there and realized that there was another island 'off Massachusetts.' Across the bay on which my windows looked, Clark's Island was the looming mass of green where, in 1620, the passengers of the *Mayflower* had held their first religious service in the new world and where, in 1958, Truman had served up *Breakfast at Tiffany's*.

Another distinguished resident was Dr. George Gardner, who received an award as the top child psychiatrist in the United States. He was head of the Judge Baker Foundation and a Harvard Professor (a chair has been named in his honor), who wrote many articles on Old Colony history, including a series on the psychological problems of the Pilgrims. His book, *The Emerging Personality: Infancy through Adolescence*, is a guideline for child psychologists.

The *Clipper* interviewed and profiled Dr. Charlotte Douglas of Edinburgh, Scotland, former Director of Child Welfare in Scotland. She stopped in Duxbury on her way home from a medical conference in Manila, and went on to spend a week with former Governor and Mrs. Sumner Sewall of Maine. Her Duxbury host was Bobbie's mother.

Ruth and Kenneth Wakefield, who owned the renowned Toll House Inn in nearby Whitman, Massachusetts, and who invented the all-famous Toll House Cookie, were among the stimulating residents of Duxbury. When the restaurant first opened in the days of prohibition, there were so many cars that the State Police suspected that liquor was being served surreptitiously. The Wakefields could tell stories about such guests as

Duncan Hines, Viscount and Lady Astor, and no end of dignitaries. The Wakefields were away the night undercooked chicken was served to Jack and Jacqueline Kennedy, who stopped on their way to Hyannis Port. When, on their next visit, Ken Wakefield expressed his regrets, JFK said he had forgotten the incident.

Here is a sequel to an incident I wrote about in *Put It On the Front Page, Please!* It concerned Sir Robert H. K. Marett, the former British Ambassador of Peru. Years ago, the *Clipper* scored a beat on all Boston dailies when it reported that "Mr. Marett was the new British Consul General in Boston." There were polite denials from embassy circles in Boston, and one angry denial from a friend of the diplomat who told us we "should check official sources before printing such rubbish." Ten days after we printed the item in the *Clipper*, radio and press confirmed the appointment of the new consul general.

We had received news of the appointment from Marett's sister, Mrs. Walter Prince, one of our Washington Street neighbors. On a June day in 1964, Mrs. Prince told us she had received a letter from her brother. It read in part:

> Just in case the news failed to get into the *Duxbury Clipper*, you ought to know that your little brother has been elevated to a knighthood, KCMG. The initials stand for Knight Commander of the Order of Michael and St. George.

Chapter Twenty-nine
SHE CAN DO ANYTHING

"Before marriage this question should be put," said Nietzsche: "Will you continue to be satisfied with this woman's conversation until old age? Everything else in marriage is transitory." And James Batcheller Sumner, Bobbie's father, had this advice: "Take the woman you want to marry on a camping trip before you propose to her. If she can take it, she'll be a good wife."

Bobbie passes both tests. In 1990, when Bobbie was seventy-three, a fortune teller could have peered into her palm and said: "Honey, you ain't done livin' yet." (This is what a palm reader told Bobbie's mother in 1956, when she was sixty-seven.)

In the almost fifty years of our marriage, I am continually amazed by the things Bobbie can do. She will try almost anything. In the fortieth anniversary issue of the *Clipper*, in 1990, Maureen Brown wrote an enlightening piece on Bobbie. Here are a few excerpts:

> She is quieter and more solitary next to John's more outgoing nature and has artistic talent that he claims barely to be able to comprehend. "She can do anything," he says with pride.
> Bobbie has hand sewn quilts and smocked little girls' dresses. She does woodworking to make mirrors and clocks, then decorates them with colorful paints. She does reverse painting on glass and rebuilds and stencils frames. She buys antique straight-back chairs and dips and recanes them, then paints or stencils them. She knows needlework and has done silkscreening and stained-glass work. And she paints dummy boards, those eye-fooling suggestions of someone at home that early Americans would prop up in their windows.
> Bobbie's studio is at the top of a converted watertower onto which the Cutlers' Surplus St. house is built. The room is reachable only by a flight of steep shallow stairs and is circular, with windows all around that let in uninterrupted daylight. The day I visited, there was a dollhouse with some tiny furnishings Bobbie had made, and further evidence of her projects—old breadboards she is painting with scenes taken from antique postcards (the

Clipper's offices have more than a dozen hanging on the walls), a tin tray she has almost finished painting in tendrilly gold against matte black.

Asked about the gift of artistic ability, she told me, "If you can do one thing, you can do a number of things. It's a matter of manual dexterity and patience." She speaks almost so as to demystify what she does, and to give implicit encouragement to others at the same time.

Bobbie can afford to be quiet about her work since the Cutler house expresses it so well. Even casual glances around the living room, dining room, and kitchen, with its little greenhouse attached, reveal her achievements, piece by finished piece. A straight chair she dipped, caned, and painted decoratively in subtle colors sits modestly in the dining room—a tip-top table won first prize at the Duxbury Art Association exhibition last year.

Painted trays hang on several walls along with valuable and valued heirloom paintings (including one of Bobbie at four, done when her father was doing research in Brussels for a year). Crewelwork pillows fill out a windowseat, and baskets she wove hang among acquired ones from the kitchen ceiling. Her collection of dolls from other countries lies in a rustic cradle next to the fireplace, which is an enormous, true hearth, and about thirty tiny cast iron pots, pans, and kettles line the mantel.

It is also a house of and for readers—a step-ladder is needed to reach the topmost bookshelves, which make up entire walls. Bobbie reads novels and short stories and especially admires Somerset Maugham, F. Scott Fitzgerald, and Ernest Hemingway. She also pores over recipes from the more than one hundred cookbooks that fill her kitchen shelves. An excellent cook, she keeps up with culinary trends and is expert at old stand-bys as well. She indeed did all of the cooking for John's seventieth birthday party, for seventy guests. . . .

"Some people buy expensive automobiles or fur coats, but I'd rather travel," Bobbie says. She and John have been to Russia, Eastern Europe, most continental capitals, Africa, Brazil—but Norway and Sweden remain to be seen. . . .

Visits with Bobbie come to a close graciously. A lively listener and hostess, helped by her husband and their poodle, François Villon, neither of whom wanders far from her. Her bright eyes don't hint that she may have more yet to do before day's end. People seem to take priority. That's no surprise to her friends and neighbors—to all of Duxbury—for it was the townspeople's doings and the workings of town government that first inspired her to take financial and other risks to put out the paper. That interest was present at the *Clipper*'s beginnings and has been essential among its various underpinnings ever since. The happy result for Duxbury for four decades has been a strong paper that continues to contribute to the town's identity and is an emblem of pride for all who live here.

Chapter Thirty
A TEMPORARY SETBACK

In 1979 I met retired Superior Court Judge Frank J. Donohue at the Harvard Club. Early in his career he had been a political reporter for the *Boston Post*, and he knew James Michael Curley intimately. I had written in *Honey Fitz* that Donohue, "as chairman of the Democratic State Committee in 1928, had been well aware of all efforts made in support of Al Smith for the Presidency. He implied that Mayor Curley's interest in Smith was insincere, prompted only by a wish to use Smith to his own personal advantage. He accused Curley, on the final night of the campaign, of having refused to take the stump for Smith."

As I entered the dining room, Judge Donohue called me over to his table. "I have read all your books on the history of the early Irish in America," he said, "including *I'd Do It Again!*, *Honey Fitz*, and your biography of Cardinal Cushing. You did a good job on *I'd Do It Again!*, but there is a lot more to the Curley story. You ought to write a more complete biography of the man. I think you're the only writer still around who could do it."

I had great respect for Judge Donohue, whom I had interviewed and frequently mentioned in my political writing. I decided then and there that my next project would be my own biography of Curley.

After several months of research, I had gathered a great deal of additional information about Curley. Particularly helpful to me was the late Francis X. Moloney, when he was assistant librarian at the Boston Public Library. Moloney gave me a key to a private cubicle in an obscure corner of the main library. It was a windowless room containing a wealth of information about Curley, some of which Moloney had obtained by taping conversations with people who had information about Curley. A few tapes were of domestics who had once worked in the Curley household in Jamaica Plain.

One morning, after spending a few hours in the cubicle, I walked from the Boston Public Library to the Commonwealth Avenue Harvard Club, where I had parked my car. As I approached Massachusetts Avenue, I suddenly felt dizzy and my right arm was growing numb. As I drove to

Duxbury, steering with my left hand, the car wobbled. I wondered whether I was having a stroke. When I pulled into the parking lot at the *Clipper* office, I came in at an odd angle and almost hit the building. Bobbie rushed out. She had warned me that morning not to drive to Boston as she had suspected something was wrong with me, but I had insisted. Only the night before, a glass I held in my right hand had fallen. That morning I could not shave easily, and at the *Clipper* office, I found I could not type. Nevertheless, I went to Boston.

Now Bobbie knew something was wrong, but she did not know what, and neither did I. She said, "We are going over to the emergency ward at Jordan Hospital." She went to the check-in desk. "I think my husband is having a stroke." A nurse quickly brought a wheelchair and wheeled me into one of the emergency sections where my blood pressure was taken and a cardiograph given. It was a slight stroke. Dr. Leslie asked me who my doctor was and when I told her she said he no longer had privileges at the hospital. Bobbie gave her the name of her doctor (Samuel Stewart, M.D.) who was chief of the medical staff. I was taken to a room and found I could not use my right arm or my right leg at all. My speech was so slurred I could not be understood. I felt that my life was over. Days went by and my speech returned. I was told after two weeks that I was being transferred to a rehabilitation hospital in Braintree. I felt so weak I cried.

When the day came to go to the Braintree Hospital, I called Bobbie. "Let's have lunch somewhere on the way." She came for me and said, "Why not go home for lunch?" She fixed me a martini, which cheered me up a bit, and after lunch we drove to Braintree Hospital. Tests followed for two weeks. I was getting stronger every day and learning to walk again. "You cannot leave until you can walk," the doctor said. I would wheel myself to the TV room, but it was full of old folks watching programs I didn't care for. I often wheeled myself onto a porch and sat enjoying the sunshine. Finally, I was able to walk about the grounds by myself and was discharged. That was a happy day for me and for Bobbie, who had been running the *Clipper* by herself.

Gradually I worked myself back into the routine of the *Clipper*. I had difficulty dictating editorials because I was not used to it. I had learned to type in my old Sixth Army Corps days and was quite proficient until I had the stroke.

I had to give up the Curley project. In my frustration, I wrote *Tips on Writing* with the help of my old friend Monroe Stearns. I dictated the first draft of the eighty-one page booklet. Monroe wrote the introduction:

In August 1948 the authors met at the Breadloaf Writers Conference, where, under the guidance of the professional writers on the faculty, they hoped to become better writers. They have been close friends ever since, even though each has from time to time been merciless in his criticism of the other's work and although each has occasionally employed the other. . . .

They conceived this book as a guide for writers by writers. It is a catalogue of those sins of literary expression, with recommendations and sometimes commands to help all writers avoid them, correct them, and structure their prose so that it will be concise, clear, colorful communication.

In the June 14, 1982, issue of the *Publisher's Auxiliary,* Harry Heath wrote the following review:

Those of the Strunk and White generation probably won't give this one a second look, but it's worth more than a glance. Subtitled: "A Sound, Engaging Guide to Writing." The authors have constructed a handy tool for those seeking to practice journalistic skills.

Monroe and I had no delusions of replacing Strunk and White. *Elements of Style* was primarily written for adults. *Tips on Writing* was intended primarily for high school and college students. The book, although it never gained wide acceptance, was used by students at Brooklyn College and at Wheelock College, in Boston. Among the few high schools to buy the book was, of course, Duxbury High School.

To date, three thousand copies have been sold.

In August 1980 Channel Seven, a Massachusetts television station, aired a special titled *Mayor Curley's Boston.* A television crew, including the producer, director, and two cameramen, came to Duxbury to interview me for the special. Several years later, I also appeared on a segment of the *American Experience* series that focused on James Michael Curley. The title of this show was "The Irish in America."

Then came disaster.

As I have said, our son John's death is something we shall never get over. Not a day goes by that we don't think of him or that something doesn't remind us of him.

One day in the summer of 1989, I spent the morning happily at the *Clipper* office. One of our realtors came in and said, "Here is the only house in Duxbury for under $100,000." I said to Bobbie, "Let's go see it. It might be a good investment." It wasn't much of a house and was in a neighborhood called "mosquito village," because of the shanty-like houses there. But many had been fixed up, and the neighborhood was improving. "We'll think about it," we told the realtor, and returned to the office.

Bobbie and I went out to lunch in Hanover, to a place Bobbie hated to go, for the drinks were too strong. For no reason, I became distraught on the way home, rebuking Bobbie for no apparent reason, and when I got back to the office I was annoyed with everyone. I called my son David and started giving him hell about something of no importance. Bobbie left to go grocery shopping, and I went home. When she came back to the office, she asked one of the staff where I was and was told I had gone home. I think she hesitated about going home because of the mood I was in. But she did come home and found me sitting by the pool, just outside our kitchen, with a drink.

I was sitting at a table, and I started thinking about Ricky. In fact, every time we sit there I think of all the wonderful hours we had spent at cookouts around the pool when he came home, usually bringing a friend. Often it had been Laura, to whom he was devoted, and we always had a nice time. Bobbie brought out food for the dog and went back into the house.

To this day, I cannot remember any of this. Bobbie, who had started cooking supper, happened to look out the kitchen door. To her horror she saw me lying at the bottom of the pool, in the deep end. Realizing she could do nothing to save me, she ran to the phone to call the fire department. She told me later she said, "Please come quickly, my husband is lying at the bottom of the pool, hurry, hurry!" Within minutes, they were there: the rescue truck, the ambulance, and several men. Two young firemen jumped into the pool and brought me to the surface, placed me on a stretcher, and rushed me to Jordan Hospital, giving me CPR all the way.

Bobbie jumped into her car and followed. I was in the emergency room when she arrived, and the doctor on duty called her aside into a private room. "You can't do anything in there. I must talk to you. Do you know he had a weight tied around his neck?" she said. Bobbie was aghast. Soon they carried me to intensive care, where I remained for two weeks in a coma. Bobbie had called David and he came quickly. My own doctor, soon on the scene, took Bobbie and David into a small room where he explained that I might not come out of the coma and that if I did, I might be completely gone mentally. Would it be better if they stopped all life-saving apparatus? What should they do? David and Bobbie both said that they felt I would not want to live without my brain and told the doctor to do what he felt best. But for the next two weeks, although I did not know where I was or why, I must have kept improving. I had wild dreams and later thought they had actually happened.

The day came when my doctor came in and said, "Do you know me?" I told him his name and from that day on, kept improving and was moved into a private room.

A few weeks of therapy followed at a nearby rehabilitation hospital. After a few more weeks of out-patient therapy I was as good as new, but I still don't understand what happened to me that day.

Chapter Thirty-one
CLIPPER CONTRADICTIONS

In a long writing career I have been called a historian, contemporary political biographer, and a country editor. Today I think of myself primarily as the editor of a weekly for one of the most delightful residential communities in the United States. We have no smoke stacks, no four-story buildings, no malls, and no serious traffic gridlocks.

Weekly newspapering is reputedly an exacting chore, but I find it absorbing, fulfilling, and an exciting challenge, because the product of the *Clipper* is laid before a critical public and is subject to careful analysis. Duxbury, a town of almost sixteen thousand residents, includes at least three retired college presidents, several present and past college professors, bankers, topflight stockbrokers, several retired admirals and generals, and realtors—one, the late Joseph Lund, was a former president of the National Association of Real Estate Boards. (Lund, a noted amateur ornithologist, also wrote a popular bird column for the *Clipper.*) We have eminent authors and so many distinguished physicians that Duxbury was once known as the summer medical capital of New England. Brilliant lawyers are attracted to Duxbury. The collective readership adds to the lure of weekly editing.

Professor John H. Casey, a recognized authority on journalism, suggested an answer to the lure when he taught journalism at the University of Oklahoma:

> Without its newspaper, the small-town American community would be like a school without a teacher or a church without a pastor. In the aggregate, the country newspaper determines the outcome of more elections, exerts a great influence for constructive community progress, is read longer by more members of the family, and constitutes with its millions of circulation and quadrupled millions of readers, a better advertising medium than any other group of newspapers or periodical publications.
>
> When properly conducted, it cultivates so intensively its home news field that city dailies, farm journals and general magazines circulating in the same territory become only secondary.

Here in Duxbury, Bobbie and I enjoy living in a vibrant, friendly, growing community and sharing its pleasures and pain with people who are for the most part good neighbors. It gave us confidence when a person like William Allen White—once one of President Franklin Delano Roosevelt's favorite weekly newspaper editors, wrote: "The country newspaper is the incarnation of the town spirit. A newspaper is as honest as its town and as intelligent as its town, as kind as its town, as brave as its town."

During our early struggles with the *Clipper*, it also encouraged us to hear Walter Williams, when he was dean of the Missouri School of Journalism, say: "When I get through with this job, I'm going to get me a weekly newspaper somewhere, and be a country editor again. There's more fun in it than in any other thing I know."

Over the years Bobbie and I have read widely of the increasing value of weeklies. Today most public libraries, large and small, acknowledge the value of a file of the local weekly. The Duxbury Free Library has microfilmed and indexed the *Duxbury Clipper*. Listen to what our local librarian says:

> The country weekly newspaper also affects and supplements work done by all other institutions. It has a much larger congregation than the combined churches in its community. There is no community activity or institution which is not in some way served by, or is not in some way dependent on, the local paper.

Bobbie and I agree that it is the peculiar flavor of Duxbury that makes our job so much fun. We recall in the early 1960s that one of the shelter magazines listed Duxbury among the ten best residential communities in the United States. The list included Rockport and Camden, Maine; Americus, Georgia; Carmel, California; and Natchez, Mississippi.

A weekly newspaper must be parochial and relentlessly local to succeed. It must be published in a vibrant community, because if it is to be a bright mirror there must be sparkle to be reflected. All your wit, humor, subtlety, and wisdom would be wasted on listless readers. "A book," said C. G. Lichtenberg, "is a mirror; if an ass peers into it, you cannot expect an apostle to look out." A weekly newspaper is a mirror, too. It is also the first draft of history.

A successful country editor must do what he thinks is the greatest good for the greatest number, as Jeremy Bentham wrote in 1857. He must always keep in mind that what is good for the swarm is good for the bee. In a growing community especially, and more especially in a town like Duxbury, which prides itself on its rural charm, he must support proposals that add to its ambience. There are four particular areas in which the *Duxbury Clipper* has helped the community.

The Town of Duxbury today owns more protected open space and conservation land than any other community in Massachusetts. Duxbury was the first town in the Commonwealth to adopt a wetland enactment. It was one of the first communities to adopt equitable zoning requirements and a building code. It was the first town in the nation, according to a 1973 issue of *House and Home*, to enact impact zoning.

One Sunday afternoon in November of 1971, five civic-minded citizens gathered in our living room. The group included the moderator, the chairman and one other member of the planning board, one selectman, and the town counsel. At the time, impact zoning was an idea waiting to happen. There was some question as to whether the town would accept the radical change at the annual town meeting in March. We decided to launch a massive educational campaign in the *Clipper* during the following few months.

House and Home featured Duxbury in the December issue of 1973 and based its editorial on what happened. Here are a few excerpts from the *House and Home* editorial:

> *H & H* Associate Editor Natalie Gerardi tells why and how Duxbury adopted a new bylaw based on impact zoning in this issue. Her story—"The town that said 'no' to no-growth"—is heartening for a number of reasons:
>
> Partly because it shows that citizens of all stripes can face reality and then compromise their differences for the common good. Even the people who worked the hardest to develop the new bylaw and to get it passed would have preferred no-growth, reports Ms. Gerardi. But they knew growth was inevitable and the best they could do was to direct it on Duxbury's terms.

A few excerpts from the illustrated *House and Home* article:

> When the opening of a new expressway drew historic Duxbury, Massachusetts, into Boston's commuting orbit, the 345-year-old town was suddenly confronted with two typical suburban problems: growing tax rates and shrinking open space.
>
> But, Duxbury, which already had one-acre zoning, rejected the usual no-growth panaceas and decided instead to take a closer look at its land and its goals. The upshot was a new zoning bylaw—the first in the nation to be

based on impact zoning—in which the town set up the machinery to sit down and negotiate with developers.

Far from no-growth, Duxbury's new bylaw actually encouraged higher densities—provided that the developer sets aside open space and provided he can prove that the taxes from his project will offset its cost to the town in schools and services. Here is how it came about. . . .

An inset showed Bobbie and me in the *Clipper* office. The caption read: "Newspaper editors John and Roberta Cutler gave the new bylaw a big push with articles and editorials in the weekly *Duxbury Clipper*. 'Without them we wouldn't have had a snowball's chance of success,' says John Rahenkamp."

The town meeting that discussed impact zoning convened on a Saturday, but the new bylaw did not come up until Monday night. The vote finally came Thursday night. "In between were eleven hours of debate. It was touch and go all the way."

The *Clipper* helped put through the concept of impact zoning, but it was Edmund Dondero, a selectman at the time, who clinched the narrow victory. He made a five-minute speech in which he said, "Duxbury has been the best kept secret on the South Shore. . . . To keep it the way it is, we need new tools. . . . Impact zoning will give us those tools." He received a two-minute standing ovation.

It was one of the longest debates on any issue in the history of Duxbury Town Meeting, with formidable speakers on both sides, including Charles Davis, president of Stone and Webster, who vehemently opposed impact zoning. The bylaw required a two-thirds vote for approval. The actual count was 517 to 214.

Natalie Gerardi, who wrote the article, spent her first night in Duxbury at our house. At the end of her seven-page illustrated piece she wrote: "And the people of Duxbury, those who were for the bylaw and those who were against it, agree on one thing: They want it to work."

And it has worked.

At the annual meeting of the Duxbury Rural and Historical Society in 1980, Cecil Atwater paid us an unexpected compliment: "In the history of Duxbury there are four persons who have most influenced the Town of Duxbury. They are Myles Standish, Nathaniel Noyes, Percy Walker, and John Cutler." (By "John Cutler," of course, Mr. Atwater meant the *Duxbury Clipper*.)

Chapter Thirty-two
TRAVELS WITH BOBBIE

Bobbie has always had a yen for traveling. When the children were small we had no money or time, but as they grew older and left home, we have traveled at least three times a year.

Our first trip was a week in London and a week in Paris. In London, in 1960, we stayed at a hotel near the Marble Arch. In Paris we stayed at a lovely small hotel, the Louvois, with a pretty little square just outside, near the Opera House. We often would buy a bottle of wine, some cheese, and bread and have lunch in our room. Across the way we could see women ironing with those old-fashioned triangular irons that had to be heated on a stove at intervals. We often dined at a nearby restaurant where for twenty-three francs we had a full-course meal with wine. (Years later we returned to the same restaurant to find the price quadrupled and the food not so good.) We went to the follies to see the topless dancers, saw some of the sights, and had a great time.

The next trip came a few years later, when our son Ricky was eleven. That summer Francis Russell, a classmate and an author, and his fiancée of twenty came on a picnic with us to Saquish Beach in Plymouth in our Boston Whaler, piloted by Ricky. Francis told us of a Harvard trip due in the fall—a two hundred dollar round-trip air fare to Brussels. We signed up and took Ricky along.

Starting in Brussels, we went to Coblenz by train, down the Rhine for a day, sipping German beer and eating while listening to the Lorelei on the loudspeaker as we passed treacherous rocks. I was annoyed at the waiter who brought us a whole duck instead of the German fare we wanted. We docked near Frankfurt, Germany, for a night.

Next morning we left for Switzerland. In Lucerne we stayed at a lovely inn with excellent food. Then to Italy, Venice, and Florence, the Leaning Tower of Pisa, where Ricky and I climbed the winding steps, leaving Bobbie at a sidewalk cafe below. When we got down Ricky said, "Look Dad, we didn't quite get to the top. Let's go back." But I had had enough.

In Rome we stayed at the Hotel de Ville on the Via Sistina and toured the city. Bobbie's brother Ted lived in Rome with his wife, Sarah, and three daughters. Not realizing the value of a lira, Bobbie tipped the taxi driver only three lire (a fraction of a cent) when he drove them to Ted's apartment one night for supper. Ricky earlier had proudly handled money, figuring out the exchange, but when it came to lire, he was puzzled. "Dad, why do they use so many thousands of lire?" That trip ended in Paris, and again we stayed near the Opera House, so we got to know that neighborhood well.

Of course, we traveled in this country also, especially when our daughter Gail went to All Saints' Episcopal School in Vicksburg, Mississippi, where her mother had gone for two years. We took Ricky with us. We often stopped to see Bobbie's Uncle John Ricketts, in Greenville, South Carolina. He was a perfect southern gentleman. We dropped in on him one Saturday morning, when he was not planning to go to his law office downtown. He came to the door at seven-thirty in the morning fully dressed, with stiff collar, tie, and coat.

After that, our trips abroad were more frequent. One was a Harvard-sponsored trip to Athens with Robert and our neighbors, the Edward Huttons, along. Also, we spent eight days in Romania, first in Brazoff, then in Bucharest. Romania is a dreary place, and if you see anyone smiling, you can bet he is a tourist. One night in a hotel bar, I said to a young man sitting next to me, "You're the first person in Bucharest whom I have seen smiling." His smile widened. "Next week," he said, "I am going to San Francisco to get married to an American girl. We will live in California."

Even police officers had an apprehensive, almost frightened demeanor. One morning I saw two brown-uniformed police officers standing in a doorway in Bucharest. On an impulse I said, "What are you doing here—get to work." To my amazement, they hurried off in different directions. Maybe they thought I was a commissar or one of Ceausescu's secret agents.

We stayed in one of the best hotels in Bucharest, but when I asked for ice to be sent up to the room, I was told it was "impossivel." Robert bought a pack of cigarettes in the lobby and had to cross a busy street to buy matches.

On a rainy Sunday morning, Robert and I took a walk and were amazed to see an unkempt, shawled old woman sweeping gutters with a broom made of a stick with tree branches attached to it. When Bobbie and I went into a store to buy a rug, the only employee we could find was a sullen and dowdy-looking woman sitting at her desk who refused to unroll any rugs. Why should she? She had no incentive to make a sale.

That afternoon we went to the Intercontinental Hotel, a few blocks away, and sat in a dark lounge for a drink. Suddenly we heard a voice—

259

"John Henry Cutler." It was Charles Armey, a friend from Duxbury, who was in Bucharest setting up a shoe factory. It was a profitable venture because labor was so cheap there. Armey invited us to lunch at the hotel the following day. He advised us to order spaghetti with plenty of butter. During lunch there was a commotion in the hall. In came Marvin Kalb leading a retinue of reporters. "Where is Henry Kissinger?" I asked, knowing he was expected. "He's staying at some other place," Kalb said.

Robert accompanied us on our next trip to Vienna, Austria. We took with us a recent *Gourmet* magazine, which had recommended the best restaurants in Vienna. The waiter at The Three Hussars said we were sitting at the same table where Robert Kennedy and Pierre Salinger had sat a few months earlier. We could walk back to our hotel from the restaurant through one of many beautiful parks in Vienna. On Sunday we visited three churches, including the famed St. Stephen's Cathedral. We also enjoyed a wonderful performance of the Lippizaner Horses in a hippodrome.

Our room wasn't ready when we arrived the first morning at our hotel, so we had to wait in the lobby. I went around the corner to buy a bottle of soda water and stuffed it in my raincoat pocket. Reentering the lobby I dropped my raincoat and the exploding bottle sounded exactly like a gunshot. All over the lobby doors opened and frightened-looking clerks came out. One employee rushed over as if to arrest me until I showed him the shattered pieces of glass. I was asked to pay ten shillings to clean up the mess.

A trip to Sicily with Robert and Ricky was fun. We stayed at the Torre Normana Hotel just outside of Palermo, where an elevator took you down to a beach. One day Bobbie and I went off on a tour to Cefalo and wandered into a jewelry store. She bought a necklace of blue stones, and the clerk handed her a ring with the same stone. She admired it and thought it went with the necklace. We handed him our American Express card, signed it, and wandered down the street, stopping in shops here and there before getting on the bus to go to a restaurant where they cooked pizza over an open fire and served delicious wine with it. Suddenly in came the clerk of the jewelry store with two carabinieri. Pointing at us, the clerk spoke so fast in Italian I could hardly make out what he said. "These people are thieves. Arrest them." He pointed to the ring on Bobbie's finger. We were both bewildered since we thought the ring had been paid for. Everyone stared at us. We gave back the ring. That evening, we walked down the steep hill to a bar for a drink. Given a modicum of vodka in a large glass, I complained, whereupon the clerk took the vodka bottle and practically emptied it into my glass. I left most of it in the glass.

Occasionally we traveled in the U.S., once to lovely Sanibel, Florida, for two weeks, and once to Daytona Beach, where we exchanged houses with a former Duxbury teacher. We could drive our car right onto the beach and have sandwiches for lunch.

I like cruises, because you unpack for a week or two and can do nothing or take part in everything that is offered. One of our favorite trips was to the Greek Islands. We went on the *Navarino*, a beautiful ship that touched on many islands, including Crete. We made friends with a charming lady and her granddaughter Jill, from San Francisco. She later sent us a book she had written, *San Francisco, Martinis, and Me*, in which she described memories of the earthquake. In Dubrovnik, Yugoslavia, we toured in a new Mercedes, the driver eagerly accepting a drink we offered him in one hotel. He said, "The next drink is on me." So we stopped. We were frightened as he drove faster and faster around cliffs with no barriers. "I drive better when I have a drink," he said. We were happy to get out finally, safe and sound.

Another trip to the Greek Islands, with Ricky along, started in Mount Sunion at a seaside hotel. We had a small cottage on a hill and he had to bring me dinner every night as I could not manage the climbing down and back to the dining hall.

Next, we went to Athens aboard the *Orion* for an island cruise. There weren't many passengers on board until we got to Israel where many Jews boarded. At dinner, they put on their yarmulkes and held a religious ceremony, so we all had to wait to be served. In Jerusalem, we saw the sights, and Ricky was most impressed with the Wailing Wall, where Jews put written prayers in the cracks. At one church, the guide said, "The Last Supper was held here and Christ sat over there." Exactly how did he know? We stopped in Egypt, of course, and drove to Giza to see the pyramids. Ricky promptly started to climb one. An Arab kept motioning him to descend and he, thinking it was against the rules, came down. All the Arab wanted was for him to take a camel ride, which he did, while Bobbie and I laughed at his antics. In the hotel for lunch, as we had been warned not to drink water or uncooked vegetables, we ordered a bottle of soda, saying, "Bring it and open it here." The bus ride back to the ship was interminable, especially as one bus broke down and we had to take its occupants aboard our bus, crowding us. Finally the cruise came to an end, and we stayed in a hotel in Athens for a few days, saw the sights, tried to find our Duxbury friend, John McCaig, and finally came home.

Bobbie and I also took a cruise in the Western Mediterranean, stopping at Majorca, where we called an old friend, Billy Walker, only to find he was in the U.S. We stopped in Palermo, Naples, Genoa, and spent a few days at the magnificent Loew's Hotel in Monaco, where we of course lost money at the famous casino. Then on to Madrid, where dinner is not served until 10 P.M., and home again.

Bobbie and I have been on many Caribbean cruises. The Royal Caribbean Cruise Line is our favorite because of its Norwegian cleanliness, wonderful food, and creature comforts. We have touched on most of the islands in the Caribbean. Our most recent trip was on their ship, the *Viking Serenade*, which took us up the inland passage to Alaska. Bobbie, being more daring than I (she takes after her mother, whose philosophy was "when you are old . . . go ahead and be bold."), went up in a helicopter, landed on a glacier, and boarded a four-passenger plane for a couple of hours on a sightseeing tour of the mountains and glaciers.

We have been going to Bermuda every April for many years and return to The Reefs in Southampton, our favorite small resort on a lovely private beach with gourmet food and absolutely nothing to do unless we want to. Bobbie usually takes along canvases and acrylics and sits on the beach for hours painting the rocks, sea, and sky.

During the past ten years, our travels have included four river trips. On one we traveled on the Rhine River from Amsterdam, Holland, to Strasbourg, France. We were amazed to find that the Rhine River in one place was only six feet deep, which explains the flatbottom ships.

Our most fascinating river trip was from Belem, Brazil, a thousand miles up the Amazon River to Manaos. It is a fabulous city with wide paved avenues, public gardens, parks, and monuments of architectural art, all built from the proceeds of rubber.

During the lush days of the rubber boom in Brazil, one of the four-flushing barons of that era built a fountain in the patio of his swank villa—a fountain that gushed champagne when he was entertaining. This unexampled bit of vulgar display occurred just before World War I at a time when the multimillionaires of Manaos spent forty million dollars to build docks and wharfs, and another five million dollars to build an opera house. The opera house attracted such stars as Scotti and Galla Curci at a time when the trip up the Amazon took eleven days by side-wheeler from Belem. Bobbie and I toured the opera house, which I had heard so much about during my Naval service in Brazil.

This "Teatro Amazonas" was built in this tropical Babylon in 1896. It is a gaudy structure modeled on the Opera House of Paris. Anna Pavlova received a thousand dollars per performance for appearing before the rubber barons and their ladies. Metro-Goldwyn-Mayer for a time contemplated transposing the Teatro into a movie house, but changed its mind when the rubber boom collapsed.

Another river trip took us on the *Mississippi Queen* from New Orleans to Vicksburg, where Bobbie hired a car to go to All Saints' Episcopal School, where she was warmly greeted by the faculty. Of all the river trips we took, one poignant incident remains in my memory.

When our ship docked at Nikopol, Bulgaria, I walked a couple miles along a narrow dusty road lined with ramshackle business establishments. On the way I saw a grizzled old man bumping along the road in a donkey cart, a familiar scene in Communist countries like Bulgaria.

On my way back I passed a Bulgarian youth who appeared to be about fourteen or fifteen years old. I nodded pleasantly to him and kept walking. Now and then I looked back and saw him standing in the same spot where I had first seen him, and as I continued to head back toward the ship, he remained in the same place with a look of wonderment on his face as if I were some kind of specter. Was he thinking that I came from a world he would never know? Would he, when he grew old, be driving a donkey cart in some cheerless run-down neighborhood?

For me, it was the most touching moment of the whole trip—one that still remains in my memory.

Chapter Thirty-three
AWARDS AND REWARDS

The *Duxbury Clipper* was launched on May 11, 1950. On May 16, 1990, it observed its fortieth anniversary with a 104-page edition that included selected historical excerpts from the *Clipper* over the years.

At the Annual Town Meeting on April 28, 1990, Town Moderator Allen Bornheimer took time before lunch to honor the Duxbury Free Library in its centennial year and also to honor the *Clipper* in its fortieth. Bobbie and I received standing ovations before and after remarks made by the Reverend Canon Robert Merry, who presented us with a resolution.

Bobbie told the assembly that the *Clipper* would not be the *Clipper* if it were published in any other town. I quoted Yogi Berra, who told fans at Yankee Stadium on his retirement: "Thank you for making this occasion necessary."

The May 16, 1990, edition of the *Clipper* reported:

Two Duxbury "institutions" were honored with special birthday celebrations on Friday, May 11, highlighted by musical tributes from the eighty-five member Duxbury High School band.

School Superintendent Donald Kennedy personally organized the special tributes complete with invited guests, birthday cakes, and renditions of "Happy Birthday" and the "Thunderer."

The yellow school bus pulled up at the *Clipper* office on South Station Street at 9:45 A.M. Editors and publishers John and Roberta Cutler were invited outside and were greeted by about 130 people and applause from town officials and old friends.

Kennedy escorted Roberta to a small podium and handed her a "straw hat," asking her if she had ever skydived, taken a ride in a hot air balloon, or led a brass band. He handed her the baton. "Now you have an opportunity to conduct a band."

The Reverend Merry, Leo Egan and Jack Post—all *Clipper* columnists—then noted a few highlights of the *Clipper*'s history.

"Forty years ago our *Clipper* slid down the ways in the waters of Duxbury," Post said. "You know what? She got stuck in the mud—never got out of the harbor. Thank God she's still stuck in Duxbury, like us, a little older, a little heavier, but still setting sail every Wednesday to voyage as far as the post office and into all our lives. . . . "

As the ceremonies were drawing to a close, the phone rang. The call was from Albuquerque, New Mexico, inquiring about the price of a classified ad, a typical interruption in our weekly routine, reflecting the unexpected diversity of our readership.

Duxbury's local cable television station was on hand to record the events.

It continued to be a *Clipper* year. The climax came when Bobbie and I were chosen to be marshals in the annual Fourth of July parade.

Did we think we would ever fail when starting the *Clipper*? Of course not. Here is what Cid Ricketts Sumner wrote as a forward to *Put It On the Front Page, Please!*:

Frankly, I was stunned. After nine months abroad, I was rejoicing to be home again and to find the children and grandchildren well and happy. Then, before I had even sat down, Bobbie thrust a newspaper at me and John stood aside watching as if I had just been handed a bomb and he wasn't sure whether it or I would blow up.

"What's this?" I said, somewhat taken aback. For the last thing I wanted at the moment was to read a paper, even if it was, as I saw at first glance, a local one started no doubt by some foolhardy friend or neighbor with more money than brains. After my long absence, I wanted to hear family news, all the small things that never get into letters, much less into newspapers.

"Read that," Bobbie said, pointing.

I read, "John H. Cutler, Publisher and Editor." That was when I had to sit down, and quickly. "Well, well!" was all I could say. But thoughts aplenty were racing through my head. . . . Good heavens! What were they doing, starting a newspaper in Duxbury, of all places? And how in the world were they going to support it, not to mention their four children?

This was just too much. I hadn't said a word when they bought that plush new Pontiac station wagon instead of a sensible second-hand car; I'd even held my tongue when John gave up a splendid, safe college position for free-lance writing, and every time I had sat down to a delicious meal in their house I had refrained from suggesting tactfully that with the mortgage payment overdue, wasn't this rather a lavish dinner they were giving me?

Luckily, I didn't have a chance to speak for a little while, because John and Bobbie, both talking at the same time, were telling me how the notion had just struck them out of the blue, how they had plunged right in, the comical blunders they had made and what fun it all was.

I had to laugh in spite of myself, at some of their stories, even while I was thinking, "Poor dears, there's a tough time ahead of you, if you only knew it." Then it occurred to me that after all, they were young and resilient; maybe they could make it, maybe it would be good financial discipline for them. Maybe this younger generation needed to face hard times in what was more important than mere comforts and conveniences—or than even a roof over their heads.

Then, as I listened, my anxiety and exasperated resignation gave way to something else. A kind of wonder came over me. They were talking as if the idea of failure had never entered their minds, and every triumph—such as someone's paying in advance for a five dollar ad—was recounted with as much glee as if it actually amounted to something. If they were going to attempt the impossible with such spirit. . . . Well, it might turn out to be possible, after all; and who was I to dampen their enthusiasm? I had done a few risky things myself.

So at last I arrived at speech. "The *Duxbury Clipper*, may the wind blow fair!"

I expect the wind will continue to blow fair as, firmly at the helm, we approach the golden anniversary of the *Clipper*.

266

INDEX